Archives of Authority

translation
TRANSNATION

SERIES EDITOR **EMILY APTER**

A list of titles in the series appears at the back of the book.

Archives of Authority

Empire, Culture, and the Cold War

Andrew N. Rubin

Princeton University Press
Princeton and Oxford

Copyright © 2012 by Princeton University Press
Published by Princeton University Press, 41 William Street, Princeton, New Jersey 08540
In the United Kingdom: Princeton University Press, 6 Oxford Street, Woodstock, Oxfordshire OX20 1TW

press.princeton.edu

Jacket illustration: Jenny Holzer, *Xenon for Bregenz*, 2004, photo by Attilio Maranzano, courtesy Jenny Holzer/Art Resource, NY, © 2012 Jenny Holzer, member Artists Rights Society (ARS), New York

All Rights Reserved

Library of Congress Cataloging-in-Publication Data

Rubin, Andrew.
  Archives of authority : empire, culture, and the Cold War / Andrew N. Rubin.
    p. cm. — (Translation/transnation)
  Includes bibliographical references and index.
  ISBN 978-0-691-15415-2 (hardback : acid-free paper) 1. Criticism—History—20th century. 2. Cold War in literature. I. Title.
  PN94.R83 2012
  801'.950904—dc23   2011049576

British Library Cataloging-in-Publication Data is available

This book has been composed in Verdigris MVB Pro

Printed on acid-free paper. ∞

Printed in the United States of America

10 9 8 7 6 5 4 3 2 1

In memory of Edward W. Said

Contents

Acknowledgments ix

INTRODUCTION 1

CHAPTER 1
Archives of Authority 11
   The Archive and the Juridical 12
   States of Exception 13
   States of Criticism 17

CHAPTER 2
Orwell and the Globalization of Literature 24
   Communist Crypts 28
   The "Communist Menace" 34
   The Translation of Authority 37
   Translation and Modes of Domination 44

CHAPTER 3
Transnational Literary Spaces at War 47
   The Sun Never Sets on the British Writer 47
   The Time of Translation 58
   London Calling 60
   Literary Diplomacy 65

CHAPTER 4
Archives of Critical Theory 74
   Accommodations 80

CHAPTER 5
Humanism, Territory, and Techniques of Trouble 87
   Terrain of Philology 90

Notes 109

Bibliography 141

Index 167

Acknowledgments

THE IDEA OF WRITING A BOOK on the subject of the U.S. and British government's support and promotion of various writers, poets, and intellectuals abroad during the Cold War owes its origins to the encouragement of Edward W. Said. For their intellectual generosity and constructive criticism, I am grateful to George O'Brien, Mark McMorris, Carolyn Forché, Jonathan Arac, Ammiel Alcalay, Emily Apter, Norman Birnbaum, Eric Foner, Jean Franco, Andreas Huyssen, and Bruce Robbins. I owe special thanks to my editor, Hanne Winarsky, whose patient understanding made this book possible in many ways. I am also grateful to Emily Apter, whose support and criticism were entirely indispensable over the years. I also wish to thank Kelly Malloy for her thorough assistance, vigilance, and enthusiasm for the project. I am particularly grateful to Penn Szittya, Jason Rosenblatt, and Kathryn Temple for their support, encouragement, and understanding throughout my years at Georgetown. In the final stages, the manuscript benefited enormously from the meticulous attention of Mary Taveras, Elizabeth Gibbens, Amy Margolin, Brenda Werth, and especially Cathy Slovensky.

I have benefited from the kindness and generosity of many institutions. I especially wish to express my gratitude to the Lannan Foundation for their generous support, which gave me the time and space to write large portions of the manuscript. In particular, I would like to thank Patrick Lannan, Jo Chapman, Chris Abani, Dinaw Mengetsu, and Martha Jessup for their kindness and spirited interest in the project. I owe a special thanks to Georgetown University Graduate School for its generous assistance. Georgetown's Department of English provided me with invaluable time to research and write much of this book, and I am thankful for the several occasions when they did so. The librarians at Butler Library at Columbia University were of critical assistance in helping me with the Trilling Papers. The staff at the Joseph Regenstein Library at the University of Chicago assisted me with the Congress for Cultural Freedom Papers. Without the support of the Stern Fellowship, much of the research on Orwell at the University College of London would not have been possible.

I must gratefully acknowledge the critical interest of colleagues, friends, and students whose questions and discussion sharpened the text to a considerable degree. George O'Brien and Mark McMorris played an enormous role in helping me reshape the manuscript as a whole. They were remarkable interlocutors, and I cannot fully express my debt to them for their tireless interest and investment in the realization of this book. I also wish to especially thank Bruce Robbins, Jonathan Arac, Eric Foner, Rob Nixon, Akeel Bilgrami, Jonathan Cole, Gayatri Spivak, and Mariam Said, who provided a great deal of encouragement in Edward's absence. I also must acknowledge the tireless work of my research assistants, Julia Lovett and Kathryn Lewis, who were indispensable in many ways. For her commitment to this book, I wish to express my gratitude and appreciation to Christina Frohock, who generously agreed to represent me pro bono in my efforts to procure much of the material I discuss in chapter 1.

For their incredible friendship and understanding, I am extremely grateful to Zaia Alexander, Alex Forman, Lecia Rosenthal, and Matthew Specter, who helped to refine many of the book's main arguments. The project was sustained in great measure by the encouragement and friendship of Phyllis Bennis, Jacqueline Loss, Brenda Werth, Louis Bernard, Sabina Zeffler, Katy Bohinc, and Aiyah Saihati. My parents, Harriet and Allen Rubin, in addition to Leslie Rubin, Joseph Viroslav, Norman Birnbaum, Jacqueline Loss, Lecia Rosenthal, and, most of all, my grandfather, the late Charles Shifrin, were a constant source of encouragement after a catastrophic injury interrupted the writing of this book.

Though he did not live to see the completion of the project, Edward W. Said was the inspiration for this book. My memory of his encouragement, commitment, and example gave this project the momentum that helped to bring the book into the world. His intellectual generosity, enthusiasm, and excitement for the discovery of new knowledge, and his humor, intellect, and friendship, are what bind these pages together. My greatest regret is that he never had the chance to read the completed book in its entirety. I wrote many of these pages, especially the final chapter, in his memory in my hopes that in my own way I might help to keep his ideas alive.

Washington, D.C.
August 2011

Archives of Authority

Introduction

> On the fantail of a boat to Europe, T. S. Eliot was reclining with several passengers in deck seats, blue cloudy sky behind, iron floor below us. "And yourself," I said, "what do you think of the domination of poetics by the CIA? After all, wasn't [James] Angleton your friend? Didn't he tell you his plans to revitalize the intellectual structure of the West against so-to-speak Stalinists?" Eliot listened attentively—I was surprised he wasn't distracted. "Well, there are all sorts of chaps competing for dominance, political and literary... your Gurus for instance, and the Theosophists, and the table rappers and dialecticians and tea-leaf-readers and ideologues. I suppose I was one such, in my middle years. But I did, yes, know of Angleton's literary conspiracies, I thought they were petty—well meant but of no importance to literature." "I thought they were of some importance," I said, "since it secretly nourished the careers of too many square intellectuals, provided sustenance to thinkers in the Academy who influenced the intellectual tone of the West ... After all, ... the government through foundations was supporting a whole field of 'Scholars of War'... the subsidization of magazines like *Encounter* which held Eliotic style as a touchstone of sophistication and competence... failed to create an alternative free vital decentralized individualistic culture."
>
> —"T. S. Eliot Entered My Dreams," Allen Ginsberg[1]

ARCHIVES OF AUTHORITY investigates a historically decisive period in the literary and cultural interstices of the Cold War and decolonization. Contributing to a growing body of scholarship that places a renewed emphasis on transnational literary history by analyzing the particular historical and cultural determinants that structure the emergence of dominant literary formations, *Archives* engages recent efforts to develop new paradigms for comparative literary historiography that have aimed to reconceive the ideal of *Weltliteratur*. A concept first articulated by Johann Wolfgang Goethe in 1827 in a conversation with his secretary Johann Peter Eckermann, Goethe's term did not refer to world literature as a collection of world masterpieces; rather, it pointed to the emergence of the multiple modes of articulation through which nations communicated the particular experiences and peculiarities they embodied. When Goethe first used the expression, he was making the observation that *Weltliteratur* was merely in the "process of formation."[2] The widening circulation of journals, such as the *Edinburgh Review*, *Eco*, the *Foreign Review*, Mme de Staël's *De l'Allemagne*, and *Le Globe* were gradually establishing the basis for different modes of recognition, understanding, and tolerance between the nations of Europe. Together these journals reconstituted the general contours as well as the limitations of a historically specific form of restrictive and Eurocentric cosmopolitanism. *Le Globe*, for example, had risen to Goethe's defense against the vicious and hypernationalist attacks of the writer Wolfgang Menzel. These journals were not simply a way for Goethe to develop new and multiple perspectives of his own work but a way of becoming familiar with the works of other writers in English, French, and Italian as well.

Even if *Weltliteratur* could have persisted as a mode that was not disrupted by the corrosive forces of totalitarianism, nationalism, provincialism, racism, and imperialism, Goethe's notion of *Weltliteratur* was never meant to suggest the full and complete realization of a universal literature, since if such a mode of understanding were to one day be achieved, *Weltliteratur*, as Goethe understood it, would be abolished. At the very most, *Weltliteratur*, as a mode of mutual understanding and coexistence between nations, was a distant potential. Goethe saw the development of these modes and the awareness that they generated as belonging to a "gradual" process. He spoke about *Weltliteratur* tentatively; he said that there "was talk of it." He "ventured to announce it." He saw "hope of it" emerging. It was "in the process of formation."[3] As the not-yet present that pointed to the future, *Weltliteratur* was, after all, a historically specific mode of cultural transmission articulated within and bounded by the specific project of German Romanticism. Geographically limited to Europe, *Weltliteratur* designated a process of translation and dissemination that at once depended on the particularities of national difference as much as it enabled an enlarged awareness of the shared, but discrepant experiences between nations.

Yet in spite of the historical impediments and challenges that *Weltliteratur* has encountered over the past two centuries, it has nevertheless often remained uncritically central to the aspirations of comparative literature.[4] While its geographical limitations have been widely rejected, it has retained its strength as a concept to justify a practice of incorporation and appropriation that has threatened to undermine the historical and cultural contributions and achievements of postcolonial studies. Many of its most ambitious accounts have appropriated and intertextually juxtaposed texts across vast expanses of time and geography, apparently in an effort to align themselves with an imaginary cosmopolitan avant-garde while overlooking the historical determinants of the concept as Goethe had used it. Advancing the illusion of a cosmopolitanism that is unaware of its own historically situated displacement, many of these works fail to question the false unity implied by the world it claims to represent.[5] They manage to do little else but reinscribe neoliberal assumptions that maintain the illusion that world literature is real, which permits *Weltliteratur* to harmonically accompany the rhythms of globalization to which it is dutifully attuned.[6] No discernible interest in the historical conditions and situation of the writers, the frameworks that structure their attitudes, the historical modes that shape their circulation, the cultural forces that determine their translation, or the social and political realities that structure the constitution of the reading publics, is evident in these accounts.[7]

Yet if we are to comprehend so-called world literature as a mode of circulation, we are often left to wonder, what are the precise modes to which *Weltliteratur* might refer to today?[8] How do these modes intersect, overlap, and interact? How have these modes become the means through which forms of understanding and knowledge are expressed? Or have these modes of *Weltliteratur* been replaced by modes of *Weltkultur*? What are the conditions through which texts are transmitted and not transmitted via these modes? How do we take into account the multiplicity of these sites? What are the actual limits to linguistic exchange, and where are they located?[9] What silences do they help to conceal? On the face of it, the nation and market *appear* to interact along the neoliberal rhythms of the global economy to produce recognizable international literary figures. Writers such as J. M. Coetzee, Gabriel García Márquez, Ahdaf Soueif, Nadine Gordimer, Salman Rushdie, Kazuo Ishiguro, Michael Ondaatje, Seamus Heaney, Derek Walcott, and Wole Soyinka, among others, appear to belong to the field of so-called world literature. Yet the notion that Orhan Pamuk represents "the Turkish Writer" more fully than any other Turkish writer entails the marginalization of yet untranslated writers such as Hasan Ali Toptaş.[10] A great many writers are rendered invisible by the seemingly totalizing circuitry of world literature, and upon closer scrutiny it becomes evident that their absences are the very conditions of possibility of world literature.

Many of the recent and rather original and elegant models that have provided the broadest and often most theoretically sophisticated accounts of literary history have hardly uncovered or excavated any of the silences produced by what Michel-Rolph Trouillot has described as the "North Atlantic universal."[11] Lost in the muddle of abstract theories and models borrowed from historians of the Annales School, such as Marc Bloch and later Fernand Braudel and others whose theories and methods traveled only to become diluted into a set of rules and laws, the texts of an untold number of writers are concealed, overlooked, or buried by concepts such as the *longue durée*, which vastly expands the scope of historical analysis to segments of time that can span centuries.[12] As part of a general attempt to provide a theory that offers a unified account of the evolution of literary forms, these ambitious studies are driven by a yearning for totality, a desire to provide a total history, *une histoire tout court*.[13] Not since Lukács's *Theory of the Novel* has there been a theoretical attempt to provide an account of a "new literary universality."[14] Yet even Lukács acknowledged that the historical and philosophical realities that the literary forms had confronted were not sufficient to provide the synthesis to which his theory of totality and historical development of literary forms aspired.[15] Nevertheless, abstract assertions about the actual existence of a "world literary space"—a "parallel territory" of literary space that has a time of its own—are made in so sweepingly transhistorical movements that it would be hard to discern that the literature of this realm has anything to do with secular human history or even the specificities of experience and realities of human beings.[16] As a result, the relationship between the overlapping aspects and the intermingling of cultures—those mutually shared and discrepant experiences that are the basis for the production of new modes of mutual understanding and coexistence—are undermined.[17] A significant amount of theoretical work that developed in the wake of Said's *Orientalism* and *Culture and Imperialism* is essentially dismissed, marginalized, ignored, or forgotten.[18] What remains, however, is a disavowal of the way culture is entangled with power, even though many of these methods use metaphors of domination and marginalization. The interpretation of other cultures is seen to operate within the realm of an ahistorical vacuum—one that is pliable enough to permit interpretation to stand for a universalism devoid of any real social attachment. Said's notion of contrapuntal criticism—so central to an awareness that metropolitan history is narrated against those histories upon which the dominating discourse acts—faces the renewed challenge that a theoretical vantage point exists that is extricated from its own engagements and entanglements with the world.[19] We must be reminded that "we are, so to speak, *of* connections, not outside or beyond them" (emphasis in the original).[20]

The ongoing activity of providing an inventory of the interpellation of culture by empire has been contested most directly by Pascale Casanova. In her effort to develop a theory that relates the particularity of the literary text to the concept of literature as a world, Casanova wants us to understand that to restore the "lost bond" between literature, history, and the world, we must abandon textually based criticism (which institutes a break between the text and the world) and, at the same time, reject the idea that literature and history are identical. The limitations posed by postcolonialism, she asserts, is that it "posits a direct link between literature and history, one that is exclusively political." Textually based criticism, she says, is internal; it is too narrowly focused on the text to see that it is part of the world. Postcolonial criticism is external; it broadly conflates literature with history. A question that initially appears to be posed in terms of a relationship between the particular text and the general concept of the whole world suddenly finds itself confronted with a different set of categories: an irreconcilable opposition between the internal and the external. Why these two practices of criticism cannot operate together as an ensemble Casanova does not say.[21]

The compulsive drive to detach oneself from the circumstances of the present and its connection to the past has diminished *Weltliteratur* into an instrumental mode of *Weltkultur* that has, in exceptional instances, played a defining role in establishing the zones of warfare and translation. Beginning in 2005, the U.S. Defense Department began embedding teams of cultural anthropologists within military units to function as cultural analysts of those subjects under military occupation. Described as the "Human Terrain System" (HTS; now referred to as the HTS Project), the operation recruited and mobilized teams of social scientists to produce an archive of knowledge about the Afghan, and later the Iraqi, populations and culture to supply the military command with more effective strategies to administer, manage, and control its subjects. The impetus behind the Defense Department's initiative came from a small body of pseudoscholarship that claimed that the acquisition of cultural knowledge about the adversary would make military engagements a more effective and efficient means to subjugate a restless and resistant population.[22] In 2008 the *Joint Force Quarterly* published an essay entitled, "The Military Understanding of an Adversary Culture," which asserted that

> The changing nature of warfare requires a deeper understanding of adversary culture. The more unconventional the adversary, and the further from Western norms, the more we need to understand the society and underlying cultural dynamics. To defeat non-Western opponents who are transnational in scope, nonhierarchical in structure, clandestine in approach, and who operate outside the context of nation-states, we need to improve our capacity to understand foreign cultures.[23]

The subjects became a "terrain" to be analyzed, examined, documented, and transmuted into the dehumanized objects of anthropological, sociological, and cultural knowledge. In the *Counterinsurgency Guidance Source*, issued in October 2008, General Odierno declared that the "Iraqi people are the 'decisive terrain' . . . The environment in which we operate is complex," he wrote, "and it demands that we employ every weapon in our arsenal, both kinetic and non-kinetic. To fully utilize all approaches, we must understand the local culture and history."[24]

Not since Napoleon's conquest of Egypt had so many scientists and scholars been mobilized to record, analyze, and study the culture, geography, and history of a people who had not invited such scrutiny and invasion from abroad. In his project to dominate Egypt, Napoleon sent his army with teams of surgeons, archaeologists, linguists, chemists, and antiquarians as part of an enormous effort to incorporate Egypt's values and its connections to a tradition that included Homer, Lycurgus, Solon, Pythagoras, and Plato. The results of this scrutiny were recorded in the *Description de l'Égypte*, a twenty-three-volume tome written between 1808 and 1828. Napoleon's project was a disciplinary practice, a mode of knowing, and a mode of understanding that was inextricably connected to power, according to Edward Said:

> To institute new areas of specialization; to establish new disciplines; to divide, deploy, schematize, tabulate, index, and record everything in sight (and out of sight); to make out of every observable detail a generalization and out of every generalization an immutable law about Oriental nature, temperament, mentality, custom, or type; and, above all, to transmute a living reality into the stuff of texts, to possess (or think one possesses) actuality mainly because nothing in the Orient seems to resist one's powers: these are the features of Orientalist projection entirely realized in the *Description de l'Égypte*, itself enabled and reinforced by Napoleon's wholly Orientalist engulfment of Egypt by the instruments of Western knowledge and power.[25]

Yet there is an important distinction to be made between an Orientalism that is situated on the terrain of war and the textual Orientalism to which Said is referring. While both forms of knowledge about the Other are placed in the service of power, the Defense Department's HTS Project entails the militarization of knowledge and the refinement of the techniques of a specific kind of biopower—a discipline and power that regulates human life itself.[26] The "terrain of operation" becomes a dehumanized place, a topos that is replete with references, quotations, observations, and citations—essentially figurative constructions that are used to justify and legitimize the exercise of power in advance, to establish order, and to provide a logic that transforms the human subject into a "terrain" to be colonized, reworked, and occupied; yet at the same time, it becomes the very means through which violence is avowed or disavowed. According to a 2009 report from the American Anthropology Association, the advisors use

> a wide range of conventional ethnographic activities and techniques for data collection. Data collection, therefore, has been reported to include at least the following techniques: surveys, snowball sampling, semi-structured individual and group interviews with both "ordinary Iraqis"

(or, presumably, Afghanis) and elites, the elicitation of oral-history narratives, kinship and genealogical analysis, as well as diverse "assessments," all of which typically includes the use of interpreters as full research partners. Depending on the circumstances and objectives, these techniques are applied in different proportion and with different degrees of depth. Sometimes a given technique is simply impractical or impossible to use, as is true of field work everywhere.[27]

The strategy develops its own epistemological framework through which the "terrain of insurgency" is made into an entity over whose destiny the United States believes it has some sort of unquestioned entitlement to rule, control, and govern. The strategy of analyzing the cultural disposition of subjects who live under foreign rule exercises power so that each aspect of human behavior can be reduced and objectified into particular categories that can be administered, observed, controlled, and manipulated. These ethnologists and social scientists are agents of total observation, although what they produce are hardly anything but stereotypical figures who possess a certain "mind-set" that can be measured, recorded, archived, inventoried, and objectified to serve the ends of a power that transmutes the field of human social activities into a zone of military conquest. In this respect there can be no consistent, coherent, intelligible "adversary" without the discourse of "counterinsurgency," through which the discipline of biopower not only eliminates life but also regulates it.

In this crucial respect, it is not irrelevant that teams of embedded anthropologists that are mobilized by the HTS Project shape the very attitudes that indirectly inform the decisions in the chain of military command. These ethnographers of warfare have not simply been enlisted in the service of the military to provide knowledge for the purpose of power, which of course is by no means new,[28] but they have become incorporated into the technologies of violence in radically new ways. The militarization of the disciplinary practices of anthropology in the service of biopower is implicated indirectly in decisions regarding who is permitted to be killed and who is allowed to survive in the context of these lethal zones of cultural translation. If the mission of anthropology is to produce knowledge and understanding for its own sake, the techniques of militarized ethnography generate kinds of knowledge that are used belligerently in the very realm of armed conflict. "There is after all a profound difference between the will to understand for the purposes of coexistence and humanistic enlargement of horizons, and the will to dominate for the purposes of control and external enlargement of horizons, and the will to dominate for the purposes of control and external dominion."[29]

I am emphasizing these iterations of militarized Orientalism and the function that it has continued to serve in these military zones of rapid cultural translation because it not only shows how brazen the connection between power and knowledge has become in our culture but also because it evinces how profoundly the modalities for understanding have become instruments of power. In many ways, *Archives of Authority* is an engagement with this reality insofar as it traces the genealogy of this view in the early years of the Cold War by describing the formidable structures and conjunctures of cultural domination, as well as the cultural mechanisms by which the United States rearticulated the discourse of British colonialism through the institutions and discourses of anticommunism. Both of these forces had very real effects on what is considered *Weltliteratur*. U.S.-sponsored Cold War organizations, such as the Congress for Cultural Freedom (CCF), did not leave the canon untouched, but rather helped to shape it, define it, regulate it, administer it, co-opt part of it, and in some cases silence and marginalize writers, particularly those whose dissenting practices threatened to undermine the episteme upon which the Cold War was based—a seemingly relentless conflict between "totalitarianism" and the "free world."[30] In 1952, the philologist Erich Auerbach had, it appeared, already grasped the general contours of the problem:

> All human activity is being concentrated either in European-American or into Russian-Bolshevist patterns; no matter how great they seem to be, the differences between the two are comparatively minimal when they are contrasted with the basic patterns underlying the Islamic, Indian, or Chinese traditions. Should mankind succeed in withstanding the shock of so mighty and rapid of a process—for which the spiritual preparation has been poor—then man will have to accustom himself to an existence in a standardized world, to a single literary culture, only a few literary languages, and perhaps even a single literary language. And herewith the notion of *Weltliteratur* would be at once realized and destroyed.[31]

Goethe's conception of *Weltliteratur*—what Auerbach understood to mean "the human as a product of the productive exchanges between cultures"—thus assumed a degraded form in the aftermath of World War II. As he observed, the cultural activities of governments, institutions, and other Cold War organizations had effectively obstructed and limited the discourse of mutual understanding and coexistence: "There is no more talk now—as there had been—of the spiritual exchange between peoples, of the refinement of customs, and the reconciliation of races. Certain distinguished individuals, small groups of highly cultivated men always have enjoyed and will continue to do so. Yet this sort of activity has little effect on culture or the reconciliation of peoples: it cannot stand the storm of vested interests—and so its results are immediately dissipated."[32]

Through bodies such as the British Council and the CCF, the British and U.S. governments enlisted a particular group of postwar public writers and sent them abroad as cultural emissaries. Figures such as T. S. Eliot, W. H. Auden, Arthur Koestler, Ignazio Silone, and Isaiah Berlin, among others, came to occupy multiple transnational positions. They found their essays, poems, and short stories translated with greater speed and published in multiple magazines in cities such as Paris, Rome, London, Berlin, New Delhi, Mexico, and Beirut. The CCF—one of the most influential cultural institutions funded by the United States during the Cold War—published an international array of sophisticated monthly magazines, such as *Cuadernos* (Mexico City), *Cadernos Brasileiros* (Rio de Janeiro), *Encounter* (London), *Forum* (Vienna), *Der Monat* (Berlin), *Preuves* (Paris), *Quadrant* (Sydney), *Quest* (Mumbai), *Tempo Presente* (Rome), and *Transition* (Kampala). A disingenuous cosmopolitan montage, these magazines of culture and politics made unlikely juxtapositions between writers of different nationalities, positioning, for example, an essay by the German writer Thomas Mann adjacent to a short story by the Mexican writer Juan Rulfo, not only in one language but also in several languages and multiple publications and places concurrently.

The emergence of transnational institutions such as the British Council and the BBC helped to mobilize national literary figures abroad, and, in doing so, fundamentally altered the relationship between public writers and their readers. Essays by critics such as R. P. Blackmur and Lionel Trilling renegotiated the expansion of American power and expressed a heightened awareness of the nation's seeming boundlessness. Cold War magazines and institutions such as *Encounter*, *Transition*, *Black Orpheus*, the Ford Foundation's *Perspectives USA*, and the BBC's *African* and *Caribbean Voices* and its *Third Programme* established new regimes of consecration—a literary and cultural order through which certain authors became specifically identifiable as world authors in a new kind of international literary system. New technologies of transmission placed both writers and readers in different orders of circulation. A whole ideology and mode of world literature underwent a historically decisive transformation during the Cold War.

Instead of mutually recognizing the intertwined histories and experiences between peoples, however discrepant those experiences may be, the dominant structural and cultural conditions that cohered in the aftermath of World War II were largely defined by new and increasingly efficient modes of transmission, translation, and dissemination. As an investigational genealogy of the Cold War and its intersections with decolonization, *Archives of Authority* provides a critical and interpretative account of the forces that established a conjuncture between the numerous modalities available for diffusion and the writers who were incorporated, mobilized, and sometimes co-opted as part of the divisions, hierarchies, and epistemological practices of the Cold War. A dominant group of writers enjoyed what had become by the mid-twentieth century new modalities of articulation: the accelerated transmission and translation of short stories and essays published from multiple sites of transmission. The analysis of these practices contributes not only to the study of the emerging cultural features of globalization and its relation to the history of modernities but also to the inventory of the asymmetrical flow of translations that were directed and shaped by organizations such as the CCF. In this respect, in the early phase of globalization (and the process of decolonization that marked its new stage), the idea of *Weltliteratur* was largely defined by the frameworks of the Cold War, not only within Europe but in Africa, Asia, and Latin America as well.[33]

If *Archives* provides an account of the circulation of the public writer in the age of technological replication, then it does so in order to allow us to document the cultural determinants of the absences that are the conditions of possibility of *Weltliteratur*. If these absences have forced us to conceive of *Weltliteratur* in negative terms, then a particular analysis of the specific historical conditions through which *Weltliteratur*'s silences are deposited permits us to apprehend the idea of *Weltliteratur* in the most materialist sense—as an "Idea which is in the process of its own actualization." As Slavoj Žižek argues:

> What the notion of the Idea as a product of itself makes visible is . . . not the process of self-engendering, but that materialist fact that the idea exists only in and through the activity of the individuals engaged with it and motivated by it. What we have here is not a historicist/evolutionist position . . . , but something much more radical: an insight into how historical reality itself is not a positive order, but a "not-all" which points to its own future. It is this inclusion of the future as the gap in the present order that renders the latter "not-all," ontologically incomplete, and thus explodes the self-enclosure of the historicist/evolutionary process.[34]

As a work of investigational criticism, and cultural and literary historiography, my overriding intention is that this book's analysis of the modalities through which cultural authority was exercised in the aftermath of the Second World War produces a critical awareness of how *Weltliteratur* was implicated in a historical world that is made by human beings, and can be unmade and remade by them as well.

CHAPTER 1

Archives of Authority

> I used to marvel that the letters in a closed book did not get mixed up and lost in the course of night.
>
> —*Jorge Luis Borges*

IN MAY 2000, I wrote what was to be the first of several letters to the Central Intelligence Agency and requested, under the Freedom of Information Act, that it release all available information in its possession about the English poet Stephen Spender (1909–95). While I had no hard evidence proving that Spender was an intelligence agent, I was confident that he had played a direct role in the various institutions that emerged in the early years of the Cold War. From 1953 to 1967, Spender had served as the co-editor of *Encounter* magazine—the flagship journal published by the Congress for Cultural Freedom. One of the most significant institutions in the Cold War, the CCF was funded by the Central Intelligence Agency to essentially administer, control, and manage the various discourses of the Cold War.[1]

When I submitted the request, I did so on the basis of an emerging body of scholarship that examines the relationship between American postwar ascendancy and "cultural diplomacy" in the early years of the Cold War and decolonization.[2] While much of the existing research focuses on how the U.S. government, through the CCF, funded symphonies, performances, musical competitions, literary prizes, exhibitions, festivals, and many scholars and writers,[3] few studies have considered how its underwriting reshaped and refashioned the global literary landscape, altered the relationships between writers and their publics, and rendered those whom it supported more recognizable figures than others.[4] While many of these endeavors arose in the absence of a defined cultural strategy to legitimize American postwar ascendancy,[5] these practices were nevertheless conceived as part of an orchestrated imperial effort to occupy a global public space that by 1948 had been largely dominated by the socialist rhetoric of the Communist Information Bureau (Cominform).

In 1948, a National Security Directive (NSC-10) authorized the Central Intelligence Agency to develop a cultural strategy to undermine the Soviet Union's "peace offensive," and shortly thereafter, the CCF became one of the most important projects and institutions in the imperial rivalry between the two superpowers. Through any number of its journals—*Cuadernos* (published in Paris but distributed in Latin America from 1956 to 1965), *Cadernos Brasileiros* (published in Rio de Janeiro from 1959 to 1970), *Encounter* (published in London from 1953 to 1974), *Forum* (published in Vienna from 1954 to 1965), *Der Monat* (published in Munich from 1949 to 1971), *Preuves* (published in Paris from 1951 to 1975), *Quadrant* (published in Sidney from 1956 to 1967), *Quest* (published in Mumbai from 1955 to 1976), *Tempo Presente* (published in Rome from 1956 to 1967), and *Transition* (published in Kampala from 1961 to 1967)—the CCF had a significant impact on the changing conditions of humanistic practice from 1950 until 1967, when the *New York Times* and *Ramparts* magazine reported that the Central Intelligence Agency had been secretly funding the CCF, along with its exhibitions, performances, poets, novelists, theater companies, dancing troupes, and student associations. All these energies and resources, it was revealed, were enlisted to legitimize and culturally sustain the transfer of imperial power from Europe to the United States in the aftermath of the Second World War and refashion and reinvent the idea of world literature.

The Archive and the Juridical

When I submitted my Freedom of Information Act (FOIA) request in the spring of 2000, I expected that the response to the inquiry would supply a complete account of the process of selection, inclusion, and exclusion that governed the congress's cultural strategy, particularly as it related to *Encounter* magazine, of which Spender was the more influential and older coeditor (above Irving Kristol). I had hoped that such information, if released, would provide a more comprehensive understanding of the intertwining of culture and power in the early years of the Cold War and decolonization. The full disclosure of the relationship between the CCF and the U.S. government would not only explain how new techniques and modes of articulation had radically redefined the position of public writers in postwar culture but would also reveal which writers were selected for marginalization, how they were chosen, and why. We know very little, for example, of the CCF's efforts to discredit and delegitimize writers such as Pablo Neruda, John Berger, Frantz Fanon, and Jean-Paul Sartre. Did this absence of a positive cultural strategy extend to other writers? The endeavor also addressed a larger shift in global alignments and accommodations: the cultural strategies that were part of the transfer of imperial authority from Britain and France to the United States in the aftermath of World War II, the history of which has been largely overlooked.[6] Mapping the whole network of relationships, assemblages, and organizations that constituted the CCF's endeavors would establish the conditions for the development of new forms

Archives of Authority • 13

of nondominative knowledge, just as it would document the historical conditions through which *Weltliteratur*'s silences are deposited. Because Stephen Spender was an editor of *Encounter*, and quite an itinerant one at that, my request thus focused on him as much as it aimed to acquire knowledge about what one might call the concealed *institutional and disciplinary mechanisms of dominant culture*, the better to be able to grasp the historical determinants of its archive.[7]

Several months after I made the inquiry, the agency requested that I provide evidence that Stephen Spender was, in fact, no longer alive. Shortly after submitting his obituary from the *New York Times*, I received a brief letter from the agency indicating that it would "neither confirm nor deny" the "existence or nonexistence" of any available information on Stephen Spender for reasons of "national security."[8] The decision did not come as a complete surprise, but it seemed alarming that the cultural policies carried out shortly after the Second World War could conceivably remain classified half a century later. The Berlin Wall had fallen in November 1989, the Soviet Union no longer existed, and a whole new way of thinking had replaced the episteme of the Cold War. The intricacies of the CIA's involvement in international and domestic cultural politics and the origins of the CCF had been made public by *Ramparts* magazine in 1966 and then by the *New York Times* in 1967.[9] Intelligence officials such as Tom Braden had already written and spoken openly about the CIA's administration of the CCF. In a strident, unapologetic defense, whose underlying irony seemed to escape him, Braden wrote:

> I remember the enormous joy I got when the Boston Symphony Orchestra won more acclaim for the U.S. in Paris than John Foster Dulles or Dwight D. Eisenhower could have bought with a hundred speeches. And then there was *Encounter*, the magazine published in England and dedicated to the proposition that cultural achievement and political freedom were interdependent. Money for both the orchestra's tour and the magazine's publication came from the CIA, and few outside the CIA knew about it. We had placed one agent in a Europe-based organization of intellectuals called the Congress for Cultural Freedom. Another agent became an editor of *Encounter*.[10]

STATES OF EXCEPTION

The CIA based its refusal to comply with my request upon its interpretation of the National Security Act of 1947, which had established the Central Intelligence Agency. The act held that the CIA was not required to confirm the existence of any material that could possibly reveal its "sources and methods" of collecting intelligence.[11] The act stipulated that the CIA, unlike other government agencies, such as the Security Exchange Commission or the Department of Labor, was exempt from releasing any material that could be "reasonably" construed "to result in damage to national security":

> The Central Intelligence Agency can neither confirm nor deny the existence or nonexistence of any Central Intelligence Agency records responsive to your request. The fact of the existence or nonexistence of records containing such information—unless it has been officially acknowledged—would be classified for reasons of national security under Sections 1.5 (c) [intelligence sources and methods] and 1.5 (d) [foreign relations] of Executive Order 12958. Further, the Director of the Central Intelligence has the responsibility and authority to protect such information from unauthorized disclosure in accordance with Subsection 103 (c)(6) of the National Security Act of 1947 and Section 6 of the CIA Act of 1949.... By this action, we are neither confirming nor denying the existence or nonexistence of such records.[12]

In a challenge to the government's decision in the spring of 2001, I filed a complaint in the U.S. District Court in the Southern District of New York, claiming that the agency had improperly withheld information about Spender in violation of the Freedom of Information Act. Given the historical nature and the obscurity of the query, I thought I stood a relatively strong chance of persuading the court of the importance of the request. Why, after all, should a scholar of English literature have to enjoin the government to release historical texts about a deceased British poet? The casuistry of the government's position seemed, to me at least, extraordinarily transparent, and I assumed that any reasonable judge would concur that the government had withheld information from the public in violation of the Freedom of Information Act.

The Freedom of Information Act was codified as a federal law in 1966. Later amended in the 1970s shortly before the Church Committee hearings disclosed the scope and ruthlessness of the CIA's various operations abroad (the then secret overthrow of governments in Guatemala, Iran, Chile, and the Congo; the attempted assassinations of Jawaharlal Nehru and Fidel Castro; the failed ouster of Sukarno in Indonesia; and the fixing of Italy's elections of 1948, among other activities),[13] the Freedom of Information Act provides access to U.S. government records, documents, cables, texts, decisions, and memoranda.[14] Yet, as a statute that regulates the release or suppression of official forms of knowledge, the law contains nine provisions through which the government is exempt from upholding the general spirit of the law. In my case in particular, the agency contended that the law could be suspended in the interest of upholding national security.[15]

The agency invoked two exemptions, claiming the information remained classified for reasons of national security and that revealing that information would disclose procedures and sources of intelligence that the director of the CIA has the responsibility to protect under the National Security Act.[16] The first exemption, based on an executive order issued by then president Bill Clinton, held that the information was classified because the very fact of its "existence or nonexistence" was itself classified. The agency was therefore permitted to "refuse to confirm or deny the existence or nonexistence of requested information whenever the fact of its existence or nonexistence is itself classified under Executive Order 12,958."[17] The second exemption was based on the principle that the disclosure of the information—whose "existence or nonexistence" it had already insisted would undermine "national security" under Clinton's executive order—was the responsibility of the director of the CIA, who had a duty to "protect [such knowledge] from unauthorized disclosure." In other words, the language of the act emphasized that the director is charged with the obligation to prevent any *unauthorized* acts of disclosure—an action that he and only he can authorize. If this reasoning suggested that the National Security Act required that the director has the duty to protect its records, it also implied that the very act of releasing them belongs to a class of unauthorized disclosures that have simply escaped the director's attention.

The relationship between these two exemptions raises questions that are relevant to understanding the mechanics of power. To begin with, how can information that belongs to the realm of "nonexistence" be protected? What kind of power can claim authority over both the nonexistent and the existent? While there is a rationale to protecting sources and methods from unauthorized acts of disclosure, how can the director prevent the disclosure of nothing at all? What, if anything, is there to protect, if there is nothing but a void? What kind of authority organizes itself in this zone of indifference? Is the power to neither affirm nor negate what it may possess or may not possess a power that suggests that all forms of knowledge might possibly be under its control? Or instead of revealing the possible scope of this power, might it reveal something more about the nature of power upon which the state relies? Is the *indeterminacy* of the archive the absence or void upon *which state power rests*, since it is not simply a matter of the suspension of the law itself but *the concealment of a zone of indifference* that has become the very condition of possibility of authority in the first place?[18] Much like Kafka's character in "Before the Law" who wants to enter the law but cannot be assured for himself that there is a law behind the series of guarded doors to begin with, the only law visible to him is the demand to remain *before* it.[19]

In November 2001, the Federal District Court in New York did not question the legitimacy of the exemption or the logic of the relationship between the two exemptions or its application. Deciding in favor of the agency's motion to dismiss my case, the court maintained that the agency had compelling reasons to protect the "appearance of confidentiality," which was "essential" to exercise United States authority abroad.[20] The Federal District Court determined that the CIA had provided a "reasonably detailed explanation" as to why it refused to either confirm or deny "the fact of the existence or nonexistence" of records germane to the request. In spite of the fact that whatever activities Spender may have engaged in or been a part of happened half a century ago, the Federal District Court affirmed that the agency had complied with the dictates of the Freedom of Information Act. The court held that "the CIA has offered reasonable explanations for why the disclosure of such information could interfere with Agency efforts to collect human intelligence in the present day, including its 'compelling interest' in 'protecting the appearance of confidentiality' so essential to the effective operation of our foreign intelligence service."[21]

The Federal District Court based its decision on a series of precedents that reinterpreted the National Security Act of 1947, which maintains that the director of the Central Intelligence Agency is obliged to "protect intelligence sources and methods from unauthorized disclosure." As the district judge observed in the decision, the Supreme Court in *CIA v. Sims* had radically extended and reinterpreted the scope of the National Security Act. In that case, the Supreme Court interpreted the National Security Act as giving the agency "very broad authority to protect all sources of intelligence information from disclosure."[22] If the National Security Act of 1947 originally gave the director of the CIA the responsibility to prevent "unauthorized disclosures," in *CIA v. Sims*, the Supreme Court broadly expanded that authority to include the protection of "*all sources* of intelligence information from unauthorized disclosure" (my emphasis), regardless of the information's level of classification, without defining precisely who or even what a "source" is.[23]

Citing the precedent, the District Court concluded that the government met its responsibility to "protect" its sources and methods from "unauthorized disclosure," claiming that its "sources" were further governed by a zone of indifference: "the existence or nonexistence" of the documents requested under the Freedom of Information Act. Not only is the Freedom of Information Act subject to a state of exception, but knowledge—which the state has the authority to "protect from disclosure"[24]—does not even have to exist for the exception to be invoked and enforced. The metaphysics of national security therefore rests on an ambivalence: to identify an "intelligence source" would be to reveal the methods that are used to determine whether a source is a source or not—itself a violation of the authority vested in the director of Central Intelligence.[25] We are thus far from enjoying the free, open, and democratic dissemination of information,[26] but are close enough to be able to see the actual meaning of the authority of the state and the archives of its authority.

STATES OF CRITICISM

The cultural process by which imperial authority was transferred from Britain and France to the United States in the aftermath of the Second World War has received very little attention in the various discussions of American culture and imperialism. The transfer of legitimacy did not simply involve the passage of imperial power from one topos to another. Instead, an entire reconfiguration of cultural relationships took place that had vast consequences for the position of the writer in society, the conditions of humanistic practice, the ideology of world literature, and the relationship between writers and the rising dominance of new and efficient modes of mass transmission. By the early 1950s, the changing conditions of literary production that the CCF oversaw had essentially become a global process, not simply of cultural reproduction but of cultural replication. While the sources of the CCF's funding were unknown to its contributors (like Hannah Arendt, Raymond Aron, W. H. Auden, Daniel Bell, Albert Camus, Cyril Connolly, Leslie Fiedler, Robert Lowell, Christopher Isherwood, Karl Jaspers, Cecil Day-Lewis, Arthur Koestler, Edwin Muir, Herbert Read, Lionel Trilling, and others), the activities of the CCF permitted their work to travel in unlikely, unexpected, and influential ways. Through its array of journals, surprising juxtapositions between writers such as Thomas Mann and Juan Rulfo were often repeated with regularity in any number of their journals, sometimes simultaneously, to the extent that their status as world authors became regulated and normalized in the different iterations of their writing.

The articulation of discourses of "democracy" and "cultural freedom" involved a set of disciplinary mechanisms and practices that placed the texts of Auden, Arendt, Camus, Faulkner, Koestler, Silone, Wright, and others in an assemblage of publications in several languages simultaneously—in Arabic, English, French, German, Italian, Japanese, Korean, and Spanish. In this way, the CCF and organizations like it reconstituted the conditions of humanist practice. It consolidated and reframed writers' associations and affiliations; it secured some reputations; it tried to ruin others;[27] it upheld an illusion of the literary world outside of politics; it certified figures;[28] and it gave them tremendous visibility. The CCF and other institutions effectively used the cultural world as a kind of disguise that certified that specific public writers were permitted to politically engage in a social system from which others were implicitly—and at times explicitly—excluded.

In the early years of the Cold War, British and American writers and intellectuals were sent abroad to diverse and unlikely places; their articles were juxtaposed with the articles of writers of different nationalities, ranging from German (Thomas Mann) to American (William Faulkner), from French Algerian (Albert Camus) to Russian British (Isaiah Berlin), and from British (Kingsley Amis) to Polish (Czesław Miłosz). From this conjuncture of new and emergent cultural forces arose an entirely new and powerful episteme that was irreducible to the antimonies of the Cold War—and often seen as a ceaseless war of rhetoric between totalitarianism and democracy. This new organization of knowledge had effects that were multiple, vast, and global. They included numerous government institutions and organizations that promoted art exhibitions, dance performances, symphonies, writers' congresses, and scholarly conferences, which brought about a tectonic shift in the intellectual culture that followed the Second World War. New forms and modes of articulation, reproduction, and replication accompanied these developments. Of all the forms that were widely available to create a profusion of opportunities, radio was one of several modalities of transmission that dramatically altered the relationship between writers and their audiences. With the cultural expansion of radio, audiences were no longer spoken to directly; instead, writers spoke via microphones to audiences. Audiences no longer listened. Instead the microphone did the listening, and the radio speakers delivered the conditions of hearing the voice of the disembodied writer.[29]

After the cessation of hostilities in World War II, the postwar world underwent a massive shift in cultural and intellectual terrain, with the development of newer and more efficient modes of articulation, duplication, and transmission that restructured the relationship between the writer and the public. The imperatives of new global alignments—the emergence of nearly one hundred decolonized states after World War II—brought about a major shift in the emphasis of the study of languages and literatures.[30] Disciplines were partitioned, divided, and separated into *areas of study*, even before the National Defense Education Act of 1958 constituted "Area Studies."[31] Managed and administered by new types of periodicals of culture and politics, by new orders of literary organization and affiliation, the discourse of cultural freedom provided innumerable opportunities for the persistent enforcement and reinforcement of dominant structures of attitude and reference, ideas ultimately bereft of variety, diversity, and history. New international alignments and accommodations brought about the personification of nations: "our friends" and "our brothers." Complex conceptions about the social reorganization of life were likely to "spread," according to George Kennan, at the behest of the "Kremlin."[32] Writers and critics no longer traveled for the sake of experience or to promote their books, but at the behest of organizations such as the British Council or the CCF. Their coordinated movements constituted different, wider, unknowable audiences, while writers became recognizable outside the domestic national spaces to which they and their work had for the most part been confined. Indeed, it was not until after the war that Cyril Connolly's journal *Horizon* (1940 to 1949) published an "all-American issue."

Often presented by the faceless figure of the Western observer writing home, as if always by hand, to share his or her personal but generalizable experience of social life abroad, "Letters from London," "Letters from Moscow," and "Letters from Kenya" gained currency as one of several generic conventions through which the "foreign" was represented, assimilated, and disseminated with greater and greater frequency. The shifting technical developments in transmission realigned the conventions of Orientalism toward the discourse of development and modernization. There was no dearth of essays in *Encounter* with titles such as "Looking for India," "Letter from Norway," "At Vecherinka," "A Sentimental Traveler in Japan," and "World Cities: Calcutta."[33] It was then, with the emergence of monthly journals such as *Encounter*, that the pressures of form and economy further accelerated the disappearance of the little magazines of modernism. Other developments ensured the synchrony, symmetry, and duration of thought. Journals and magazines were drop-shipped transnationally with greater velocity by air. Writers working in faraway places were read at new proximities in both time and place. New means of reproduction and replication overcame geographic distances. In "Marrakech," a text George Orwell published in *New Writing* in 1939, he wrote, "When you walk through a town like this—two hundred thousand inhabitants, of whom at least twenty thousand have nothing but rags they stand up in—when you see how people live, and still more easily how they die, it is always difficult to believe that you are still walking among human beings."[34]

Translated, distributed, reproduced, and, in the case of more abbreviated forms, replicated in multiple languages nearly simultaneously, the new monthlies, such as *Cuadernos, Encounter, Der Monat, Preuves, Tempo Presente*, and others inaugurated a new historical phase of writing: the essay form from abroad became a mode of social and political analysis in a world whose productive and massively destructive forces diminished the value of the category of human experience and restructured the passage of time to an always imminent state of emergency, while a rhetoric remained radically discrepant with the actual lived realities and experiences of human beings. The titles of the magazines were allegorical: Britain had to face the new terms of *Encounter*, in Paris they needed *Preuves*, Italy was returned to the present (*Tempo Presente*), in Mexico writers filled up their notebooks (*Cuadernos*), in Berlin they kept track of the months (*Der Monat*) of Soviet and American occupation, and Africa was in *Transition*.

Spheres of influence, barbed wires, airlifts, zones, crypto-communists, fellow-travelers, the bomb, covert actions, propaganda, neutralism, nonalignment, free world, un-American activities, Sputnik, arms race, peace dividend—a whole new battery of language and rhetoric refigured one of the most seemingly incurable imperial rivalries, whose violent effects and actual human and environmental devastation were experienced and endured in the Third World, as Vijay Prashad has shown in *The Darker Nations*.[35] New vocabularies of imaginary geographies arose. Out of Asia came "areas"; terrains were spatialized by new signals of distance and orientation; "Middle East," "Southeast Asia," "South Asia," and "East Asia" replaced the "Near East" and the "Far East."

The emergence of governmental and nongovernmental institutions—the British Council, the CCF, the United States Information Agency, the Information Research Department (IRD; a secret division of the British Foreign Office), the Rockefeller and Ford Foundations—had historically decisive effects on the relationship between the public writer and his or her audience. These new cultural formations that mobilized writers to unpredictable places abroad not only fundamentally reconstituted the relationship between the writer and their public but redefined the very modes of domination, subjugation, and subordination. No longer the object of imperial desire, the physical occupation of territory was replaced by the occupation of literary and cultural space.[36] A global public space had replaced the physics of colonial presence; the public space had to be saturated by signals that were interchangeable with the new cultural order.

The chapters that follow will demonstrate how the emergence of and cooperation between organizations such as the IRD, the CCF, the British Council, and the Ford and Rockefeller Foundations served a critical function that constituted new patterns of administration and dominance. They will show how, in the face of the development of organized movements for national independence and liberation, America's postwar ascendency involved the development of new strategies and methods to suppress and eliminate dissent. The spread of different forms of mediation—the growing transnational importance of radio and the writers' presence on programs such as the BBC's *Third Programme*; the global expansion of the British Council; the appearance of new types of journals of culture and politics (*Perspectives USA* and *Encounter*); the emergence of new strategies and techniques of duplicating translations that accompanied these practices; and the changing realities facing the public writer, whereby certain writers acted as cultural emissaries abroad—were, I argue, among the efficient modalities that became the altered basis of humanistic and literary practices in the early years of the Cold War. The following chapters will also show how so-called world writers were subjected to new regimes of consecration and authorities that arbitrated the recognition of some authors over others. Revising Pascale Casanova's claim that an international literary law emerged that owed nothing to political fiat, this book interrogates this claim by analyzing an archive of relations between authors and the interrelated cultural activities of the British and American empires.[37] Viewing these relations as an analyzable formation, I argue that this archive of relations places new kinds of critical demands on the practice of literary historiography, particularly in the framework of the present.

The five chapters of the book and the twelve sections into which the book is divided are intended to facilitate an exposition of the changing basis of humanistic practice after World War II. If this chapter summarizes the dimensions of the subject both in terms of historical time and the dimensions of the subject, and in terms of its major philosophical and political themes of the archive, chapter 2, "Orwell and the Globalization of Literature," traces the development of specific postwar modalities of transmission that articulated, adapted, translated, and recontextualized Orwell's *Nineteen Eighty-Four* and *Animal Farm* in order to describe a set of devices and techniques that gave a new momentum to transnationalization of Orwell's works. Chapter 3, "Transnational Literary Spaces at War," characterizes the new relations and circumstances that writers experienced after the Second World War by emphasizing the emergence of what were not simply the new modes of literary "reproduction" but new and increasingly efficient modes of "literary replication"; that is to say, a faster, more efficient, increasingly instantaneous and synchronic practice of translation, whereby an essay by T. S. Eliot might appear next to a short story by Jorge Luis Borges, not only in one single language in one single monthly but also in several languages in several monthlies. The nearly instantaneous translation of texts by George Orwell, Thomas Mann, W. H. Auden, Arthur Koestler, Ignazio Silone, Czesław Miłosz, Stephen Spender, Richard Wright, Mary McCarthy, and Isaiah Berlin, among others, into interrelated journals— *Encounter* (London), *Der Monat* (Berlin), *Preuves* (Paris), *Tempo Presente* (Rome), *Quadrant* (Sydney), *Transition* (Kampala), *Black Orpheus* (Lagos), *Jiyu* (Tokyo), and *Hiwar* (Beirut)—effectively transformed writers, critics, and intellectuals into easily recognizable, transnational figures while excluding alternative figures of particularity and dissent. I underscore the importance of the emergence of new forms of mediation that radically transformed and reoriented the relationship between writers and their publics in the interstices of the Cold War and decolonization, and elaborate on, for example, how radio broadcasting was not simply a relatively new mass mode of reproduction and one-way transmission but also a way of securing and establishing the authority, visibility, and recognition of intellectuals, public writers, and literary movements in this decisively new and historical phase of literary, cultural, and humanistic practice. The purpose of this analysis is certainly not to reduce these generic and formal effects to the endeavors of the organizations, governments, foundations, and institutions that I examine, nor is it to say the government completely administered cultural life, but rather it is to focus on what has until now been a mostly unexamined cultural and literary terrain that underwent enormous changes in the years immediately following the Second World War.

Chapter 4, "Archives of Critical Theory," returns to the subject of the political archive by examining the FBI's surveillance of Theodor Adorno and the rhetorical codes subsequently registered in texts such as Adorno and Horkheimer's *Dialectic of Enlightenment* and Adorno's *Minima Moralia*, both of which were written in exile. By placing an equal and related stress on the context of the surveillance of Adorno and the logics involved in Adorno's aversion to empirical radio research and his critique of empiricism and positivism in general in the context of his exile in the United States, I highlight the political constraints on Adorno's thought in the domestic context of anticommunism in order to emphasize that the discourse of cultural freedom advanced abroad was part of an interrelated process of censorship and surveillance at home. Having drawn on Adorno's work, in chapter 5, "Humanism, Territory, and Techniques of Trouble," I argue that Adorno advances a critical model that serves as the basis for Edward Said's negatively dialectical view of a humanism that is rooted in philology. It is in this view of humanism that I finally identify what makes *Archives* a work of investigational literary historiography that is critical to challenging the epistemological limits of the archives of authority that increasingly define the conditions of modernity.

What is being proposed in this book is the thesis that these institutional relationships between intellectuals and the state, as well as its related institutions, had a profound effect not only on the identity of a corpus of cultural work but also, as Edward Said observed in *Humanism and Democratic Criticism*, on the basis of humanist praxis. Although the government did not fully program cultural life, much of the work that was promoted abroad was the object of anticommunist hysteria and censorship at home.[38] Indeed, there is a decisive shift in the way that the idea of *Weltliteratur* was conditioned, not only by the relationships between a group of intellectuals and the institutions of anticommunism but also by the development of transnational modes of communication, translation, and transmission, which fundamentally altered the basis of literary and cultural production. If the government's manipulation of the cultural archive has partially prohibited the critical examination of the relationship between culture, the state, and humanistic practice, the responsibility of the critic and the intellectual is nothing less than the demand for democracy, for democratic criticism. This does not mean, as Alain Badiou has suggested, maintaining a distance from the state.[39] To the contrary, the place of power is empty, captured by the CIA's refusal to "neither confirm nor deny the existence or nonexistence" of the traces of it power. By revealing the gap between the emptiness of this power and the authority that exercises its hold on the void, the following chapters provide a symptomatic account of the relays of power in order to give us a better understanding of its function in the interstices of the Cold War and decolonization.

CHAPTER 2

Orwell and the Globalization of Literature

PERHAPS NO BRITISH WRITER of the late imperial period has left as deep an impression on the literary and political consciousness of subsequent generations as George Orwell.[1] His work, in particular *Homage to Catalonia*, is esteemed for its intellectual honesty and historical acuity.[2] His columns on popular culture for the *Tribune* contributed to the emergence of cultural studies in England.[3] His novels of the 1930s—*A Clergyman's Daughter*, *Keep the Aspidistra Flying*, and *Coming Up for Air*—influenced a subsequent generation of bilious and bitter male writers of the 1950s.[4] His writings on language have continued to shape many ongoing debates about the responsibilities of the writer and questions of language.[5] His colonial works and stories, such as *Burmese Days* and "Shooting an Elephant," have been taken as exemplary, liberal critiques of colonialism.[6]

Orwell's late fiction, *Animal Farm* (1945) and *Nineteen Eighty-Four* (1949), helped to define and structure Western political and cultural conceptions of totalitarianism.[7] Architects of the Cold War, such as George Kennan, have asserted that Orwell's vision of totalitarianism in *Nineteen Eighty-Four* was somehow more representative of life in the Soviet Union than the apparent reality the former American ambassador had known in Moscow. "The fictional and symbolic images created by . . . Orwell," Kennan wrote, represent totalitarianism more adequately than the Soviet picture, "as I have known [it] in the flesh." In *The Captive Mind*, Czesław Miłosz also remarked on Orwell's incisive understanding of Russian culture and politics. "Even those who know Orwell only by hearsay," Miłosz wrote, "are amazed that a writer who never lived in Russia should have so keen a perception into its life." In the *Partisan Review*, the critic Philip Rahv wrote that *Nineteen Eighty-Four* was "the best antidote to the totalitarian disease that any writer has so far produced."[8]

As John Rodden has illuminated in his two major accounts on the construction of George Orwell as a cultural icon, the author of *Animal Farm* and *Nineteen Eighty-Four* has become an entirely reified figure.[9] Beginning with Bob Dylan's "The Thin Man" (1965) and its lyrics, "Because something is happening here / But you don't know what it is / Do you, Mister Jones?," Orwell's *Animal Farm* has been adapted to almost every possible medium. The musician David Bowie composed two songs, "Nineteen Eighty-Four" and "Big Brother," about *Nineteen Eighty-Four*; the film about the futuristic dystopia, *Brazil*, was originally named *1984½*; in 2005, the

Royal Opera House produced *1984*; the libretto was written by J. D. McClatchy and Thomas Meehan and the music was composed by Lorin Maazel, who also conducted the performance. In 2009, Joe Tantalo staged a dramatic production, *George Orwell's 1984* at the 59E59 Theater in New York.[10] In 2004, a satire of surveillance programs directed by the U.S. Department of Homeland Security, *America 2014: An Orwellian Tale*, appeared under the pseudonym "Dawn Blair." Norman Podhoretz invoked Orwell's legacy to advance George W. Bush's "War on Terror" as a defensive war on behalf of Israel.[11] After the collapse of the Berlin Wall, Rupert Murdoch proclaimed that the free market had prevailed over the very kind of "totalitarian" regimes that Orwell had imagined. The former British prime minister John Major invoked Orwell as a figure who stood for the British values embodied in *The Lion and the Unicorn*.[12] *Animal Farm* was made into several films, animated cartoons, and variously performed as a musical, an opera, and even as a rock opera, in cities ranging from Jakarta to Barcelona. Orwell has become such a hackneyed figure in the United States that Tea Party demonstrators have carried placards declaring, "STOP. YOU'RE STARTING TO SCARE GEORGE ORWELL."[13]

Animal Farm and *Nineteen Eighty-Four* have been translated into more languages than many Anglophone authors of the twentieth century, including Malayalam, Telugu, Gujarati, Indonesian, Icelandic, Estonian, Latvian, Farsi, Burmese, and Vietnamese, among others. The historian Timothy Garton Ash has asserted that, "Orwell was the most influential writer of the twentieth century."[14] His neologisms—"Big Brother," "thoughtpolice," "newspeak"—though descriptive of a vastly different set of historical and political circumstances than those we face today, remain embedded in contemporary discourse, often with very little attention to or discussion of what the terms signified and concealed in a work of literature. Some critics have even justified their interpretations of Orwell's works on grounds related to their visibility. Murray Sperber concluded an essay on *Nineteen Eighty-Four* by suggesting that the success of the work was what accounted for its importance: "Orwell wanted to break through the noise and claptrap, especially government propaganda of his age, and he chose a most extreme rhetorical form as his vehicle. The success of *Nineteen Eighty-Four* validates the wisdom of his choice."[15]

Yet in the summer of 1996, Orwell's reputation came under a very different form of scrutiny than his texts had endured in 1984 over the battle of its interpretation. Under the Open Government Act, Britain's Public Records Office disclosed that George Orwell had provided the names of thirty-five "crypto-communists and fellow-travelers" to a secret unit of the British Foreign Office known as the Information Research Department (IRD).[16] While the Foreign Office maintained that these names were a matter of "state security," the disclosure nevertheless instituted a new discourse around Orwell's status as writer and intellectual: Was he complicit? Did he collaborate with the Foreign Office? Was the list of names he shared with the secret division of the Foreign Office a blacklist? If it was not intended as a blacklist, did the IRD use it as one? If so, how did it function as a blacklist? If not, how did it function at all? In what ways does it even matter that Orwell had not adhered to his own counsel that "the less truck a writer has with the state, the better for him and his work"?[17]

The discussion of the government's revelation was so one-dimensional that it had the effect of observing a prolonged tennis match. In the *Independent*, Tony Benn wrote that Orwell had "given in."[18] In the *Evening Standard*, Gerald Kaufman declared, "it turns out Orwell himself was hounding those whose thoughts did not chime in with his own."[19] The historian Christopher Hill charged that Orwell was "two-faced" and "fishy."[20] Others defended him, arguing that Orwell had neither betrayed the figures on the list nor disclosed information that was not already publicly known.[21] Peter Davison argued, "Orwell was only too well aware of the threat that some people in the intelligentsia posed for the country and the common people he loved so deeply."[22] Bernard Crick situated Orwell's collaboration in contemporary political terms, recasting the "communist" menace with the political strategy of terrorism. "It is no different from responsible citizens nowadays passing on information to the anti-terrorist squad about people in their midst whom they believe to be IRA bombers," he wrote.[23] Christopher Hitchens played down the controversy and insisted, correctly I think, that Orwell had at the very most "denied job opportunities, for anti-Moscow work, to pro-Moscow fellow-travelers."[24]

Why that knowledge took half a century to surface was hardly questioned. Indeed, the response was in some ways similar to the much more serious allegation that had arisen at the same time—that Orwell's contemporary, the Italian writer Ignazio Silone, had for years served as an informant for Mussolini's police. In 1996, two historians, Mauro Canali and Dario Biocca, had brought forward what seemed to be incontrovertible evidence that Silone, one of the several founders of the Italian Communist Party in 1921, had acted as an informant for the Italian police from 1920 to the early 1930s, even before he became a major figure of the postwar anti-Stalinist left and author of *Bread and Wine*.[25] Basing their claims upon documents that had been curiously released by the police only days before the announcement of the 1996 Silone Prize, Canali presented Silone as a remorseful and melancholic informant for Mussolini's police.[26]

In all the debates within the British press about Orwell and Silone's activities, it was interesting how little critical discussion there was of the conditions, procedures, mechanisms, and circumstances that governed the suppression of knowledge of that information in the first place. The closest one came to this line of inquiry was in a polemic with one of Silone's apologists, when Canali argued that the importance of the documents he cited was not what they demonstrated about Silone's intentions and motivations but rather "that they existed at all."[27] No one questioned why that material about Silone and Orwell took so long to come to light in the first place. Why were such "secrets" *secret*, and what interest did the state have in concealing its past affiliations with writers, particularly if Silone's *Bread and Wine* appears as an attempt to work through what amounted to his betrayal of his brother, who was in the Italian Communist Party? By engaging in these lines of inquiry, it should be said in advance that I am not at all suggesting that literature like *Nineteen Eighty-Four* is reducible to public writers' affiliations with the government or its institutions. Nor is it to promote the reevaluation, reassessment, and reconsideration of the value of literary and cultural texts in light of these disclosures. What I am suggesting is that whether or not their role as oppositional intellectuals is questioned, the forces that continue to actively manipulate the archive of possible knowledge remain an active component in our culture and society. They are powers that largely circumscribe our own procedures of investigation, inquiry, and criticism up until this day.

No better evidence of this is how after the tragic attacks of September 11, 2001, *Nineteen Eighty-Four* acquired a new valence in the face of the government's suspension of the law. There was no dearth of comparisons between the oppressive elements described in *Nineteen Eighty-Four* and the Bush administration's War on Terror.[28] The violation of rights guaranteed by the Constitution, the infractions against international law, and the secret "extraordinary renditions" of "enemy combatants" to other nations that disregarded the Convention against Torture shared a general tendency that was portrayed in *Nineteen Eighty-Four*. The flouting of the Geneva convention in the prison camps of Guantanamo, Abu Ghraib, and Bagram, where the United States has held "enemy combatants" without habeas corpus, were, as Paul Krugman writes, "all very Orwellian. But when Orwell wrote of 'a nightmare world in which the Leader, or some ruling clique, controls not only the future, but the past,' he was thinking of totalitarian states. Who would have imagined that history would prove so easy to rewrite in a democratic nation with a free press?" In the *Guardian* in 2003, Margaret Atwood wrote that she could imagine the horrors portrayed in *Nineteen Eighty-Four* occurring *anywhere*.[29]

Yet do we require a novel written in 1948 under a vastly different set of circumstances to provide a fully critical account of the present? How have we arrived at a historical moment when a novel such as *Nineteen Eighty-Four*, a work of the human imagination, structures not only our attitudes but also our points of reference to the present? Why should *Nineteen Eighty-Four* itself serve as a critique of society in lieu of an actual, critical account of the present—one that need not rely on a novel for its authority? What kind of cultural work is being done and *has already been done* to make *Nineteen Eighty-Four* readily available for political analogies between an imagined society in a work of fiction, on the one hand, and an actual, existing reality with its own complexities on the other? Has this reification of *Nineteen Eighty-Four* incapacitated our ability to provide a dissenting description of the total social process in the present? How, too, has *Nineteen Eighty-Four* become universal? And how might our understanding of the process by which that novel was repeatedly translated, retranslated, adapted into different forms, and globalized enable us to think beyond the terms of the text and provide us with a better understanding of the cultural dimensions of the transnationalization of literature at a moment when *Weltliteratur* is enlisted in the project of *Weltkultur*?[30] In many ways, these questions require that we analyze the determinants of these translation practices and ask how these particular "zones of translation" emerged. If the zone of translation "applies to diasporic language communities, print and media public spheres, institutions of governmentality and language policy-making, theatres of war," how do these zones become sites for a particular kind of cultural activity? If, as Emily Apter goes on to argue, "the translation zone defines the epistemological interstices of politics, poetics, logic, cybernetics, linguistics, genetics, media, and environment,"[31] what kind of economies of power do these zones conceal? And what do these zones reveal about the powers that constitute them as sites of linguistic exchange? In what way do these silences serve as the conditions of possibility for the realms of linguistic exchange?

Communist Crypts

For decades George Orwell's blue quarto notebook, filled with the names of 135 "crypto-communists and fellow-travelers," languished, mostly unexamined, in the George Orwell Archive in London and attracted only passing interest from the few scholars who were granted permission by Orwell's estate to examine the material. In his 1980 biography of the author, Bernard Crick, for example, made only a brief allusion to the list, writing that Orwell worried about "communist infiltration . . . and kept a notebook of suspects."[32] Many of those listed, Crick said, "are plausible as possible underground or front members, but a few seem far-fetched and unlikely."[33] A decade later Orwell's authorized biographer, Michael Shelden, speculated that Orwell was "engaged in a continuous exercise of determining who was sincere and who was not." The notebook was "primarily to satisfy [Orwell's] own curiosity," Shelden wrote.[34]

The notebook included 135 names of those whom Orwell suspected of having affiliations with the Communist Party of Great Britain (CPGB) or sympathies with the Soviet Union.³⁵ Among them, he mentioned poets such as Stephen Spender, whom he described as a "sentimental [communist] sympathizer," "very unreliable," and "easily influenced."³⁶ George Bernard Shaw was, he wrote, "no sort of tie-up, but reliably pro-Russian on all major issues."³⁷ The historian A.J.P. Taylor was "anti-American"; Isaac Deutscher was "a sympathizer"; Richard Crossman was a "political climber" and "too dishonest to be an outright f[ellow-]t[raveler]"; J. B. Priestley was "a strong sympathizer," "very anti-USA," and, noted Orwell, "makes huge sums of money in the U.S.S.R."³⁸ The Scottish poet Hugh MacDiarmid was "probably reliably pro-Russian" and "very anti-English." Cecil Day-Lewis was "not completely reliable," and the Irish playwright, Sean O'Casey, was "very stupid."³⁹

Orwell's notebook of "crypto-communists and fellow-travelers" represented "communism" in the form of various threats to the identity of English culture. He made note of the fact that the historian Isaac Deutscher was a "Polish Jew"; that Ian Mikardo, a columnist at the *Tribune*, was "silly" and "Jewish"; that the writer Cedric Dover was "Eurasian"; that Paul Robeson was a "U.S. Negro" and "very anti-white"; that the MP Konni Zilliacus was "Finnish" and "Jewish"; that the biologist J. D. Bernal was "Irish"; that Louis Adamic was "Jugo-Slav" and "very anti-British"; that Vera Dean was "Russian"; and that the French intellectual Emmanuel Mounier, author of *La Pensée de Charles Péguy* (1931), was "slimy."⁴⁰ Indeed, Orwell once wrote to his friend Dwight Macdonald that he could "smell" a crypto-communist.⁴¹ Irish and Scottish writers, such as Sean O'Casey, Liam O'Flaherty, and Hugh MacDiarmid, were recast and refashioned as communist threats. "I think we should pay more attention to the small but violent separatist movements which exist within our own island," Orwell wrote in 1946. "They may look very unimportant now, but, after all, the Communist Manifesto was once an obscure document, and the Nazi party had only six members when Hitler joined it."⁴²

From the 135 names in the notebook, Orwell drew up a more limited list of thirty-five names that he sent to the Information Research Department.⁴³ Founded by Clement Atlee's government in 1949 as a kind of cultural branch of the British Foreign Office "to devise the means to combat Communist propaganda," the IRD was unique to the Foreign Office in that its budget and its very existence was kept secret, lest its function be compromised.⁴⁴ Its mission was to assert and project Britain's power abroad—along the lines of the British Council. In a memo from 1949 that discussed how to advance the nation's authority around the world, the British foreign minister Ernest Bevin observed, "We cannot hope successfully to repel Communism only by disparaging it on material grounds. [We must] add a positive appeal to Christian and Democratic principles, remembering the strength of Christian sentiment in Europe. We must put forward a rival ideology."⁴⁵ In other words, for Britain, the Cold War demanded that the empire reorient itself to address itself to new threats and menaces to its very existence.

Although Orwell may not have known it, he effectively turned over the names to the IRD to use for whatever purposes they chose to put them to. In fact, the list was not simply an effort to recruit writers to effectively represent British interests abroad; it was part of the development of a political and cultural response to what its leadership saw as the spread of Soviet influence in Southeast Asia.⁴⁶ The list was included in a memo drafted by an MI6 official, Lieutenant Colonel Leslie Sheridan, in which the IRD's Celia Kirwan recounted her discussion with Orwell about the government's ambitions to recruit a group of writers who would promote Britain's image abroad. According to Kirwan, the IRD aimed to publicize Soviet control of the arts.⁴⁷ She said that "Orwell was delighted" to learn about the discreet efforts of the Foreign Office. She wrote, "He expressed his wholehearted and enthusiastic approval of our aims."⁴⁸

Kirwan and Orwell discussed the office's international efforts to publish books that characterized Britain's presence and dominance abroad as benign, well intentioned, and civilized. Orwell recommended his former publisher Victor Gollancz, who, along with Harold Laski and John Strachey, had established the Left Book Club and brought out Orwell's *The Road to Wigan Pier*. He also encouraged her to recruit several writers, including Darsie Gillie, the *Manchester Guardian* correspondent in Paris, C. D. Darlington, an English geneticist, and the Austrian historian Franz Borkenau, who, as so many others, had traveled to Spain to write about the civil war.⁴⁹ Orwell did not think much of the list. "It isn't very sensational and I don't suppose it will tell your friends anything they don't know. At the same time it isn't a bad idea to have the people who are probably unreliable listed," he wrote to Kirwan.⁵⁰

This list—whose contents had remained classified by the British Foreign Office until 2003—included historian E. H. Carr, the *New Statesman*'s Kingsley Martin, physicist P.M.S. Blackett, Charlie Chaplin, anthropologist V. Gordon Childe, journalist Walter Duranty, MP Tom Driberg, biologist Cedric Dover, the *News-Chronicle*'s Stefan Litauer and Ralph Parker, the *Observer*'s Iris Morley, professor of moral philosophy John Macmurray, poets Nicholas Moore and Hugh MacDiarmid, novelist Robert Neumann, Trinidadian intellectual George Padmore, publisher Peter Smollett, novelist J. B. Priestley, and the British Royal Navy commander Edgar P. Young, among nineteen others.⁵¹ The list was arranged in three columns with three headings: "Name," "Job," and "Remarks," beneath which Orwell made comments identical to those in the notebook. He added, however, that Isaac Deutscher had become a Trotskyite because of his "sympathetic view toward the Zionist movement." Orwell suggested that Deutscher could just as easily change his position again.

The idea that threats and menaces to cultural and political authority were precisely those that were concealed only to be later revealed as a knowledge and power over that open secret was at the center of the principle and expression of crypto-communism itself.[52] Its logic worked in such a way that Orwell's representation of crypto-communist needed only to repeat and give a regularity to what was already publicly known about various writers' political affiliations in order to give the anticommunist discourse its persistent, durative quality. George Bernard Shaw, for example, whom Orwell describes as "reliably pro-Russian on all major issues,"[53] had made no secret of his visit to Moscow in July 1931 on the occasion of his seventy-fifth birthday and, like many others who were inspired by the October Revolution, misrecognized the reality for the fantasy engendered by the event of 1917. Without any trace of irony, Shaw wrote that the Soviet Union had fulfilled its utopian role: "The society which has established itself and is being worked out in Russia is a Fabian society," Shaw wrote.[54] It was precisely the wish that utopia could be realized that brought Shaw to insouciantly call for the near total elimination of an entire group of human beings. "Peasants will not do," Shaw said, arguing that Stalin's policy of forced collectivization was a way of "weeding the garden."[55] There were others whose names appeared in the notebook, but not the list, who had publicly defended the fairness of the Moscow Trials. In his report to the Fabian Society on the trial of Grigory Zinoviev, D. N. Pritt wrote in a sentence devoid of evidence that he was "completely satisfied that the accused were fairly and judicially treated."[56]

Although Shaw, who was ninety-three at the time, did not make it onto Orwell's final list, J. B. Priestley, who grasped the blindness of Pritt and Shaw, did not enjoy the privilege of nonrecognition. "Shaw presumes that his friend Stalin has everything under control," Priestley wrote of Stalin's decision to form an alliance with Hitler in the Molotov-Ribbentrop Pact of 1939. "Stalin may have made special arrangements to see that Shaw comes to no harm, but the rest of us in Western Europe do not feel quite so sure of our fate, especially those of us who do not share Shaw's curious admiration for dictators," Priestley wrote after Spain had fallen to Franco.[57]

What was of broader significance, however, was that Orwell's list was an element of a global strategy to manage the anticolonial discourse abroad, particularly critical accounts that were counterhegemonic. One intellectual, George Padmore, who had resigned from the Communist Party in 1934 after it had refused to lend its support to movements for national liberation, earned both the IRD's and Orwell's attention. Padmore's essays in the magazine *Socialist Asia* had effectively criticized British colonial policy to the extent that one official called it "thoroughly offensive." Memos from the IRD to the embassy in Rangoon discussed ways to "undermine Padmore's position" or even dissuade *Socialist Asia* from printing his essays.[58] "I think it highly unlikely that the *Asian Socialist* [sic] will drop

Padmore," an official wrote, "anti-colonialism, after socialism, is their main plank." The embassy in Rangoon was sufficiently worried about Padmore's influence that it sent Morgan Phillips, the general secretary of the Labour Party, "to see whether something could be done to undermine Padmore's position."[59]

Yet many of those whom Orwell listed were not party members, and several of them may have faced travel restrictions because of the additional attention and accumulated density of information to which Orwell contributed at that time. Paul Robeson was at no point a party member, and when he offered to join the party's ranks in 1953, the Communist Party flatly rejected his application.[60] Nevertheless, the Home Office deemed him to be a "nuisance," and from 1949 onward, the office closely followed and monitored his movements throughout England.[61] Three writers—J. D. Bernal, the *Economist* editor J. G. Crowther,[62] and the novelist Louis Golding—were also denied visas to attend the Cultural and Scientific Conference for World Peace at the Waldorf-Astoria Hotel in New York City a month later, May 25, 1949. All of this is not to say that Orwell's list directly affected the lived realities of those whom he named, but that is exactly what I am saying: Orwell's list contributed to the enlargement of the corpus of evidence, the frequency of visibility, and the repetition of negative identities that sustained the practice that certain particularities and dissenting positions were not occupied without some kind of social certification.[63]

Indeed, the nature of Orwell's list made "crypto-communist" an epithet that was applicable to nearly anyone on the Left whose ideology differed from the prevailing views about how society might be organized and transformed in the future. Yet, as Orwell saw it, those who held alternative viewpoints were precisely those who had no views of their own. Ten years before Orwell shared his list with the IRD, in his essay "Inside the Whale," he portrayed the figure of the crypto-communists as having a slavish morality:

> [The Communist Party of Great Britain is] controlled by people who are mentally subservient to Russia and have no real aim except to manipulate British foreign policy and the Russian interests. . . . The more vocal kind of communist is in effect a Russian publicity agent posing as an international Socialist. . . . [The party's] long-term membership really consists of an inner ring of intellectuals who have identified with the Russian bureaucracy and the slightly larger body of working-class people who feel loyalty toward Soviet Russia without necessarily understanding its policies.[64]

The disparaging assumptions of the lack of capacity of the working class to think independently was really no different than his view of intellectuals' blindly following the Soviet Union. The latter—"the more vocal kind"—was bound to what he later called "duckspeak" (*n.— to speak words not your own; to quack like a duck*) and the former were destined to be mute, dumb figures of a passive working class that had betrayed their Englishness for Marxism. It is not an uncommon trope in Orwell's work; one finds it in *Coming Up for Air*, *Keep the Aspidistra Flying*, *Nineteen Eighty-Four*, and *The Road to Wigan Pier*. Yet, as Raymond Williams has shown, he often misrepresented the case. In Wigan Pier and other industrial towns of northern England, there *were* "decent" working-class homes, some in which he lodged and does not mention because it would have altered the text's affect. He was disposed to exaggerate the extent to which Marxism and the CPGB was advanced in the works and writings of W. H. Auden and Spender.

There was a lot more to be said about the CPGB than that it was simply an appendage of Moscow. What distinguished the CPGB was that it was notorious among communist parties for its absence of the rigidity, uniformity, and discipline that the continental parties practiced.[65] In fact, the CPGB was more of a viable political alternative than he makes it out to be. It was not a revolutionary party, but it did represent a particular bloc of workers and middle-class intellectuals who stood to the left of the Labour Party and who often voted with Labour. In comparison to the continental parties, the British party was a relatively new political formation, and the working class never posed enough of a threat to even spawn British sociology to provide a study of itself until the publication of E. P. Thompson's *The Making of the English Working Class* in 1963. Until the 1960s, Britain, after all, had never really had a Marxist or sociological tradition as had Italy, France, and Germany. It did not have a György Lukács; there was no Antonio Gramsci; not even a Max Weber, a Vilfredo Pareto, or Émile Durkheim. Instead, it had I. A. Richards, C. K. Ogden, and Hegelians like A. C. Bradley. A Marxist avant-garde never emerged, and with the exception of Christopher Caudwell and Christopher Hill, it had few Marxist writers. Instead, it had futurism: Wyndham Lewis. And it had a range of intellectuals: T. E. Hulme, John Maynard Keynes, T. S. Eliot, Bertrand Russell, and, of course, George Orwell. If it had a socialist discourse, it mostly emerged in the peculiar and historically eccentric inflection of socialism: Fabianism, not Marxism. Burke, Mill, Bentham, and Arnold had a far greater impact on British culture and politics than Marx and Engels. In Britain, "socialist theory was in general the work of men who called themselves 'Marxists,' though each understood the term in his own way," as Leszek Kołakowski has observed.[66] In this respect, as Perry Anderson has argued, England lacked a sociological tradition that could have provided a totalizing view of society.[67] Indeed, even in the 1930s, the radical concerns of that generation were taken up by poets whose views were defined not by a totalizing view of society but by an undercurrent of liberalism and a "set of external political attitudes."[68] "British culture was consequently characterized by an absent centre," Anderson writes.

The "Communist Menace"

Whatever logic can be ascribed to crypto-communism, the significance and effect of the list was how it formed and reproduced a relationship between Orwell's works and the government. Translated, published, and then distributed by the British and American governments, *Nineteen Eighty-Four* and *Animal Farm* were disseminated in a way that reflected the transfer of postwar cultural and imperial authority from Britain to the United States. This realignment entailed a discursive shift whereby resistance to colonialism was reshaped in the form of various "communist" threats and menaces to what E. P. Thompson called "the Natopolitan world."[69] Coded in a language of subversion, insurgency, and revolution, resistance was seen as part of a global communist menace. A critical element in the emerging order of Anglo-American imperialism, this rhetoric rested on an abstract, ideological threat that could be affixed to any subject who challenged its ascendancy, just as it could be used to assert its authority over subjects who did not.[70] The forces behind the new civilizing mission no longer depended on the same inflections of racial superiority as classic imperialism; instead, its Other was now described as a collective political identity that was, in the words of George Kennan, "a malignant parasite [that] feeds only on diseased tissue."[71]

In Malaya, where Britain fought a colonial war for twelve years (1948–60), the mobilizing and distorting power of British rhetoric conjured up anticommunist terms that permitted and even sanctioned the colonial power to assert its authority over the lives of subjects struggling for liberation—or at the very least, independence. Characterizing former colonial subjects as communist threats to the imperial order enabled Britain to continue to exercise its power in concert with the U.S. strategy of containing communism. In Iran, for example, the British government surmised that the United States would be willing to support the overthrow of Mohammad Mossadegh if it labeled him as an emerging communist threat to Anglo-American dominance. "The Americans are more likely to work with us if it saw the problem as one of containing Communism rather than restoring the position of the . . . [Anglo-Iranian Oil Company]," wrote one British official.[72] The IRD conflated anticolonial resistance with movements for national liberation, labeling them both as "communist." According to the IRD's Adam Watson, Britain had to invent another menace to realign its imperial aims with those of the ascendant postwar America. "It seems very dangerous to pretend that the troubles in Malaya are not caused by Communism but only by a kind of local banditry," Watson wrote, continuing:

When wholesale military operations are required to suppress mere internal unrest, it is in some way due to bad government. This is especially so in a colony; and instead of receiving sympathy and support from American public opinion in our praiseworthy struggle to combat the well known international Communist menace, we shall merely be regarded as a bad colonial power coping with rebellions.[73]

What was previously encoded as a rebellion to British colonial rule was rearticulated as an international anticommunist threat. The fact that Greece posed precisely this kind of menace only reinsured that the contest between communism and the West would also be represented as an effort to restore the foundations upon which the West reinvented itself.[74] Second, the discourse of anticommunism was a substitute for the logic and rhetoric of "decolonization," and that language, or the more widely used term among government officials—"devolution"— described a process that continued to exclude the agency of colonial subjects, the better to portray them as passive observers to their own struggles for self-determination. The discourse of devolution was, to say the least, distorted; in its historical meaning, the word could denote "[England] conceding power to a previously subservient state and people."[75] First defined in Henry Cockeram's *The English Dictionarie; or, An Interpreter of Hard English Words* (1623), "devolution" signified "a falling down." The term was then taken up by the discipline of geology to describe the "deterration" (or loss) of land by natural causes. Later, the word developed a juridical sense that involved the transformation of England's dominion over Ireland, Scotland, and Wales to indirect rule.[76] Yet devolution masked the process of decolonization, which on the one hand signified the loss of colonial territories, yet on the other implied that its subjects were products of devolution with no real agency capable of resistance, so as not to lend credibility to the idea that independence was an achievement born of human will to unmake the colonial world and remake a postcolonial one.

Yet with its etymology, unconsciously implicit in the word "devolution" itself is an entirely different form and modality of power: "revolution." Now, "revolution" did not mean the same thing as it did in the years of the French Revolution. Instead, in the context of the collective memory of the Bolshevik Revolution of October 1917, revolution was much more closely tied to the discourse of liberation. While the discourse of devolution gave British imperial power the ability to retain the density and mass of its identity as an empire, revolution signified the emergence of new threats and menaces to the global order. Expressing the corresponding fear, Carlos Romulo, the Philippine diplomat, said at the Bandung Conference of 1955, "The Empires of yesterday, on which it used to be said the sun never set, are departing one by one.... What we fear now is the new empire of Communism, in which we know the sun never rises."[77] The strategy was to avoid the implication that resistance to colonial rule was a popular movement that sought independence and was motivated by ideas of liberation. As Victor Kiernan has written, "anticommunism" became the new "civilizing mission" after the war; it was the "substitute for ... [an] earlier imperialism."[78]

While the fear of communism realigned colonial discourse in modes that were compatible with the new and emerging conditions of American postwar hegemony, the idea that communism represented a threat to these postwar alignments was founded on a set of invented assumptions. With the exception of the Soviet Union's annexation of Azerbaijan in 1948, there was, in fact, little historical or real material evidence to adduce that the Soviet Union posed a real threat to American or British authority abroad. The Comintern had been dissolved in 1943; Stalin withheld support for the Greek communists in the civil war; the United States encountered no resistance to its manipulation of Italy's parliamentary elections in 1948; there was no Soviet resistance to Franco in Spain after 1939; and the revolutionary exceptions, Yugoslavia and Greece, were not the products of Soviet interference or intervention.[79] Stalinism, in other words, was far more about the consolidation of power within the Soviet Union and Eastern Europe than an expansionist policy aimed at the territories outside of Eastern Europe.[80]

Yet the prevailing view as expressed by George Kennan in "The Long Telegram" was quite different. He saw the Soviet Union as historically defined by the "insecurity of a peaceful agricultural people trying to live on a vast exposed plain in the neighborhood of fierce, nomadic peoples." For Kennan, it was Russia's exposure to Islam in bordering countries such as Iran and Afghanistan that allowed him to personify Russian identity as conflicted and antagonistic. Kennan argued that the "political personality" of Moscow became "neurotic" and fearful of everything foreign. The Soviet leadership was not given to reconciliation and was "unmodified by any of the Anglo-Saxon traditions of compromise."[81] The idea of communism respatialized and refigured the political and cultural identity of the postwar West.

The IRD was the primary institution responsible for the process of refiguring and refashioning anticolonial threats to the putative communist menace; and of particular concern to the IRD—as well as one of the reasons they sought out Orwell—was the perception of Soviet activities throughout Southeast Asia.[82] In a report that outlined the "Communist Strategy in South East Asia," it was argued that, "the rapid advance of the Chinese Communists southwards has greatly increased the direct threat to South East Asia during the last year [1949]."[83] The report continued,

"South East Asia presented and . . . still presents a classic example of a potentially *revolutionary* situation: politically dislocated" (my emphasis). The report described Soviet leaders as unable to distinguish between the interests of international communism and the interests of the Soviet Union. It cited the communist "infiltration" of the trade union movements in Malaya, Burma, Indonesia, and the Philippines.

Part of the process of producing these communist threats entailed disseminating texts addressed to, and therefore constitutive of, those putative menaces.[84] Using the imprimatur of publishers such as Oxford University Press,[85] Penguin, Allen Lane, and Fredrick Warburg,[86] the IRD and the British Council actively promoted such intellectuals as Bertrand Russell, whose book, *Why Communism Must Fail*, was central to their endeavor to project power and authority abroad. Under the same distinguished license, the organizations disseminated essays by Richard Crossman, a Labour MP who had edited *The God that Failed*; Harold Laski, author of *Faith, Reason, and Civilization*; and Ruth Fischer, the author of *Stalin and German Communism*.[87]

THE TRANSLATION OF AUTHORITY

Orwell's activities with the Foreign Office established what became a lasting relationship between the government and his texts, such as *Animal Farm* and *Nineteen Eighty-Four*.[88] In Iran, for example, the Foreign Office's Central Office of Information hired Ali Javaherkalam, the editor of the Tehranian magazine *Hoor*, to translate and publish Orwell's *Animal Farm* into Farsi (Enqelab Hayvanat, *The Revolution of the Animals*). In India, it was behind Janamanci Ramakrishna's Telugu translation of *Animal Farm, Pasuvuladivanam: Hkalpitmamaina Peddakatha* (*Animal Farm: A Fairy Tale*). In Kerala, India, it published and distributed a Malayalam translation by Pi Rosi (*Animal pham: Oru palankatha*).[89] In Athens, it published a Greek translation; in Indochina, it published a Vietnamese one; and in Bandung, Indonesia, *Animal Farm* was published as *Negara Binatang*.[90]

On April 4, 1949, Ernest Main of the Information Department of the British Embassy in Cairo wrote to then director of the IRD, Ralph Murray, that the embassy staff was "very enthusiastic about the idea of an Arabic translation of *Animal Farm*."[91] Rodwick Parkes, an information counselor at the embassy, elaborated to Murray, "It is generally agreed that [*Animal Farm*] would have excellent propaganda value and wide popular appeal in the Middle East."[92] With the assistance of the United States Information Exchange, the IRD located a translator, Abbas Hafez, an editor of the Arab News Agency in Cairo, who had translated Winston Churchill's speeches and *War Memoirs* into Arabic.[93] The book was published by the Al Maaref

Publishing House, a major Egyptian publisher that could distribute the book throughout the Middle East—in Beirut, Baghdad, Khartoum, Mecca, Bahrain, Aden, and throughout North Africa. Illustrated by a young Armenian artist, the Arabic translation was to "contain no references to the Information Department of the Embassy or the United States Information Exchange."[94]

If the dissemination of Orwell reinscribed the process by which both the United States and Britain methodically and laboriously constructed authority in the "Third World"—itself a Cold War concept[95]—both governments did so by adapting and rewriting Orwell's work to conform to local cultural conditions. "With a skillful storyteller, one should have thought that [*Animal Farm*] could be made into a very effective piece of propaganda down to a village-audience level," an official wrote about a cartoon version of *Animal Farm*.[96] In Malaya, where Britain fought its longest postwar conflict, there was an effort to produce a less "English" version of *Animal Farm*. In Egypt, too, where British authority faced mounting anticolonial challenges to King Farouk, the IRD viewed *Animal Farm* as particularly "relevant" to conditions there. Reducing the Arabic language to Islam, Ernest Main wrote Ralph Murray that translating *Animal Farm* "is particularly good for Arabic in view of the fact that both pigs and dogs are unclean animals to Muslims."[97] Shifting the emphasis from the representations of Soviet communism and Western capitalism, the IRD illustrated the text, portraying Napoleon as an Englishman, thus conflating anticommunism with anticolonialism.[98]

The process of dissemination additionally involved the IRD's arranging for and financing cartoon strips of *Animal Farm*, featuring about ninety panels that were to appear daily over a three-month period in local newspapers in multiple countries and in a variety of languages. The IRD purchased the rights to these in Borneo and Malaya and published translations of the cartoon strip in New Delhi, Rangoon, Eritrea, Bangkok, Saigon, Caracas, Lima, Mexico City, Karachi, Ankara, Cyprus, Bogotá, Reykjavík, Rio de Janeiro, Singapore, Colombo, Ceylon, Benghazi, and Montevideo.[99] The British diplomatic post in Singapore, "considerably interested in the project," translated these strips into Chinese, Vietnamese, Malay, and French for distribution throughout Southeast Asia.[100] In Mexico City, the cartoons were published in *La Prensa*; in New Delhi, in the *Times of India*; in Burma, in the *Nation* and *Bamakkhit*; and in Colombo, they were translated into Tamil and Sinhalese.[101]

While the encoded meaning of the various adaptations could not be decided in advance and had multiple valences in different cultural contexts, the texts themselves enabled the authorities to make certain subjects visible in new ways. After translating and distributing *Animal Farm* into the countries' vernacular languages, embassy staffs pored over newspapers and magazines to identify writers whose reviews of *Animal Farm* differed from the so-called official version. In Ankara, Bangkok, Montevideo, and Rangoon, the IRD asked its embassy staff to examine where and in what form the text produced any "resentment among Communists," not only in order to be able to identify them as possibly subversive subjects but also to identify these subjects as communist ones.[102]

In one memorandum the authorities expressed their concern that while *Animal Farm* did not necessarily have the ideological effects the government supposed it would have, its intentions of constituting anticommunist colonial subjects could be counted on to make communist subjects visible and identifiable in their reviews of the text. While the possibility of misreading was an occasion to produce other adaptations of other works that conformed and adhered more closely to the semiotics of local and indigenous cultures, the United States deployed Orwell's work as a means of controlling and extending its political, economic, and, to a lesser extent, cultural authority. In postwar Japan, which was under U.S. military occupation from 1946 to 1952 as part of the Potsdam Accords, U.S. authorities faced a vibrant and growing labor movement, which by February 1947 had posed a formidable resistance to the new terms of American economic domination. "Assisted by the intensifying food and employment crisis throughout 1946, and spearheaded by Korean and non-Japanese subjects, unions organized on an immense scale and prepared a united front for a general strike in February 1947," writes Masao Miyoshi.[103] "Although it began with the Supreme Commander of the Allied Powers' [SCAP] blessing and ended with SCAP's alarmed intervention, still it was as close as Japan ever came to [a] worker's revolution."[104]

With hopes of disciplining and containing the sentiment of the working-class movement, the American authorities adapted *Animal Farm* in the popular form of a *kamishibai*, hanging scrolls composed of thirty-three large, colorful, cartoonlike panels that narrated an abbreviated version of Orwell's satire. Under the auspices of the Civil Information and Education branch of the U.S. Army, these *kamishibai* were exhibited in corporations, factories, government offices, and in the headquarters of more than forty labor unions, including the Hitachi Electrical Workers Union, the Gunma-Ken Teachers Union, the Takasaki National Railway Workers Union, and others.[105] Exhibited prominently in the reconstructed factories, they were intended to control the labor movement by providing a significantly altered and abbreviated adaptation of Orwell's fable for Japanese and Korean workers. The pigs were represented as superior to humans. "We are troubled by the animals of lower classes, similar to you human beings struggling with labor problems," Napoleon declares.[106]

The effect of situating this version of the fable was that it dehumanized the workers as animals. To manage and administer Japanese working-class culture, the United States often never ceased to offend and create the conditions for resistance. In a report on "Reactions over the Showing of *Animal Farm*," an official wrote, "The theme of the play was expressed in animal terms. This, from the standpoint of the workers, is very unpleasant, because workers were represented by animals such as sheep, horses, and pigs. It is hard to understand why labor officials showed such a picture.... [Some workers] thought it meant [they] must get rid of [the] labor bosses."[107] As one historian has written, much of what the United States did during its occupation reflected its belief in an "old prewar, anticommunist authoritarianism."[108]

The American and British worldwide publication campaigns structured and further consolidated the relationship of Orwell's text to the government. As the IRD's Adam Watson wrote, the Orwell campaign was a means of keeping Orwell "in the picture." During the summer of 1949, though debilitated physically by tuberculosis, Orwell devoted his failing energies to arranging other similar agreements and projects with the IRD and the U.S. government. He communicated with the IRD about a Russian translation of *Animal Farm* and other initiatives involving *Nineteen Eighty-Four*, which had been published to widespread acclaim in June 1949. In August, he assembled a list of the completed translations of *Animal Farm* and submitted it to the IRD to enable the department to pursue similar projects with his more recent work. "I enclose three copies of the Telugu translation of *Animal Farm*," Orwell wrote to his agent, Leonard Moore, in a letter about the IRD plans for a similar translation of *Nineteen Eighty-Four*.[109] Although Orwell died of tuberculosis in January 1950, the process that he had helped to initiate and to which he gave momentum continued to develop and expand long after his death and with his estate's permission.

Few books in the history of English literature enjoyed such a rapid diffusion into as many languages as *Animal Farm*. By 1955, the rights to Chinese, Danish, Dutch, French, German, Finnish, Hebrew, Italian, Japanese, Indonesian, Latvian, Norwegian, Polish, Portuguese, Spanish, and Swedish translations had been procured by the British government. Rights for the Burmese edition were obtained, and, through the Orient Publishing Company in Hong Kong, Britain arranged for an illustrated Chinese edition as well.[110] Before Orwell died, he was certainly aware of the dubious political uses to which *Animal Farm* could be put. In 1946, a Portuguese publisher in Lisbon, Livraria Popular de Francisco Franco, published a translation by Almirante Alberto Aprá entitled *O Porco Triunfante (The Triumphant Pigs)*.[111] Unsettled that his publisher was tied to Franco's government, Orwell was apparently willing to overlook publishing in Salazar's Portugal, but certainly not with a press that had direct ties to a government that he had personally fought against. "I could not consider letting ... [Livraria Popular de Francisco Franco] have the book if they have any connection with Spanish fascists," Orwell wrote to Leonard Moore on November 9, 1945. "It could do me a great deal of harm in this country if it got out, as it would. I know of course that Portugal itself has a semi-fascist regime and censorship of books must be pretty strict there, but it is a different matter to be definitely used as propaganda by Franco's lot."[112]

A Dutch newspaper that serialized *Animal Farm* had political ties to a reactionary and right-wing organization. Orwell wrote to Moore, "As to the Dutch publication of *Animal Farm*, I enclose a rather alarming letter from the publishers, which you might perhaps deal with. I am sure I don't know what arrangements we made about serialization, but if anything irregular is happening, do please try and put a stop to it. As to the paper which is serialising, it being 'reactionary,' I don't know that we can help that. Obviously a book of that type is liable to be made use of by Conservatives, Catholics, etc."[113]

However, Orwell was most actively engaged in making particular arrangements with the British and American governments and various groups of exiles to get *Animal Farm* published in the Soviet Union. Of particular concern to Orwell was the distribution of Ihor Ševčenko's Ukrainian translation of *Animal Farm* (*Kolhosp tvaryn*). For that translation, Orwell took the time to write his important (and only) preface to *Animal Farm*, which is revealing in its description of the particular experience from which the story arose. Yet although the preface survives as an essential account of the fable's origin, crates of Ševčenko's translation of *Animal Farm* never reached their intended destination in the Soviet Union. Five thousand of them were seized by the American Military Government in Munich and unwittingly turned over to the officials of the Russian Repatriation Commission, who with little doubt appreciated the American military's vigilance.[114] In spite of this failure, the IRD encouraged Orwell to find a way to make *Animal Farm* available in the Soviet Union. "I am trying to pull a wire at the Foreign Office to see if they will subscribe a bit," Orwell wrote Moore in July, describing his effort to get the IRD to arrange for the translation, publication, and distribution of *Animal Farm*.[115] And it seems Orwell's cooperation with the IRD and the Foreign Office was reciprocated.

On June 24, 1949, the Information Research Department sent a communiqué to *Possev*, a magazine edited and published by Russian émigrés. The editors of *Possev* had wanted to bring out *Animal Farm* in a Russian translation by Gleb Struve,[116] a professor of Russian literature at the University of California at Berkeley. *Possev*'s editor, Vladimir Gorachek, wrote Orwell:

> It seems desirable to publish *Animal Farm* in book form and issue it through the channels that we have in Berlin, Vienna, and other towns of the Soviet Occupation zones, whence, as has been proved in practice,

Russian literature percolates into the ranks of the occupation army and through it into the USSR. We ask you please to not think that this letter has been sent to you with any mercenary motives, but exclusively in the interests of the cause of combating Bolshevism, which the cause of your book [*Animal Farm*] serves so brilliantly.[117]

By assuring him that his work would appear in *Possev*, the IRD in effect supported Orwell's relationships to other publications subvented by the government. On July 18, Kirwan wrote to Jack Brimmel, an official in the IRD, saying, "If *Animal Farm* does get through to the USSR, as *Possev* claims it would, I am sure it would be most effective and eagerly sought after."[118] In a letter to Orwell, the IRD reassured him that *Possev* was "reliable."[119] The government subsequently arranged for the distribution of *Animal Farm* through various organizations, including, most significantly, the U.S. Army, which published the magazine *Der Monat* in Germany. On July 20, Orwell wrote Moore, "It occurs to me that the American army magazine *Der Monat* . . . might be a convenient way of financing the Russian translation of *Animal Farm*."[120] Eight days later Orwell received word from the British Foreign Office that it could not finance the Russian translation. Orwell wrote Moore, "I have heard from the F[oreign] O[ffice], who of course won't help to finance the Russian translation of *Animal Farm*. . . . We can use them for help to distribute a Russian edition of *Animal Farm*, or at least for printing it. Would you arrange with [Melvin] Lasky of *Der Monat* to hold over some Deutschmarks in case they are needed for this purpose?"[121] On September 21, Orwell wrote *Der Monat*'s editor, Melvin Lasky, directly: "A Russian paper in Limburg called *Possev* has recently serialized *Animal Farm* in a Russian translation, and are now printing an edition in book form. I told Moore to ask you to pay the required amount directly to the *Possev* people."[122]

The affiliation between Orwell with Lasky and *Der Monat* was instrumental in developing a cultural strategy with the United States, and in particular, with agencies and departments such as Voice of America, the U.S. Information Agency, the State Department, and the CIA.[123] The first translations of *Nineteen Eighty-Four* were serialized in *Der Monat*, which later was to become the model for a whole series of transnational magazines, such as *Encounter*, *Preuves*, *Tempo Presente*, and many others—all of which were published by the CCF.

The serialization of *Nineteen Eighty-Four* in *Der Monat* spurred the development of an entirely new kind of transatlantic cultural formation. On November 4, 1949, Celia Kirwan wrote the director of the Voice of America, Charles Thayer, that the Foreign Office was in the process of translating *Nineteen Eighty-Four* into Italian, French, Swedish, Dutch, Danish, German, Spanish, Norwegian, Polish, Ukrainian, Portuguese, Persian, Telugu, Japanese, Hebrew, Bengali, and Gujarati.[124] Also in 1949, in Korea, the

American military published a Korean edition. In Japan, the U.S. Military High Command oversaw the transfer of royalties from Keisuke Nagashima's Japanese translation of *Animal Farm* (*Dōbutso nōjō*) to the British Embassy. U.S. Army colonel E. C. Miller Jr. wrote the head of the Bank of Japan requesting the "transfer [of] ¥14,120 from the Custody Account for Supreme Commander for the Allied Powers' Book Translation Program to the Hong Kong and Shanghai Banking Corporation for credit of [the] United Kingdom Liaison Mission and charge this to the account of George Orwell."[125] In 1951, the U.S. secretary of state Dean Acheson wrote that works like *Animal Farm* and *Nineteen Eighty-Four* "have been of great value to the Department in its psychological offensive against Communism."[126]

As a result of these transatlantic agreements and accommodations, official adaptations of *Animal Farm* and *Nineteen Eighty-Four* became immensely important to the process of developing new modes through which American authority could be exercised abroad. The Office of Special Projects (OSP), the CIA division that administered the CCF, was charged with the task of developing the cultural content of what had come to be known as "psychological warfare," the intention of which was to expose the "vicious activities of the USSR." Among the OSP's first cultural initiatives was its involvement in the production, rewriting, and distribution of the 1955 feature-length animation of Orwell's *Animal Farm*. Produced by Louis de Rochemont, a Hollywood director who had directed one of the first documentary films of the 1930s, *The March of Time*, Orwell's satire was widely acclaimed in official circles as politically and culturally relevant to furthering the aims of the cultural Cold War. "It seems to us that it would not be difficult to concoct a script embodying local touches which might provide an alternative means of making people aware of this ... very effective piece of political satire," the IRD wrote of *Animal Farm* to its posts in Baghdad, Jakarta, Cairo, Rangoon, Asmara, and Tehran.[127] The film was directed and animated by John Halas, a Hungarian, and Joy Batchelor, a graduate of the London School of Art. Though they later directed several popular television series, such as *The Addams Family* (1973), *The Lone Ranger* (1966), *The Osmond Brothers* (1972), and *The Jackson Five* (1971), as well as several corporate films for oil companies like ESSO, Royal Dutch Shell, and British Petroleum,[128] the two artists had had considerable experience working for Britain's Central Office of Information during the Second World War. They directed more than one hundred films during the war, mostly documentary animations, including the *Dustbin Parade* (1941), a navy recruitment film; *Filling the Gap* (1941), an exhortation to boost domestic agricultural production; and *Abu's Pointed Well* (1942), a wartime propaganda animation that was aimed at audiences in Egypt, Palestine, Iran, and Iraq.

Reviewing the conclusion of the Halas-Batchelor script, the Office of Special Projects, which was then administered by the CIA, found it "confusing" and "nebulous," and, under pressure from Louis de Rochemont, revised the emphasis of Orwell's critique and depicted the animals as revolting against the figures of Stalinist repression.[129] De Rochemont was receptive to the CIA's suggestions and in August arranged a viewing of the film at the CIA's headquarters. De Rochemont shortly thereafter sent a telegram to Borden Mace to reschedule the screening of the substantially revised ending, in which the farm animals rebel against the pigs. Halas and Batchelor's *Animal Farm* (1955) was revised to conform to the ideologically and methodically elaborated structures of the Cold War. The text's emphasis on Orwell's critique of both capitalist and collective forms of production was altered to exclusively emphasize the brutality of communist repression.

Both the British and U.S. governments pursued what amounted to a global campaign to give the film the widest exposure. To ensure the scope of the film's visibility, the IRD intended to "show the film in all our colonies on as wide a scale as possible."[130] Indonesia, Burma, Siam, India, Ceylon, Pakistan, and Indochina "presented an ideal audience for Orwell's warning."[131] To complement the dissemination of the film, the IRD saturated the colonies with cartoon strips to which it bought rights in Cyprus, Tanganyika, Kenya, Uganda, North and South Rhodesia, Sierra Leone, the Gold Coast, Nigeria, Trinidad, Jamaica, Fiji, British Guiana, and Honduras.[132] In the United States, the American Committee for Cultural Freedom made a concerted effort to ensure that *Animal Farm* reached the widest possible audience, particularly among the working class. It sold discounted tickets to the United Auto Workers Union and scolded the management of New York's Paris Theatre for failing to promote the film's "anticommunist message." Sol Stein wrote, "If for no other reason than in respect for George Orwell's memory, would you not agree that the public ought to know that this is a great anti-totalitarian film? The neglect of this factor in the promotion for the film is not quite understandable to us, especially in view of public concern about the threat of Soviet totalitarianism, and we wonder if there is any special reason why Orwell's vigorous indictment of our enemy should not be described as such."[133] The American Committee for Cultural Freedom, whose board included Daniel Bell, Sidney Hook, and Dwight Macdonald, placed and arranged for editorials in New York newspapers to ensure that the rewritten message remained.[134]

TRANSLATION AND MODES OF DOMINATION

Orwell's participation and collaboration with the IRD helped to establish, reproduce, and even to consolidate the relations through which his own writings were translated, adapted, and, above all, transmitted abroad. Never before in the history of literature had a work of contemporary writing been so rapidly translated in ways that fundamentally reshaped what Pascale Casanova, in *The World Republic of Letters*, called "the world literary space"—a territory of texts circumscribed by institutions, academies, awards, and, most important, the social and cultural function of the translator, who helps to consecrate and authorize certain texts at the expense of others.[135] According to Casanova, the translator operates like a foreign exchange broker who is responsible for exporting and importing texts whose literary value is determined through the act of exchange.[136] Translators, she writes, are the "great intermediaries" who possess the "immense power[s] of consecration."[137]

Yet translations of *Animal Farm* and *Nineteen Eighty-Four* belong to a different historical mode of literary and cultural production than to the modernist period. The laborious and painstaking work of translators such as Valery Larbaud before the war was, after 1945, supplemented by the emergence and development of entirely new modes of increasingly efficient and immediate translation. The changing means of textual reproduction and duplication now administered by government agencies, institutions, foundations, media corporations, and international organizations made it increasingly possible to replicate mechanical copies of texts in multiple languages in distant and remote places, nearly instantaneously, for the first time in literary history.[138]

The postwar development of what Edward Said called "new and efficient modes of articulation,"[139] thus came to occupy and dominate the global public space along radically different lines. Newly organized and collaborative endeavors among governments, international institutions, organizations, and foundations were not only part of the shifting imperial alignments from Britain to the United States, but they also engendered a process that dramatically changed the conditions of humanistic praxis, restructuring and refashioning the relationship between the writer and the public. An entirely new phase in the history of literature was established, and the reputation of internationally recognizable authors such as Faulkner, Orwell, Miłosz, Eliot, Albert Camus, and Ignazio Silone were shaped by this transnational transmission and translation of their texts.

Yet the transmission of texts was not simply about the values for which they were thought or intended to stand. Whether or not Orwell's *Nineteen Eighty-Four* was *received* as it was *intended* must not be the criteria by which the process of creating global literary figures is to be assessed or examined. Instead, emphasizing the relationships between the new means of reproduction, duplication, and replication enables us to comprehend both how Cold War culture was dominated, regulated, and controlled and how the power of transmission functioned to allow the British to transfer their imperial authority to the United States and to continue to dominate territories, minds, and public spaces without an actual colonial or physical presence.¹⁴⁰ It is often overlooked, for example, that Walter Benjamin's famous remark that "There is no document of civilization which is not at the same time a document of barbarism" was followed by the observation that "barbarism taints also the manner in which it was transmitted from one owner to another."¹⁴¹

To examine texts for their *inherent, essential,* or *universal* values alone is to devalue the tremendous power of the social means through which those values are maintained; to disregard the means of literary reproduction, transmission, and translation is to reinforce the very illusions that conceal the process by which a culture reproduces itself and ideas about itself and others. In *Cultural Capital,* John Guillory makes the following critical observation: "If canonical works do not all by themselves reproduce cultural values, it is significant—even integral—to the real social process that they are *thought* to do so. The real social process is the reproduction not of social relations. These relations consist of much more than a relation [between the] text and [the] reader."¹⁴²

These processes of cultural transmission and the development of multiple means of articulation reinforced an epistemic regime that had registered *Nineteen Eighty-Four* within the framework of the ceaseless war between totalitarianism and democracy. An epistemic *deformation,* "totalitarianism"—like "Islam," "Terrorism," or "the West"—"each possesses [its own] styles of polemic, batteries of discourse, and an unsettling profusion of opportunities for dissemination."¹⁴³ In the interstices of the Cold War and decolonization, newly developed techniques of articulation reproduced a dominant set of social relationships that reinforced itself against ongoing emancipatory challenges to it in the postcolonial world. In the broader context of these new global configurations, the investigation of these specific types of practices offer an inventory of the forces that played a critical role in providing the conditions not only through which imperial authority was transferred from Britain to the United States but also the mechanisms through which the idea of world literature was managed and administered in the context of postwar American hegemony.

CHAPTER 3

Transnational Literary Spaces at War

THE SUN NEVER SETS ON THE BRITISH WRITER

THE DIFFERENCES BETWEEN British colonial rule and U.S. imperialism were for the most part structural. Often described as an empire without a major colony, the United States exercised its postwar hegemony through brute force—military interventions, coups, and covert operations in support of groups whose interests coincided with, or did not completely threaten, the articulation of American power abroad.[1] In contrast to the European powers prior to 1945, the United States never depended entirely on the practices of direct colonial rule, even though there were several notable exceptions to this in places such as the Philippines, Puerto Rico, Cuba, Panama, and the Dominican Republic. In the aftermath of the Atlantic Charter of 1941, the transfer of imperial authority from England to the United States entailed the development of new strategies and methods of domination that substantially transformed the conditions through which the public writer addressed their audiences. The public function of the writer had changed with the development of new and more efficient modes of articulation, as the new basis of imperial authority brought about a shift in the modalities of imperial rule.

The development coincided with the emergence of new strategies of control and mediation. The establishment of the British Council in 1934, which, as Douglas Coombs has shown in *Spreading the Word* was related to the emergence of the transnational publishing industry, provided universities and schools in the emerging neocolonial world with English textbooks and the work of British authors (T. S. Eliot, Virginia Woolf, John Galsworthy, Joseph Conrad, William Butler Yeats, and George Bernard Shaw) as a way of at least maintaining the institutional and educational practices that had been consolidated in the nineteenth century. In 1935, R. A. Leeper, an official in Britain's Foreign Office, reported that "the establishment of English libraries ... would be the best possible way to spread the English language and a better understanding of British life and culture."[2]

Then chaired by poet laureate John Masefield, the British Council's board grew to include the publisher Stanley Unwin, who helped to develop a set of commercial arrangements with major British publishers to ensure and negotiate translations and copyrights throughout the colonial and emerging neocolonial world. By 1939, the British Council had developed significant holdings in Cairo, Alexandria, and Baghdad, and later expanded its operations in Jamaica, Nigeria, and throughout Latin America, ensuring at the very least the continued circulation of English literature and criticism abroad. The "Panel of Book Selectors" included the literary critic Ivor Brown, who authored *Contemporary General Literature*, and Daniel Jones, a linguist who had written extensively on English phonetics and pronunciation. The council published short introductions to a culturally dominant group of writers. To name a few, Stephen Spender's *Poetry since 1939* summarized the New Signatures movement; Rex Warner revived an interest in E. M. Forster; Edmund Blunden wrote a short book on John Keats; Herbert Read did one on Byron; and John Lehmann provided one on Edith Sitwell. John Hayward wrote *Prose Literature since 1939*.[3] The council copublished works, such as Bernard Lewis's *British Contributions to Arabic Studies*,[4] as a way of reinforcing and maintaining power amid growing anticolonial pressure.[5]

Reterritorializing the entire geography of postcolonial space, the council extended and maintained Britain's cultural domain by sending writers or books—or, as in the case of E. M. Forster, the authors' recorded voices —to places they would not ordinarily visit as representatives of English literature, culture, or language, or as writers for that matter. By the beginning of decolonization, the spaces that the council occupied were extensive. It opened offices in Kenya in 1947, Malawi in 1950, Malaysia in 1948, Pakistan in 1948, Sri Lanka in 1950, and India in 1948. The council's library system was the most extensive in the world.[6] At the end of 1956, there were ninety-five libraries in fifty-seven countries, containing about 900,000 volumes and about 10,000 periodicals.[7] The cultural presence of the council assumed many forms: institutes, centers, libraries, pamphlets, novels, poetry, manuals, magazines, auditoriums for conductors and symphonies, and spaces for exhibitions. The Sound Department of the council recorded a talk by E. M. Forster to accompany the exhibition of a large model of an Elizabethan theater that was installed adjacent to a display that provided a history of "Shakespeare in the British Theatre"[8]—all to ensure that the English culture maintained its value in what was then East and West Pakistan; or, at the very least, that England retained its imperial identity in order to exert its authority in countries it no longer directly controlled. Writers were sent to improbable places abroad where some, such as V. S. Pritchett, worried that the council was dramatically redefining the relationship between the British writer and the new transnational space the writer came to occupy. "It has become almost impossible for the English intellectual to travel abroad unless he gets on to one of the 'culture buses,'" Pritchett wrote in the *New York Times*. T. S. Eliot evinced concern over the council's commonalities with the planned economies of Eastern Europe. "[Culture] cannot be planned," he wrote, "because it is also the unconscious background of all our planning."[9]

Writers were essentially transformed into representatives and cultural emissaries—not an insignificant process for the writers themselves, however capable they were of discerning and even resisting the inherent problems of representing the entirety of a national culture. The experience abroad established different structures of attitude and frames of reference to the world; it made available new spaces that were semiofficial. Eliot, whose authority was consolidated by his eighty-three radio broadcasts on the BBC's *Third Programme*,[10] worried that these cultural arrangements would subject the writer to new pressures from the government. In "The Man of Letters and the Future of Europe," he wrote:

> There are other matters over which the man of letters should exercise constant time, and here surveillance: matters which may, from time to time, and here and there, present themselves with immediate urgency. Such are the questions which arise in particular contexts, when the freedom of the man of letters is menaced. I have in mind, not merely questions of censorship, whether political, religious or moral: my experience tells me that these issues must be faced as they arise. I have in mind also the dangers which may come from official encouragement and patronage of the arts; the dangers to which men of letters would be exposed, if they became, in their professional capacity, servants of the State.[11]

While in many cases the sending of writers as emissaries explicitly involved an intertwining of culture and power, the more salient point was that these changing conditions of cultural practice belonged to a shift in the modalities of cultural transmission, in which culture could be mobilized, possessed, and articulated. At times, these literary expeditions and adventures utterly baffled the public abroad. Robert Lowell had to be retrieved from Latin America before he caused further diplomatic damage to the cause. Faulkner, though he would exert a lasting influence on writers like Gabriel García Márquez, was by all accounts not suited for cultural diplomacy. As R. P. Blackmur observed:

> Many American authors, professors, intellectuals, add shame without apparently knowing it to their reputations among foreigners by speaking under the American aegis in as much contempt as ignorance of their audience, as much indifference to their own abilities as insolence to others. To hear a great man garble himself is a hard thing, to hear second-rate men garble and repudiate every assumed responsibility is shameful. I have heard Americans let down their audiences in a dozen countries, and I have heard, not always but often, their American sponsors express themselves as either content or ignorant that the speakers had done so. I

suspect that soon our foreign audiences will regard this misbehavior as a normal American corruption, a mere jobbery of intellect; and they will be right.[12]

Blackmur wondered what his thirty-minute broadcast on the subject of the New Criticism had to do with efforts to "combat neutralism" in Nagano, Japan.[13] What Blackmur's experience abroad did provide him with, however, was an occasion to later reflect on the new postwar functions of the American intellectual at home. In his essay "The Logos in the Catacomb," he came to recognize that the specific phenomenon in which he participated was part of a more general, structured set of practices that had placed new kinds of limitations on the American intellectual. The territories and fields that intellectuals occupied involved metropolitan modalities of articulation and different impingements that consolidated and redisposed the discourse of neutralism and anticommunism. Government support reinforced the general idea that the writer need not be concerned with speaking directly on issues of political substance, nor was he or she socially sanctioned to do so. Speaking on the radio to the people of Nagano, Japan, about the subject of the New Criticism became a means, he wrote, of "shoring up American imperial identity" to such an extent that one might have thought "that some empire . . . had been falling, where the emergencies or salvage were thought to include the New Criticism."[14] If his talk on the New Criticism helped to maintain a division between politics and art, the experience enabled Blackmur to express a sharp awareness that "Logos" was "in the catacomb."

Following the Second World War, when the United States occupied the positions previously held by Britain and France, the development of new imperial strategies were largely refashioned against various "communist" threats. Most of these methods of control and management were developed in their initial phase in the form of transatlantic and transnational relationships between critics and various organizations such as the Ford and Rockefeller Foundations, the latter of which played an immensely unsettling and subversive role in Latin America, as Jean Franco has written,[15] but also included the subventions of literary periodicals, journals of opinion, and a set of imperial arrangements that were evident in the invention by C. K. Ogden and I. A. Richards of Basic English ("British American Scientific Commercial English"), an auxiliary language of English consisting of no more than eight hundred words to ensure that linguistic differences would not pose a barrier to trade in the aftermath of decolonization.

Foundations—such as the Rockefeller and Ford Foundations—were quick to see the changing political alignments as opportunities to reshape and give a direction to the humanities.[16] In 1945 John Marshall, the associate director of the humanities division of the Rockefeller Foundation, met with T. S. Eliot in London, along with F. R. Leavis and Herbert Read, to explore ways to reinforce and sustain the corpus of English literature.[17] In 1947, the Rockefellers financed the Princeton Seminar in Literary Criticism (later named after Christian Gauss), which aimed to address, as Robert Fitzgerald wrote, "the substructures of tradition [that] had been laid bare for the United States to take account."[18] In a series of seminars that Blackmur arranged, scholars such as Erich Auerbach, Francis Fergusson, Jacques Maritain, Randall Jarrell, Herbert Read, Leo Spitzer, and René Wellek discussed Mann's *Doctor Faustus* and Dante's *Inferno*, because, as Fitzgerald recalls, "circumstances in the world at large appeared to demand a certain centering, grounding, and girding up."[19]

In order to mediate these new postwar realities, numerous magazines and journals appeared that were transnational in scope and circulation.[20] Often covertly supported by the U.S. and British governments, as well as overtly by the Ford and Rockefeller Foundations, these journals all shared a focus that extended beyond the domestic and national spaces. Through the CCF, the CIA published journals such as *Cuadernos* in Latin America, *Encounter* in London, *Preuves* in Paris, *Hiwar* in Beirut, *Jiyu* in Tokyo, *Der Monat* in Berlin, *Tempo Presente* in Rome, *Transition* in Kampala, *Quadrant* in Sydney, *Quest* in Mumbai, and *Solidarity* in Manila.[21] What distinguished these journals from their predecessors—literary periodicals like *Nouvelle Revue Française* (Paris), the *Neue Rundschau* (Berlin), the *Criterion* (London), the *Revista de Occidente* (Madrid), *Il Convegno* (Rome), and many others—was that their emergence reflected and reinforced the formidable structures of cultural domination.[22] Indeed, the cultural energies behind the little magazine, which shaped the private, individual styles of modernism, had become exhausted by the end of World War II. Even before hostilities erupted across Europe, Eliot's *Criterion* had stopped publishing in 1939; John Lehmann's *New Folio* lasted from 1940 to 1941, and his *New Writing and Daylight* ran from 1942 to 1946. Eugene Jolas's avant-garde *transitions*, which had published James Joyce's *Anna Livia Plurabelle*, stopped publishing in 1938, only to resume in 1948 under a different editor, Georges Duthuit, who published numerous translations by Samuel Beckett. British publishing quotas and the wartime paper rations ran other magazines aground. The one major publication to survive the war was Cyril Connolly's *Horizon*, which went under in 1949. *Horizon* published Orwell's "Boys' Weeklies" and his "Raffles and Miss Blandish." A sign of the shifting alignments of power, the 1947 edition of *Horizon* featured solely, for the first time, contributors from the United States: writers including Delmore Schwartz, Clement Greenberg, Alan Tate, and Randall Jarrell. But by the early 1950s, C.L.R. James lamented the end of a particular historical phase of writing.[23] The elimination of publications with more limited circulation, of course, led to the further standardization of thought.[24] In the *Hudson Re-*

view, Geoffrey Wagner described the "flattening of the periodical audience" in England.[25] There were, of course, exceptions to this, but even those were short-lived. In the summer of 1950, *Nine*, edited by Peter Russell, published the Pound-Eliot correspondence on *The Waste Land*.[26] *Arena*, one of Britain's first transnational magazines, emerged in 1949, but it ceased publication in 1952. Edited by Jack Lindsay and Randall Swingler, *Arena* brought together writers that included Pablo Neruda, Albert Camus, E. P. Thompson, Tristan Tzara, Paul Éluard, Hugh MacDiarmid, and Louis Aragon. By the early 1950s, the publishing opportunities narrowed considerably and would consolidate in entirely new ways. "Our current periodical literature has been marked, in the last year, by certain important changes. *Scrutiny* has ended publication; *London Magazine* and *Encounter* have begun," Raymond Williams wrote in 1954 in the journal *Essays in Criticism*.[27]

Among the most important of these new assemblages of transnational magazines to emerge out of this crisis in 1953 was *Encounter* magazine—a London-based magazine that was conceived of and financed by the CCF.[28] Coedited by Stephen Spender and Irving Kristol, *Encounter* was among the twenty-one transnational magazines (such as *Der Monat*, *Preuves*, and *Tempo Presente*) that were also published internationally and in near synchrony by the Paris-based CCF.[29] One of the most powerful and organized cultural institutions of the Cold War established by the CIA through the National Security Council directive NSC-10, the CCF mobilized the literary energies behind *Encounter* and its other organs to dominate and control what was widely seen as the endless, global competition between "freedom" and "totalitarianism."[30] If the United States perceived those intellectuals who took neither side in the Cold War as among the more pressing menaces facing Anglo-American ascendancy, these publications contributed to the changing conditions of humanistic practice—a Cold War discourse whose vocabulary was replete with its own supply of metaphors and metonymies, combative discourses, and styles of thought, for which the CCF afforded multiple opportunities for their dissemination through any number of its magazines, societies, conferences, clubs, or institutes.[31] Although *Encounter* was published in London, the composer Nicolas Nabokov and the secretary-general of the CCF viewed the magazine as "aimed primarily at the Far East, where neutralism is the strongest force."[32] The director of the CCF, Michael Josselson, a CIA agent and the only one who presumably knew the nature of the CCF's connections to the CIA, wrote to Stephen Spender that the magazine's primary aim was to address the so-called "communist and neutralist problem."[33] The publisher who printed the magazine on behalf of the CCF remarked "that *Encounter* is uniquely trying to do a job of the maintenance of Western culture against all forms of totalitarianism."[34]

As one of the first transatlantic magazines—with one editor housed in New York and the other in London—*Encounter* mixed the subjectivism of Bloomsbury with the anticommunism of such New York intellectuals as Mary McCarthy and Leslie Fiedler. Yet its contributors did not dwell on the subject of anticommunism, nor did it place an explicit emphasis on the absence of the autonomy of the Eastern European or Soviet writer. *Encounter* published few American writers, lest it be seen as a mouthpiece for the United States or the source of its CIA funding be revealed. Indeed, it was more interested in constraining cultural discourse and controlling what could be and could not be said about the United States than it was in providing a serious critique of the absence of cultural freedom anywhere. Its inaugural issue, published in October 1953, began with a very brief account of the uprising of East German workers in June of that year, alongside a selection of pages from Virginia Woolf's diary, which was included to suggest *Encounter*'s emphasis on a shared and inherited tradition tied to Bloomsbury. Yet it was a tradition that was oddly juxtaposed to a vastly different postwar reality of treason and the atom bomb—an essay by Leslie Fiedler on the execution of Julius and Ethel Rosenberg, who, Fiedler argued, were celebrated for a radical cause that they in no way embodied. In the same issue, Denis de Rougement was "Looking for India" and presumably found it. It included Cecil Day-Lewis's poem "Pegasus," Alberto de Lacerda's "Lake," and two poems by Edith Sitwell. Christopher Isherwood's short story, "In the Head of a Leader," portrayed the initial enthusiasm of the communist intellectual Ernst Toller in the 1930s and went on to represent his eventual disenchantment by the end of that decade. It translated and reprinted an early essay by Albert Camus about an Algerian town that served merely as a backdrop for his elaboration of existentialism. Stephen Spender wrote a spirited defense of American diction, and the historian Hugh Seton-Watson reviewed K. M. Panikkar's classic *Asia and Western Dominance*, insisting that nationalism was a "Western concept," and that it arrived ready-made in Asia.[35] There was no mention of American racism or imperialism, and the few articles it later published on subjects such as the Bandung Conference were to ensure that the relationship between the movements for national liberation in Africa and Asia and the civil rights movement in the United States remained obscure. As Mary Dudziak has argued in *Cold War Civil Rights*, the hierarchies of race and the structures of racism did anything but weaken the Communist Information Bureau's (Cominform) critique of American expansion, especially after W.E.B. DuBois took the initiative at the United Nations to charge the U.S. government with crimes against humanity for slavery.[36]

When certain writers were permitted to contribute to any one of the CCF's publications, it was to maintain the existing structures of attitude and reference. In *Encounter*, which was devoted to the subject of "Literature, Arts and Current Affairs," Isaiah Berlin wrote on Vissarion Grigoryevich Belinsky, but not on Grigory Yevseevich Zinoviev. Robert Graves wrote on Sor Juana Inés de la Cruz. The CCF published letters from D. H. Lawrence to Samuel Koteliansky, the business manager of John Middleton Murray's magazine the *Adelphi* and a friend of Leonard and Virginia Woolf's. On the whole, the magazines published by the CCF ensured that only certain writers were socially certified to comment on political affairs. It rarely censored its writers, because for the most part, it did not need to do so; their positions were chosen in advance. It would publish Albert Camus, not Jean-Paul Sartre; Richard Wright, but not Frantz Fanon, C.L.R. James, or W.E.B. DuBois; Wole Soyinka, but not Derek Walcott; Edith Sitwell, but not Doris Lessing; Isaiah Berlin, but not Charles Taylor or C. Wright Mills; Lionel Trilling, but not John Berger; Hugh Seton-Watson, but not Eric Hobsbawm, Christopher Hill, or V. G. Kiernan; Tosco Fyvel, but not Konni Zilliacus; Raymond Williams, but not E. P. Thompson; W. H. Auden, John Wain, and Dylan Thomas, but not Christopher Logue, Nicholás Guillén, or Nâzim Hikmet. That it would publish someone like Raymond Williams (1921–88) and not E. P. Thompson (1924–93) suggested something of the magazine's rarity. Yet there were distinct differences between the two. Williams wrote in a very different kind of political register. Furthermore, Williams, at the time, was still writing within the orbit of Leavis, whereas Thompson, who remained in the Communist Party until 1956, started the *New Reasoner* with John Saville in the aftermath of the Soviet Union's invasion of Hungary.[37]

What was critical about the power of the CCF over a whole corpus of thought was that it effectively and comprehensively prevented, or at the very least manipulated in complex ways, the emergence of alternative and dissenting discourses. When the CCF explicitly interfered in editorial matters, it would censor its own editor for his negative portrayal of the United States. Shortly after Dwight Macdonald stepped down as the American co-editor of *Encounter*, he submitted an article to *Encounter* entitled "America! America!," which inveighed against popular culture in the United States, stressing its vulgarity, its "lack of style," and its "ugliness."[38] America, he wrote, was "shapeless"; it did not have the form or national character that defined, for example, the English. He saw American culture as homogenized and leveled to the extent that everybody was "equal" in the sense that "nobody appears to respect anybody else unless he [sic] has to." This self-interested and self-serving individualism was, he argued, ill-suited to fulfill the demands and so-called responsibilities of the American imperium. "Americans," he wrote, seem to be "more gross and sentimental, immature and tough, uncultivated and hypocritical." Alluding to John Foster Dulles, he described the American diplomat as a figure who appeared civilized on the surface but was brutish in his actions. "I can deal with gangsters or with Boy Scouts," he wrote, "but I admit that I am at a loss with Boy Scouts who act like gangsters."

According to Macdonald's account, which was published in *Dissent* with the original essay, the CCF demanded that the article be removed from *Encounter*, lest it unsettle its American benefactors at the Farfield Foundation. The irony that the CCF, which putatively advanced the cause of cultural freedom, would censor its own editor was apparently lost on its leadership. Norman Birnbaum took the occasion to write an "Open Letter to the Congress for Cultural Freedom":

> The Congress for Cultural Freedom has for some years been lecturing the intelligentsia on the indivisibility of freedom. It's right: freedom is indivisible, it has to be fought for on issues large and small, and extended against a hundred dogmatisms and petty tyrannies—not least apparently those of its self-appointed champions.... It talks liberty, and then acts as if liberty consisted in the recognition of Mr. Dulles's necessity.[39]

Of course, the CCF did not impose conformity, though there were many who viewed *Encounter* as anachronistic and a lifeless reenactment of prewar writing. Its silence on certain subjects allowed many to come to the conclusion that it had nothing to do with cultural freedom but was more interested in consolidating an international bloc of Natopolitan intellectuals. In the *Hudson Review*, a magazine initiated by two of Alan Tate's former students at Princeton in 1947, Geoffrey Wagner summarized the critical reception of *Encounter*'s first issue:

> In *World Within World*, Spender confesses to having been a card-carrying member of the Communist Party, though attempting to whitewash the action; this information is totally redundant after a glance through the first issues of *Encounter*. So wholly were the critical articles in the first issue of this magazine devoted to drop-the-bomb-now liberalism that Cyril Connolly, in *The Sunday Times*, and Philip Toynbee, in *The Observer*, and the lead writer of *The Times Literary Supplement* (possibly Alan Pryce-Jones), all independently protested against *Encounter*'s preaching to the converted. Connolly thought Leslie Fiedler's essay on the Rosenbergs a "gloating account," while looking back over the first four issues Philip Toynbee found them obsessed by "obsessive literature." *Encounter* hit back in the Editorial to Number 4, signed by Irving Kristol, indicting *The Times Literary Supplement* with fellow-traveling, with "one of those unwitting, familiar concessions to Communist ideology," and this in turn Toynbee called "depressingly reminiscent, this, of the Communist pugnacity, which assumes that all who are not with me must be enemy

agents." As for the creative side of *Encounter*, with its Woolf diaries, Yeats letters, and so on, even Connolly admitted that the literary section of Number 1 "might well have appeared about 1938."[40]

A similar recrudescence was evident in John Lehmann's *London Magazine*, which published works by Eliot, Bowen, MacNeice, and Rex Warner—writers who had, Toynbee said, "come to their literary maturity twenty years ago."[41]

Yet *Encounter* was one element of the several transnational practices available to ensure that the structures and available modes for cultural domination remained an active component in the persistent regulation of which public writers would be mobilized for transnational consumption and which ones would be denied access to the multiple opportunities afforded by the CCF. As one mode in the sustained effort to negate the achievements of the historical avant-garde, which had made the institutionalization of art apparent as a process,[42] *Encounter* must be seen in the wider framework of its relation to a transnational assemblage of journals, of which it was only one part. What distinguished CCF's magazines from their precursors was that their emergence reflected a set of transnational practices of translation and recognition that was an inherent part of consolidating and maintaining control over political discourse.[43] The assembly of magazines developed the modes of articulation, as well as what Foucault describes as "the modes of circulation, valorization, attribution and appropriation."[44] This group of journals not only retained its identity as a corpus and gave a density to the separation between aesthetics and politics but at the same time structured the domain of transnational culture so that certain writers more than others would become recognizable as "world" literary figures by their established relationship to others. In other words, it was not their mere visibility and presence in different languages and different places that counted, but the relationship of their presence and proximity to other authors that seemed to matter; their authority was established as a relation.[45] "The bait that *Cuadernos* offered to Latin American writers was a readership outside the boundaries of their national communities," writes Jean Franco. "Their work was published in the same journal as 'world' writers, such as Thomas Mann, Benedetto Croce, and Upton Sinclair."[46]

In this respect, the role that translation plays in consecrating literary authority is, in this period at least, much less esoteric than Pascale Casanova's analysis would suggest. While Casanova is certainly on solid ground to claim that the translation of, for example, the Argentine Jorge Luis Borges and the Serbo-Croatian writer Danilo Kîs into French established the conditions for their literary consecration, it is by no means enough to say that what she calls their *littérisation* (the transcription or translation of a text into a dominant language) sufficiently explains why their works acquired the prestige of literariness. We must also take into consideration the fact that literary value is relational, and that culture works by instituting discriminations, hierarchies, and divisions of inclusion and exclusion that are at the same interrelated, interdependent, and intermingled, and not divisible into watertight categories such as the "major" and "minor" characteristics of language.[47] What I am concerned with, in other words, are the institutional and disciplinary mechanisms and techniques through which power and cultural authority get redisposed, and by whom or by what and on whom they get dispersed within the transnational domains of writing.

The improbable juxtapositions and "worlding" of writers such as Rulfo and Mann were not restricted to the endeavors of *Cuadernos* but extended to the entire consortium of magazines that the CCF published worldwide in a new kind of transnational space with different national arrangements and alignments. In its inaugural issue, *Preuves* published essays by Jorge Luis Borges (Argentina), Bertrand Russell (England), and Franz Borkenau (Austria). *Encounter* also made oblique juxtapositions with its selections. In its second issue it published fourteen letters by Yeats to his father; a travel essay by Rose Macaulay on the "Pleasures of Palaces"; articles by the Italian intellectual Nicola Chiaromonte; the German philosopher and son of Thomas, Golo Mann; the Indian novelist Raja Rao; and Stephen Spender on "Literary Movements."[48] The West German magazine *Der Monat*, which was the first magazine to serialize George Orwell's *Nineteen Eighty-Four*, published selections from Faulkner's novel *A Fable* adjacent to Czesław Miłosz's "Murti-Bing" in one issue,[49] and Faulkner, Benedetto Croce, and Arthur Koestler in another.[50] In 1954 *Preuves* published Richard Wright ("Deux portraits africains"), Roger Caillois ("Socialisme et militarism"), Richard Lowenthal ("La secession du proletariat"), Lionel Trilling ("Sur Bouvard et Pécuchet"), Niccolò Tucci ("Les vandals de la Voie Appienne"), Julian Gorkin ("Le 'drame de l'Amérique' et l'expérience du Guatémala"), and Hugh Seton-Watson ("L'Empire colonial soviétique").[51] What was significant about these juxtapositions was not their mere presence, but the projected affiliation among writers: Wright (African American, United States), Caillois (France), Trilling (United States), Tucci (Italy), Gorkin (Spain), and Hugh Seton-Watson (England).

Their techniques of distribution permitted groups of national writers to reach new international audiences with regularity, consistency, and apparent variety. It subsequently brought about a historically decisive shift in the alignment between the writer and the public. For the first time in literary history, the process of immediate translation and rapid circulation was part of the changing conditions of literary and cultural production and transmission. Establishing affiliations with writers from France, Argentina, England, Japan, Germany, Lebanon, India, Australia, Nigeria, Kenya, and Mexico, the CCF rendered these relations and affiliations visible in multiple languages in a wide array of magazines simultaneously and in concert with one another. Its transnational activities introduced a whole set of differently aligned relationships that effectively rearticulated a historically specific idea of world literature.[52] The process that the CCF administered, managed, and sustained thus marked a definitive historical phase of intellectual and humanist practice. Yet at the same time, on the surface, the idea of world writers appeared to be undergoing a major upheaval, partially as a result of the expansion of the transnational magazines of politics and culture: *Preuves, Tempo Presente, Encounter, Der Monat, Cuadernos*, and others already mentioned. Together, these journals made visible, in all the European languages, a group of writers, intellectuals, and critics who seemed to represent the best of contemporary thought in their national traditions. Their appearance and reappearance marked a significant stage in the history of literary and cultural production. Not only did the various organs of the CCF help to consecrate writers through the sheer repetition and translation of their work, but they invented and regularly reconstructed affiliations between writers in multiple languages and incorporated others, thus conferring related authority onto those whom it published and reprinted in numerous locations, which afforded the writer opportunities to occupy multiple positions at the same time.[53] A central feature of this strategy was to establish both cultural capital and legitimacy through the regular appearance of writers such as Raymond Aron, W. H. Auden, Isaiah Berlin, Albert Camus, Cyril Connolly, Nicola Chiaromonte, Richard Crossman, Leslie Fiedler, Tosco Fyvel, Arthur Koestler, Melvin Lasky, Herbert Lüthy, John Lehmann, Salvador de Madariaga, Golo Mann, Ignazio Silone, Stephen Spender, Herbert Read, Hugh Seton-Watson, Philip Toynbee, and Lionel Trilling—all in order to maintain a new kind of dominance over them by publishing their work on certain subjects and not on others.

The Time of Translation

The magazines as a whole had largely relied on technical innovations that enabled the essay, short story, poem, and generic "Letter from Abroad" to not simply be mechanically reproduced but *replicated synchronically*; that is to say, a faster, more efficient, increasingly instantaneous practice of translation, whereby an essay by Thomas Mann might appear next to work by Juan Rulfo, not only in one language in one monthly but in several languages in several publications at the same time.[54] Never before had there been an active *transnational imaginary* articulated in quite this way. The initial forms of simultaneous translation belonged to the juridical domain: the Nuremberg Trials in 1945 and later to the United Nations General Assembly. Among one of the most remarkable and historically original achievements of the CCF, however, was its ability to translate and *replicate* articles in its wide array of journals almost simultaneously in multiple languages, which established not only a hold over what could or could not be said but over the mediated passage of essays from one language to several or multiple ones. It also controlled the flow of authors and texts inside and outside the languages in which they were published. If translation was once a slow and time-consuming specialty, practiced patiently by figures such as Valery Larbaud, postwar technical innovations in printing and distribution dramatically altered the conditions of cultural transmission. Essays from *Encounter*, *Preuves*, *Tempo Presente*, and others were translated and retranslated into different languages and distributed from multiple sites of transmission. The Korean journal *Sasangge*, for example, reprinted essays from *Der Monat*, *Preuves*, and *Jiyu*. This structured and established new hierarchies for the production and reception of so-called world writers, who in many ways no longer knew exactly for whom they were writing.

What this meant was that the passage of an essay from one language into another was no longer subjected to older rhythms and forces of reproduction; the accelerated transmission of essays and the short story meant that there were newly efficient ways of respatializing world literary time. T. S. Eliot's work, for example, was translated into Arabic and printed in *Hiwar* (*Dialogue*) in Beirut alongside the work of the Palestinian poet Tawfiq Sayigh, who later translated Eliot's *Four Quartets* into Arabic. In its first issue, *Hiwar* published an essay by Albert Hourani on Taha Hussein that was simultaneously printed in *Cuadernos* and *Preuves*.[55] Not only was the replication of the monthly essay affected by the changing conditions of cultural practice but various institutions coordinated the strategy and procedures of transmission in often complex and circular ways. Wole Soyinka's drama, *Dear Parent and Ogre*, was first produced by the Mbari Writers Club (which was supported by the CCF), reviewed in *Transition* (a CCF magazine edited by Rajat Neogy), and then promoted in *Encounter* magazine, which had introduced Soyinka to its readership by previously awarding a literary prize to *The Dance of the Forest*. Further aggregating Soyinka's reputation, it awarded an accolade to *Dear Parent and Ogre* on the occasion of Nigeria's independence. The self-reflexive, self-aggrandizing, and self-serving activities of the CCF saturated and subsequently shaped the limits of a whole generation of postcolonial Anglophone writing in Africa. In this respect, the CCF was most effective in fashioning the discourse in the developing world, particularly in Africa, where it had established ties to *Black Orpheus* in 1957, and several years later to *Transition*. The ramification of these modes of appearance and articulation were critical in Africa and the Caribbean: "The function of periodicals in nurturing the new literatures of Africa and the Caribbean cannot be overstated. They represent necessary documentary proof of fashion and growth. Their function is not so much to preserve as to link. Often they stand at the very beginning of the development of local literature, setting up standards and providing a literary market for buyer and seller."[56] Yet the way this literature was assigned value was through processes of constraint. Fanon apparently had witnessed the process itself: "As soon as the native begins to pull on his mooring and to cause anxiety to the settler, he is handed over to well-meaning souls who in cultural congresses point out to him the specificity of Western values."[57]

Established partly in response to the emergence of *Présence Africaine* in Paris, *Black Orpheus*, which was named after Sartre's essay on *négritude*, made the works of Aimé Césaire and Léopold Sédar Senghor available for the first time in English. "In London the names of Césaire and Senghor barely are known," Janheinz Jahn (a translator of Césaire and Senghor) reported in *Black Orpheus*. "In countries like Nigeria, Ghana or Jamaica they have not been heard of, although their writings are full of meaning and significance for the peoples of those territories."[58] *Black Orpheus* introduced a whole range of African, Haitian, and Cuban writing to English readers. It translated the work of Léon Damas, the Cuban writer Nicholás Guillén, Aimé Césaire, Léopold Sédar Senghor, Felix Tchikaya U'Tamsi, Flavien Ranaïvo, and Jean-Joseph Rabearivelo. In many respects, *Black Orpheus*, and later *Transition*, was a way to regulate, sanitize, and co-opt the literature of decolonization, as it would publish these writers on certain subjects and not others.

"Soon enough," Wole Soyinka recalls in his memoir,

> we would discover that we had been dining, and with relish, with the original of that serpentine incarnation, the devil, romping in our postcolonial Garden of Eden and gorging on the fruits of the Tree of Knowledge! Nothing—virtually no project, no cultural initiative—was left unbrushed by the CIA's reptilian coils. The first All-African Congress of Writers and Intellectuals in Makarere, Uganda, after the winds of independence blew across the continent, had been sponsored by the Congress for Cultural Freedom and *Encounter*. The same source infiltrated *Transition* magazine, the pioneering journal of ideas in postcolonial Africa, under the editorship of an East African Indian of Brahmin extraction, Rajat Neogy. That a certain U.S.-based Farfield foundation, which lavishly expended its resources on the continent's postcolonial intellectual thought and creativity, was a front for the American CIA![59]

London Calling

With the postwar expansion of new occasions for transmission and translation, as well as the emergence of new forms such as the "radio magazine," the relationship between the writer and public underwent further transformations that would decisively expand and constrain cultural space. Working for the East Indian Division of the BBC, Orwell produced a series of radio talks from 1941 to 1943. Entitled *Voices*, the radio program brought together a group of Anglophone writers to read and discuss their poetry and prose on the air. In London, the BBC's *Third Programme*, which began broadcasting in September 1946, performed a critical function in establishing a dominant culture and community, thus securing the reputation of Isaiah Berlin and T. S. Eliot as public figures and intellectuals. Isaiah Berlin, for example, delivered numerous addresses on the BBC's *Third Programme*. T. S. Eliot was broadcast on more than eighty occasions on the *Third Programme*, for which he recorded his British Academy lecture on Milton.[60] Edward Sackville-West speculated that the *Third Programme* would become "the greatest civilizing force England has known since the secularization of the theater."[61] What was significant about these institutions is the way that they appeared to inadvertently interact and overlap with the CCF and the various organizations it had established in London, Paris, Berlin, New York, and Rome. The first comptroller of the BBC's *Third Programme*, Herman Grisewood, served as the treasurer for the British Society for Cultural Freedom; Michael Goodwin, the secretary of the Society for Cultural Freedom, was the editor of the *Twentieth Century*, the successor to the *Nineteenth Century and After*, among one of the first publications that the CCF sponsored before it launched *Encounter* in 1953.

This is not to say that these coincidences were anything more than a conjuncture of power and authority. They were more significant in that they constituted new and effective techniques of articulation that transformed a fundamental relation between the writer and the public, the writer and the private, and the writer and the world in dramatic ways. "In 'Poetry and the Microphone,'" George Orwell observed, "millions may be listening [to the radio], but every one is listening alone."[62] If radio transformed the relation between the writer and the public, the concepts of private and public would undergo changes as well. "The authority of radio increases the more it reaches the listener in his privacy," Adorno writes.

> The more strongly this voice is coming from the personal sphere of the listener and the more it appears to stream from the cells of his intimate life, the more he has the impression as if his own cupboard, his own phonograph, his own bedroom were speaking to him as a personal friend or enemy: the more perfectly he is ready to accept *in toto* whatever he hears. His own sphere of existence becomes the messenger of the outside world. His privacy at the same time sustains the authority of the radio voice—because it is "his" apartment, a language of which he cannot escape—and helps to hide it by making it no longer appear as if it were coming from the outside.[63]

This historical and technical development of radio profoundly altered the conditions of literary practices, authorship, and culture in the newly reconstituted sphere. Indeed, during war, many of the British writers of the generation who came of age in the 1930s had the formative experience of writing, producing, and editing for the BBC, its World Service, its East Asian service, and its Indian service, or working for the Ministry of Information. William Empson, for example, held a post in the Eastern Division of the BBC. Isaiah Berlin, who was later to play a crucial role in shaping the ideology of the CCF, worked for the Ministry of Information. Spender reported for the Foreign Office's Political Intelligence Department, and later joined the historian Noel Annan at the Allied Control Commission in Germany. The historian Hugh Trevor-Roper worked for British Intelligence. The translator Arthur Wiley and Cecil Day-Lewis served for the Eastern Division of the Ministry of Information. Louis MacNeice worked for the BBC.

Their participation with these institutions left a lasting impression on them, and would in many respects shape and help to define their view of institutions of power and authority from which they were excluded prior to the war. That this was the generation of intellectuals who had shared the collective experience of disappointment, disillusionment, and disenchantment in the 1930s—a generation that saw the defeat of the Spanish Republic, witnessed the sham of the Moscow Trials, and felt betrayed by the Hitler-Stalin Pact—only accentuated the meaning of these structures of cultural transmission. The aftermath of the Second World War witnessed the ascendance of writers such as Stephen Spender, Ignazio Silone, and Arthur Koestler, who were culturally charged with reasserting and reinforcing their disenchantment with communism, which made anticommunism a persistent and ironic source of political renewal. Although Spender, Koestler, and Silone would play important roles in the 1950s as intellectuals and members of the CCF, there were major discrepancies between their experiences and the expressions of those experiences in literary form. Both Koestler and Silone wrote about their political encounters with communism in novels such as *Darkness at Noon* and *Bread and Wine*. Spender, however, had provided no such account of his involvement in the Communist Party of Great Britain, save for the essay he wrote for the collection of *The God that Failed* and a mention of it in his autobiography, *World Within World*. Unlike Spender, Koestler and Silone's experiences were shaped by their membership in European communist parties that were illegal and had gone underground in countries where fascist governments were already in power. Spender, however, had no such political experience, save for his two years in the Communist Party, which he joined solely, it seems, to defend the Spanish Republic.

The coadunatory forces that were crucial to their transnational positions after the war concerned their attitude toward—and in many ways their representation of—the United States. Spender had come into the fold of anticommunist intellectuals largely through his writing an editorial in the *New York Times* that claimed that "We Can Win the Battle for the Hearts and Minds of Europe."[64] Spender's essay announced that there was a vast cultural divide between the United States and Western Europe, which exacerbated the cultural anxieties and insecurities of a group of American intellectuals who perceived that the United States lacked the cultural authority to manage and administer the postwar settlement, and assume the role of a superpower. "Even the most disaffected intellectual must nowadays respond, if only by way of personal interestedness, to the growing isolation of his country amid the hostility directed against it," Trilling wrote. "He had become aware of virtual uniqueness of American security and well-being, and, at the same time, of the danger in which they stand. . . . He now also responds to the fact that there is now no longer any foreign cultural ideal to which he can possibly fly from that American stupidity and vulgarity, the institutionalized awareness of which was once the mainspring of his intellectual life."[65] As Trilling suggested, American popular culture and the United States' distance from the rest of the world would undermine its imperial mission. At a symposium organized in 1952 by the *Partisan Review* on the subject of the American intellectual's attitude toward the United States, Trilling asked, "Where in American life can artists find the basis of strength, renewal, and recognition, now that they can't depend upon Europe as a cultural example?"[66] While Trilling also thought that America's identification with European culture was largely responsible for the diffusion of Marxism in the United States, other intellectuals were bent on inventing cultural strategies to contest European hostility to American culture. Articles in the *Partisan Review* and a number of books appeared that lamented Europe's anti-Americanism and America's lack of imperial culture.[67] The philosopher Sidney Hook warned that "the French public, by and large, is shockingly ignorant of American life and culture." Hook feared that

> [France's] picture of America is a composite of impressions derived from reading the novels of social protest and revolt (Steinbeck's *Grapes of Wrath* is taken as a faithful representative account), the novels of American degeneracy (Faulkner) and inanity (Sinclair Lewis), from seeing American movies, and from exposure to an incessant Communist barrage which seeps into the non-Communist press. The informational re-education of the French public seems to me to be the most fundamental as well as most pressing task of American democratic policy in

France, towards which almost nothing along effective lines has been done.[68]

Hook was concerned that Europe's perception of America had been undermined by the novels of Faulkner, Steinbeck, and Lewis. The philosopher James Burnham argued that it was precisely American identification with Europe that gave the West the power and identity to recognize itself as the antithesis of communism. In *What Europe Thinks of America* (1953), Burnham wrote, "There is no surgeon skilled enough to cut Europe and us apart," Burnham continued. "If Europe dies, then we will not have long to live. Alone before a massed world of alien civilizations armed, organized and aroused to absolute hostility by Bolshevism, we would soon be crushed and absorbed."[69] The appeal of Spender's editorial was that he wrote of the need to affirm the values of American culture in Europe, warning that postwar Europe had grown cynical and defensively divided between the two superpowers. He urged that the United States "take part in showing Europeans its greatest contemporary achievements in education and culture." Spender's rhetoric of incorporation provided a means to sustain the discourse of intellectual freedom and, at the same time, provided the United States with an imperial identity that was based on the United States' integration with "the West, not as a politics or a strategy, but as a civilization."[70]

Unable or unwilling to work through the inconsistencies, contradictions, and failures of the 1930s, writers like Spender, Koestler, and Silone suddenly found themselves socially sanctioned to comment on politics as they once had done under entirely different, marginal conditions. The public positions the war had made available to them introduced them to new mechanisms of transmission and different means of cultural redistribution, which permitted them, with the assistance of various government agencies, to redispose a discourse of anticommunism. Collections like the CCF's *The God that Failed*, which included contributions by Stephen Spender, Richard Wright, Ignazio Silone, Arthur Koestler, André Gide, and others, provided a collective account of the emergence of this new political formation of writers, critics, and scholars whose identities and positions in culture and society depended on the repeated assertion of the failure of their former ideals. Their cultural authority strangely rested on the discourse of confession, a kind of assimilation into a dominant culture that found it much easier to imagine the outbreak of nuclear war than alternatives to the persistence of the discourse of anticommunism.

Yet Richard Wright's position in this formation in many respects lies outside the boundaries of the shared kind of experience to which the other contributors to *The God that Failed* belonged. Although Wright, like the other contributors, had been a member of the Communist Party, he left the party for its failure to organize and mobilize against the structures of racial discrimination. From 1947 until his death, Wright lived in a kind of exile in Paris, where he not only escaped the escalating racial violence in the American South, but developed important, though critical affiliations with a group of African and Caribbean intellectuals who had advanced the cause of "*négritude*"—figures such as Léopold Senghor, Alioune Diop, and Aimé Césaire, who saw in *négritude* the possibility of reviving a precolonial African past that had not been distorted and silenced by European colonialism. Although Wright grew increasingly critical of the movement's essentialism, he played a crucial role in encouraging Sartre to lend his support to their journal, *Présence Africaine*, largely to protect it from the French laws that made it illegal to speak or write on behalf of Algerian independence.

Yet Wright's involvement with the CCF was ambiguous, and there is little doubt that the leadership of the CCF exploited him for both his writerly gifts and identity. In 1955 he was commissioned by *Encounter* to report on the Bandung Conference in Indonesia, a historically decisive moment that brought together representatives of the nonaligned nations of the Third World. In "What Africa Means to Me," he wrote in *Encounter* that Africa was not a meaningful source of his identity because it never provided him the concrete terms by which he could account for the experience of his existence. "My problem," he wrote, "was how to account for this 'survival' of Africa in America when I stoutly denied the mystic influence of 'race,' when I was as certain as I was of being alive that it was only, by in large, in the concrete social frame of reference in which men lived that one could account for meaning being what they were."[71] In this respect, his association with the anticommunist ideologies was far more complex than the narratives of confession of Koestler, Silone, Spender, and others who were unable to work through the failure of a radical politics to bring about new forms of community, belonging, and social change. Indeed, the appearance of *Présence Africaine* largely prompted the CCF to initiate coverage of African writing in journals such as *Transition* and *Black Orpheus*, which would not only publish writers such as Césaire and Senghor into English for the first time, but would also, over time, manage and administer the visibility of certain African writers like Chinua Achebe and Wole Soyinka.

LITERARY DIPLOMACY

In December 1947, only several months after the communist parties of the Soviet Union, Hungary, France, Italy, Poland, and Yugoslavia established the Communist Information Bureau (Cominform), the National Security Council issued a directive (NSC-4) calling for the "Coordination of Foreign Information Measures,"[72] in order to counter the "vicious psychological efforts of the USSR, its satellite countries and Communist groups [that sought] to discredit and defeat the aims and activities of the United States and other western powers."[73] Shortly thereafter, the U.S. Congress drafted legislation of its own, the Smith-Mundt Act, which expressed the need for "the preparation, and dissemination abroad, of information about the U.S., its people, and its policies, through press, publications, radio, motion pictures, and other information media, and through information centers and instructors abroad . . . to provide a better understanding of the U.S. in other countries and to increase mutual understanding."[74]

Critics such as R. P. Blackmur, novelists such as William Faulkner, and poets such as Robert Lowell were subsequently recruited, mobilized, and exported in a historically decisive way that altered the situation of the transnational postwar writer and his or her public.[75] The effect of these movements and influences was by no means nugatory. In many cases, their texts opened up the realm of new possibilities that had, until the arrival of their work, been utterly unimaginable. As Jameson says, "The phenomenon of influence or imitation . . . simplify a very complex process, namely the way in which an event, a text, a concept, in a distant and sometimes utterly marginal land, can suddenly open up new possibilities in a domestic situation in which such possibilities had been hitherto literally unthinkable and unimaginable. We may say that the immense worldwide influence of Faulkner was of this kind, whose work suddenly showed writers all over the world that you could do something else with land, deep memory, defeat, and historical passion."[76]

In 1945 John Marshall of the Rockefeller Foundation commissioned R. P. Blackmur to examine the effect that the culture industry had on the identity of English literature. In his report on "The Economy of the American Writer," Blackmur observed that "there is no country in the world in which there is at this time, or likely to be in the future, either a dominant class or dominant institutions which assert a high aesthetic value against either the market system or its evident successor, the monopoly system."[77] What undermined the division between high and low culture was the international expansion of the culture industry, the expansion of American markets, that country's films, and its commodities in service of what he called the New Illiteracy. Blackmur's concerns were part of a larger set of fears he attributed to mass culture. In 1947, Eliot observed that even the "humblest material artifact . . . is an emissary of the culture out of which it comes."[78] Yet Blackmur was less concerned with this early phase of globalization than with the threat to the very divide between high culture and "illiteracy" culture—a division that he saw as central to the identity of the so-called West. The very maintenance of that distinction was what was at stake in the imperial contest. For Blackmur, the New Illiteracy not only involved the expansion of the culture industry beyond the United States, but it meant that the dictates of imperial conquest would further weaken the great divide at home. Describing the erosion of English, he lamented how popular culture "was spreading the greatest damage to the available fund of general intelligence.... Thus we get the Franklin Press going to the Arab world with the products of our own illiteracy.... Thus we find the United States Information Service in Tel Aviv competing against Russia with the Tarzan books as an indicator of the American way of life and all its superiority to the Russians, who came bringing Tolstoy."[79]

In response to these pressures, which were exerted by an increasingly transnational culture industry, the Ford Foundation recruited James Laughlin, the former editor of *New Directions*, to edit *Perspectives USA*. Developed "in part as a response to the sense of isolation the American artist feels, separated as he is by the *oceans* from an important section of his *natural* public" (my emphasis),[80] *Perspectives USA* represented its aims in largely Arnoldian terms and refashioned its interests as a defense of the best that has been known and thought. "If we publish good American writing and still fail," wrote Hayden Carruth, a poet and one of *Perspective USA*'s editors, in a letter to Lionel Trilling, "then it is either because good American writing is not good enough (which I should be distressed and surprised to find out), or because the foreign reader himself is too pig-headed to accept good writing even when it is readily accessible."[81] What passed for "good American writing" was structured by the very idea of what was "foreign" and other to American culture. "We have all agreed that we will do nothing to select or tailor our contents simply to meet what we fancy to be the foreign susceptibility, we will give them only what we think is good American writing. But the foreign reader is the reason for our existence," continued Carruth.

The effects that these cultural expeditions had on the structure of attitudes cannot be underestimated.[82] Blackmur, for example, who guest-edited *Perspectives USA* alongside Lionel Trilling, Jacques Barzun, and Perry Miller, described the activity of literary criticism in the rhetoric of endless horizons, and a limitless, yet unsettled modernity: "Not an inch measure, nor a yardstick, but a compass bearing: the focus of scope, great enough initially to absorb any amount of attention, wide enough eventually, one thinking, to command a full horizon," he writes.[83] If Blackmur described the changing field of the critic's disposition in metaphors of a "full horizon"—one that extended to Egypt and Lebanon—he describes the experience of this "horizon" as if he were hearing the polyphony of languages. He recalls editing the pages of *Perspectives* in Italy, England, France, Egypt, and Lebanon as he listens to "the sound of foreign thoughts and tongues whirring in the ears." The excursion abroad brings with it "alien modes of thought and idioms of expression impossible of intimacy echoing just at the threshold of perception."[84] He "reads [the] proofs of different articles in different cities with the buzz of different tongues in the ear."⁸⁵ The shift in experience is not just a development of a new mode of movement, experience, and expression, but, for Blackmur, a critical category: a new way of living, a modus vivendi from which "spring the values of the intellect—like poppies in the Italian wheat field or anemones in Lebanon."⁸⁶

This new structure of experience, and the attitudes attached to it, was inextricably tied "to a sense of American responsibility for the world after the dismantling of the old imperial structures."⁸⁷ Blackmur was trying to make coherent sense of a new reality, however alien, strange, and unwelcoming it appeared. If the experience was translated into anarchic energy and "mobile awareness,"⁸⁸ it was a way to render the changing global reality into endless horizons, brought together aesthetically by the critic in history. In this manner, Blackmur's description of a new modus vivendi provides an account of a modernity whose terms of dominance remain unsettled and unsedimented, while they are brought together through a new kind of literary and cultural expedition that had not been available to critics of an earlier generation.⁸⁹ In his description of a modus vivendi of criticism, Blackmur observes how "the intellect and the imagination everywhere struggle always in the quicksand," a predicament that marks the limits of mutual understanding and coexistence.⁹⁰ The "quicksand" upon which Blackmur's "intellect" and "imagination" rests develops into an extended metaphor that is represented as "the ever-suspended mud of the Nile."⁹¹ However, "no Babel," he claims, "is to be understood except by the angel of the imagination."⁹² Observing a river dissolved in mud, Blackmur transposes the metropolis's "whirring sounds" and "alien thought" in relation to American culture and reinscribes the ideals of exceptionalism. The sounds and words are not those of the Arabic or Turkish languages but are ultimately for an American, and it is his or her responsibility to make sense of them and place them in order. "Listening to its Babel all at once, one realizes how many wars—how many journeys and how many forms of pity—cry in the *one* American voice. One sees why America is at the same moment both evangelic and frivolous, full of decorum and abandon, sober purpose and free humor, moved by traditions it does not know how to acknowledge and driven by immediate response, looking to uniformity and acting in diversity."⁹³

Though he would enjoy the blandishments of the U.S. government to a greater degree than Blackmur, Lionel Trilling underwent a similar set of experiences that redefined his identity in his reflections on how to represent the United States to his European readers. Indeed, his criticism reached audiences it would not have otherwise found were it not for endeavors of the State Department, the United States Information Agency (USIA), and the CCF. For example, he became a recognizably public figure partly through his ties with the Department of State, the USIA,[94] and the Farfield Foundation, which also served as the front through which the CIA financed the operations of the CCF.[95] Multiple organizations contributed to the new and geographical positions Trilling was able to occupy as a critic. Grants from the American Committee for Cultural Freedom, the CCF, the U.S. Army,[96] and such literary organs as *Perspectives USA*, *Encounter*, *Preuves*, and *Der Monat*, helped to make Lionel Trilling a recognizable figure.[97] *The Liberal Imagination*, which, in his own words, was an account of "the dark and bloody crossroads where literature and politics meet," was translated into and published in Korean, Hindi, and French by the U.S. government.[98] This helped Trilling's volume to sell more than one hundred thousand copies.[99] In 1956, the provost of Columbia University, John Krout, informed Trilling that the director of the USIA, Theodore Streibert, had "very definite designs on [his] services."[100] The Department of State arranged Trilling's visits to Europe.[101] The U.S. Embassy in Rome put together a series of lectures for him in January 1958.[102] The essay "Contemporary American Literature in Its Relation to Ideas," which explored the relationship between literature and liberal democracy, was translated by the State Department into Japanese.[103] Trilling's essay "Outlines of Psychoanalysis" was reprinted in the Department of Defense's *Die Amerikanische Rundschau*.[104] The Farfield Foundation was directed by his former student John Thompson,[105] who funded a series of lectures that Trilling delivered in Poland, Rome, Athens, and Berlin.[106] Selections from Trilling's collection *The Opposing Self* were translated into Arabic, Spanish, and Portuguese by the USIA.[107] Shortly after learning that the USIA had translated the *Opposing Self* into Arabic, Trilling wrote to James Meader, the head of the USIA, "I am sure I needn't tell you how gratified I am to see the book in a language so distinct from our tradition—nor how bewildered I am by speculation to what my sentences will mean to the Arabic reader."[108]

Among *Perspectives USA*'s first guest editors, Trilling elaborated and defined his role as a critic through these emerging and transnational forms. He describes his activity as part of a lived tension that was embodied in his experience of writing on behalf of an American perspective for readers whom he does not know and who speak languages he cannot even read. In *Perspectives* he establishes a distinction between the function of a "cultural ambassador" on the one hand and "the writer" on the other. The "cultural ambassador," he writes, represents "a harmonious unity," whereas the writer or critic regards culture as "embroiled in something like civil strife."[109] The "ambassador" reconciles and consolidates the tensions within culture by "compounding differences," as if "all sides [are] shaking hands after the battle."[110] The ambassador shares the outlook "of the foreign observer" and sees "culture" as an "undifferentiated mass." The critic, in contrast, will understand ... that sometimes a foreign work has the power to refresh an old native impulse—he will understand, for instance, that Dreiser or Steinbeck may speak to the French of the possibility of violent energy and the intense representation of social reality in a way that perhaps Balzac or Stendhal cannot at the given moment command.... But when the American writer has made these acts of comprehension, he looks again at the list and remarks that, as for himself, it really means nothing.[111]

Trilling embraced the "vital difference" that he saw as inherent to the unity of American culture. Unlike Blackmur's vision of a "full horizon," however, his view was more limited and narrow; there were certain political differences that needed to be eliminated from American culture in order for it to survive. Yet Trilling's liberalism was ultimately illiberal; they concealed his tacit sympathies with McCarthyism by praising the diversity of American culture. By turning himself quite literally into a character with his own standpoint in the figure of the American "writer," Trilling conveys a collective mood and attitude toward "his" own culture in such passages as this:

Behold us! We are a divided people. We do not agree with each other. We hold each other up to scorn for our opinions. What a mess! And how right that this should exist! ... As for me and my allies, we are not trying to represent the American Spirit or the American Quality—we are only trying to solve our problems, or put our questions, under the aspect of eternity and daily necessity.[112]

It is not hard to see that Trilling is doing exactly what he says he is not able to do. His first words issue an order—"Behold us!"—which immediately establishes a demand and an identity that is defined by whoever "us" represents. He proclaims that "we" are divided, that there is real disagreement, and that intellectual discourse has become vituperative. "Behold us!" is an imperative that the "we" must be taken as it is, because there are divisions in American society. Yet the anaphoric use of "we" conceals differences of class, race, gender, and sexuality, all of which are reduced to a "messy" disagreement. The mess is not inchoate; it appears through his introduction to the volume as "complexity of general life" and not a "simple, simple thing."[113]

If Trilling found America difficult to portray as a way of abandoning an engagement with reality, he knew how *not* to represent it. When asked to remove a statement that *Perspectives USA*'s board of directors—which included James Laughlin and William Casey—found troubling, he wrote the young editorial assistant and poet Hayden Carruth that, at the time, there was no real interest in developing ties with the dominant bloc of intellectuals in France. He wrote, "The political situation of France, the commanding position of Stalinism in French cultural life, does not prevent our having the old affinity with certain elements of that life, but it does make the artistic and intellectual leadership of France at present unthinkable."[114] These negative fears were not so different from his response to Mary McCarthy, whose essay unsettled him for its negative portrayal of America. He revised her essay, "America the Beautiful," to advance a less critical image of American life and culture, and to focus its critical attention on Simone de Beauvoir's "America Day by Day."[115]

Although McCarthy shared Trilling's view of American complexity, her criticism was far more grounded and material in that it addressed the threat of atomic warfare in the context of American reified life: "The inalienable rights to life, liberty, and the pursuit of happiness," she wrote, "appear, in practice, to have become the inalienable right to a bathtub, a flush toilet, and a can of Spam."[116] For McCarthy, it was not the culture industry itself but commodity fetishism that had become an unrealizable desire. "We are a nation of twenty million bathrooms, with a humanist in every tub."[117] Yet there is no pleasure in standardization, and "Americans don't enjoy their possessions, because enjoyment was not [the] object, except for social outcasts, such as Jews, African Americans, racketeers, and homosexuals," who, she wrote, have no difficulty evincing the "the love of fabrics, gaudy shows, and rich possessions."[118] If McCarthy displaces the commodity fetish through these marks of racial, religious, and sexual difference, it is to extend the reification of life to a majority who are not only condemned not to find pleasure in things, but who live a mode of life that fails to grasp that the United States is itself a consumer and a producer of atomic weapons. Those deprived of the joys of consumption are, she suggests, unable to realize what the United States produces because they find no pleasure in consumption; they consume blindly. "The nation with its new bomb is little different from the consumer with his new Buick," she writes.[119] The real threat, she argues, is not the American consumer or the figure of the salesman, but the collective ignorance of the actual reality of *another* atomic war.

The screen of fantasy is so inscribed within American culture, as the Frankfurt School pointed out in its revision of ideology, that the fantasy is inscribed within reality itself: reality is simply a projection of our wishes and experiences. "The very mode of American life—the asceticism of its national character," she argues, permits society to be blasé about the reality of the bomb, while at the same time, it prevents any position of thought from emerging that might question its necessity. Culture has led to acquiescence. "Movies, radio, the super-highway" have softened us up to the atom bomb. If McCarthy's essay is a response to Beauvoir's memoir of her travels throughout the United States, the different registers in which they write are less a cultural disagreement than an epistemological one over the absence of a general existential philosophy.

In *America Day by Day*, Beauvoir criticizes the culture industry on existential grounds: the American fetish for the commodity is a belief in the essences of things, not in the existence of the subject, since the value of the subject is derived from the essence of things themselves. The American, she generalizes, views "the source of values and of truth in things, not in themselves. Their own existences are things of chance to which they attach no importance. That is why they are interested in net results, and not in the spirit that engenders them."[120]

The variety of writers Trilling included in his *Perspectives* was by no means unconventional. McCarthy may have provided a kind of rebuttal to Beauvoir's observations about the failure of French existentialism to grip American readers, but it was a backhanded one. If Beauvoir had suggested that the American fetish for the commodity precluded the development of a critical existentialism, McCarthy's response was not simply to dismiss the notion that the United States had an obsessive attachment to the essence of things, but to suggest that its subjects, with the exception of its minorities, really had no felt attachments to anything at all. By denying that most Americans gained no pleasure from the world of commodities, she transcribed that lack of feeling onto a general apathy over the capacities of the country to destroy itself—and the world. Yet those who experience enjoyment in the commodity fetish are precisely those who are marginalized in American culture. They cannot reflect on the conditions of their own existence because reality for them is simply the projection of their desires, which have been manufactured by culture. They are situated in the social world and yet unreflective, whereas the dominant culture is detached and actively apathetic. This idea, however, is contested in an interesting way in Trilling's decision to reprint James Baldwin's "Everybody's Protest Novel," which made Baldwin's critique of Richard Wright's *Native Son* one of the most widely reprinted and visible essays on criticism; it had already appeared in the *Partisan Review, Zero, Encounter*, and now alongside a story by Saul Bellow, "The Einhorns," and was preceded by Richard Gibson's writing on the subject of the literature of protest.[121] Baldwin argues that the pleasure to be discovered in the "protest novel" is the realization that the misery is the protagonist's and not the reader's. In his analysis of *Native Son*, Baldwin sees Bigger Thomas not as a symptom of society, as his first name might suggest, but as a reflection of a social viewpoint that has accepted the social and racial hierarchies that render him inferior.

For Trilling, both McCarthy's and Baldwin's essays embody the affirmation of the "complexity" and "vitality" of the United States. He argued that the nation's dynamic vitality was a way of "solving our problems." What problems these were, Trilling never explicitly stated in that essay. Yet as several critics have observed,[122] this was largely a way for Trilling to express his lasting preoccupation with what he mistook for an element of Stalinism in American life: that the act of belonging to the Communist Party was in itself an act of intellectual control. Trilling helped draft the guidelines for Columbia University's cooperation with the federal and state investigations of "un-American" activities. "A refusal to testify must not be automatically condemned, but also a refusal to testify must not be automatically condoned," Trilling wrote.[123] In a letter to the *New York Times* in 1953, he wrote that "membership in Communist organizations almost certainly implies a submission to an intellectual control which is entirely at variance with the principles of academic competence as we understand them."[124]

Yet the framework must be expanded beyond his negative attitudes toward communism. The scope of his criticism was transnational, although it has its obvious European limitations. He wrote about figures such as Gide, Kafka, Freud, Arnold, Flaubert, and Austen, and did so in a way that managed to evince an apparent sophistication and refinement that was part of a dominant view that English literature and the humanities in general were to be distanced from political concerns. Politics, this view implied, was the domain of the specialist and expert; literature, the domain of a passive tolerance and liberalism. If we are to understand his function as well as Blackmur's in their particular function abroad, we begin to notice how the United States in its relationship toward the world generates a certain anxiety in both of them. Both critics transform this structure of feeling into a distinct sense of national purpose. Blackmur traverses national borders, trying to make sense of the unsettled boundaries, which permits him to speak not only in terms of a full horizon but of an American singularity. Yet this form of writing, which he calls a modus vivendi, was structured by the new rhythms of movement in which the relationship between national identity and humanistic practice was renegotiated. He transposed his national anxieties and incorporated them into a vision of a full horizon—the imperial sublime.

CHAPTER 4

Archives of Critical Theory

ACCORDING TO DOCUMENTS RELEASED under the Freedom of Information Act, the Institute for Social Research (or the Frankfurt School, as it has come to be known) was the object of a widespread surveillance operation by the FBI as early as 1934. Almost without exception, nearly every member of the Frankfurt School in exile—Theodor Adorno, Max Horkheimer, Herbert Marcuse, Henryk Grossman, Leo Lowenthal, Karl Wittfogel, Frederick Pollock, Franz Neumann, and several others—was policed and investigated; their mail and telegrams were opened and read, their telephones wiretapped, their apartments burglarized, their private affairs scrutinized, and their income taxes audited, all for the slightest sign of any radical, left-wing political activity.[1]

As Alexander Stephan has shown in his powerfully documented and argued book, *Communazis: FBI Surveillance of German Émigré Writers*, beginning in 1934, the FBI began to monitor the activities of many German exiles who had immigrated to the United States after Hitler's takeover of the Reichstag in 1933.[2] "Few exiles suspected that their telephone conversations were being recorded and their mail not only open and read but translated, summarized, cataloged, photographed, and passed to other government bureaus," Stephan writes.[3] Mobilized by a confluence of anxieties about Germany, communist threats, and other fears that contributed to the domestication of American national culture, FBI director J. Edgar Hoover branded these exiles "communazis."[4] Their German identity and their fate as exiles were seen as a double threat. Figures such as Thomas Mann, Heinrich Mann, Lion Feuchtwanger, and others were the object of censorship and harassment, and were faced with possible deportation. Anti-Nazi organizations, like the Free Germany Movement and the Council for a Democratic Germany, were systemically observed to such an extent that the FBI could "justly be called the head of the world's first center for German exile research."[5]

Felix Weil, whose grain fortune in Argentina largely helped subsidize the Frankfurt School for many years, was under constant FBI surveillance. Hoover urged the New York division of the bureau to conduct a "thorough investigation concerning Weil's communist connections."[6] An FBI case report claimed that "Weil had used his large fortune to finance the Communist Party of Germany and was presently financing an economic research organization in New York City connected with Columbia University which served as an economic report center for the Comintern."[7] The institute's economist, Arkadij Gurland, was described as "posing as a refugee scholar" and "one of the Soviet's top economic reporters in the United States."[8] Henryk Grossman was probed while vacationing on Cape Cod. "He has all kinds of data regarding the location of harbors," a police official wrote Hoover. "It is believed that part of his identification is phony and he is being checked with Fifth Column activities."[9] As part of its investigation of Hanns Eisler, the composer with whom Adorno collaborated and who was eventually deported in 1947, Adorno's movements in Los Angeles were closely scrutinized by the bureau. According to one FBI memo, Adorno owned a green 1936 Plymouth with license plate "5E5507."[10]

By as early as 1943, Adorno, as well as the rest of the Institute for Social Research, were no doubt aware of the FBI's presence. The FBI interrogated Adorno in 1943,[11] and the institute retained a lawyer to defend against allegations that they were a communist front.[12] The FBI's surveillance had visible effects on the idiom of their work. Sensing the pressures of anticommunism and all the more wary of any incendiary rhetoric,[13] Adorno and Horkheimer revised the language of *Dialectic of Enlightenment* in order to conceal any superficial evidence of its political tendencies. In its first published edition (1947), the mention of "capitalism" was changed to the infinitely vaguer and euphemistic expression "existing conditions."[14] "Class society" was substituted with metaphors of "domination" and "order."[15] "Capital" was abstracted and became "economic system."[16] "Capitalist bloodsuckers" was replaced with the more dignified expression "knights of industry."[17] Gone was any mention of the "ruling class." That class had become quite simply, in the 1947 edition, "rulers."[18] Even the mention of "classless society" was suppressed.[19]

Far from being part of the Frankfurt School's long-standing "tradition" to censor itself, as Rolf Wiggershaus has asserted,[20] the new metaphors and euphemisms disclose the pressures that these exiles confronted upon arriving in the United States. In fact, the altered rhetoric effectively eluded the censors. To the literal-minded analysts of the FBI, according to one bureau report, the Institute for Social Research evinced little sign of "communistic" thought. "It is to be noted," an FBI agent wrote with some frustration to FBI director J. Edgar Hoover, "that nowhere ... have the authors themselves mentioned Communism or indicated their attitude toward Communism. Furthermore, no explanation was offered as to the reasons for this omission, in spite of the fact that the ideas expounded ... appear to coincide in many respects with what is being practiced in Russia today."[21]

Indeed, the FBI had enormous difficulty in grasping exactly what kind of communication it was monitoring. Memoranda and telegrams sent from Horkheimer to Adorno that discussed the philosophy of Nietzsche were redirected to confounded cryptographers and analysts on the grounds that the two critics were writing to each other in cipher. J. Edgar Hoover thought the mention of "Nietzsche" and "[German] Expressionism" could "possibly be code."²² What exactly "Nietzsche" and German "Expressionism" was code for, Hoover did not say. Nevertheless, the very names signified the national, ethnic, and political fears that were mobilized to monitor the activities of German exiles in the United States—and to later deport figures like Hanns Eisler, Bertolt Brecht, and C.L.R. James. Max Horkheimer, for example, signed his telegrams "Alright," an apparent parody of American complacency, yet in the inventive minds of the FBI, the name suddenly became both a pseudonym and thus a sign of possible subversion.²³ Indeed, at first the bureau thought that the Frankfurt School was a group of Nazis who were tracking the movements of Jewish refugees, when, in at least one instance, they were trying to get a visa for Walter Benjamin so that he could leave France and come to the United States.²⁴

But exile was much more than the experience of the impingements of American culture. It was not the text that was damaged, but life. Written to his friend Max Horkheimer on his fiftieth birthday, *Minima Moralia: Reflections on a Damaged Life* is, of all of Adorno's writings, arguably one of the most illuminating accounts of the cultural pressures on exiles in the United States, where Adorno would eventually enjoy the company of Mann and the protection of a community of exiles who were centered around Lion and Marta Feuchtwanger, who owned the beautiful villa Aurora in the hills of the Pacific Palisades in California.

Yet exile for Adorno also meant an unhappy confrontation with the ideals and practices of positivism and empiricism:

> The past life of émigrés is, as we know, annulled. Earlier it was the warrant of arrest, today it is intellectual experience that is declared nontransferable and unnaturalizable. Anything that is not reified, cannot be counted and measured, ceases to exist.... Reification spreads... to the life that cannot be directly actualized. For this a special rubric has been invented. It is called "background" and appears on questionnaires as an appendix, after sex, age and profession. To complete its violation, life is dragged along the triumphal automobile of united statisticians, and even the past is no longer safe from the present, whose remembrance of it consigns it a second time to oblivion.²⁵

That Adorno was monitored and investigated was only one element that defined the experience of exile. For Adorno, exile also entailed working against a series of assumptions about the value and objective of social analysis. Shortly after his arrival in New York, Adorno was hired by the Princeton Radio Research Project, an initiative supported by the same division of the Rockefeller Foundation that had lent its support to Blackmur. Yet if Blackmur was consulted to examine the spread of the "New Illiteracy," Adorno was recruited to assess the "tastes" and "preferences" of radio audiences. Working out of an abandoned brewery in Newark, New Jersey,

Adorno devoted his critical attention to the study of the "improvement of the standard of listening attitudes."[26]

Directed by the psychologist Hadley Cantril, Frank Stanton (later president of CBS), and Paul Lazarsfeld, the project was a major undertaking in the social sciences and was designed to develop the means of collecting audience information and the techniques for measuring the data in order to improve the quality of radio. The title of the grant was "The Essential Value of Radio for All Types of Listeners."[27] In Cantril's words the study was determined to investigate and analyze "the value of radio to people psychologically, and the various reasons why they like it."[28] As Paul Lazarsfeld wrote, the project intended to investigate "psychological and social factors which determine the trend and limitations of radio's influence."[29] The project had wider implications than the mere assessment of what was for Adorno a way to examine the structure of radio music.

Adorno, however, questioned the very assumptions underlying the study. His main concern was how the formal elements of radio music had fundamentally transformed a true understanding of music into nothing more than an appreciation for it. For Adorno, it was not simply the content, but the very nature of the media itself that lent itself to critical scrutiny. As he argued in "On a Social Critique of Radio Music," listening was driven by an enjoyment whose real and only basis was that listeners be satisfied that the sounds that they expected to hear in advance were heard. What was being heard was no longer music at all, but melodies, a series of notes, a phrase, a fulfillment of an expectation. "Retrogressive listening to the symphony," he writes, "is listening which, instead of grasping the whole, dwells upon those melodies, just as if the symphony were structurally the same as a ballad."[30] What he called the "promotional bias" in radio inherently prevented radio music from being *fully* understandable to the listening subject, who hears only melodies and phrases and not, for example, symphonies as a whole. Radio music was the appreciation of music, and that meant music was enjoyed merely in the cognitive act of recognizing its identity. Furthermore, Adorno argued that there could never be any meaningful survey of listener attitudes and tastes without understanding how listening patterns are conditioned by society as a whole. The very nature of listening to radio music in social isolation meant that listeners were under the illusion that the music was being broadcast for them and for them alone. If the recognition of a piece of music was the enjoyment of identifying several bars of a Beethoven sonata, what was being heard was no longer music at all, but a series of notes, a phrase, a manufactured, self-fulfilling desire.

Adorno's argument challenged the dominant assumptions of the project's director, the sociologist Paul Lazarsfeld. Adorno argued that the popularity of a piece of music was not something that could be subjected to social analysis and measured; rather, he contended that what was popular was "a functional term" that necessarily "depended on the structure of the object of art that is supposed to be popular as much as on the structure of the people with whom it is supposed to be popular."[31] Adorno's Princeton work—"A Social Critique of Radio Music," "On Popular Music," and "The Radio Symphony"—did not meet the stipulations of the project.[32] According to Lazarsfeld, Adorno showed a "disregard for evidence and systematic empirical research." He charged that Adorno had "confused ethical and esthetic judgments and questions of scientific fact." He claimed that Adorno's writing possessed a "dishonest tinge" and displayed a "lack of candidness." Overall, Lazarsfeld implied, Adorno was reluctant to submit to the dictates of American empiricism and positivism.[33] John Marshall, the Rockefeller official responsible for the Princeton Radio Research Project, wrote that Adorno seemed "psychologically engaged at the moment by his ability to recognize deficiencies in the broadcasting of music to an extent that makes questionable his own drive to find ways of remedying them."[34] Partially as a result of Adorno's unwillingness to acquiesce to the project's assumptions, the Rockefellers cut the project's funding in the summer of 1940.

Adorno's intransigence was well founded in ways that went beyond his critique of Lazarsfeld's method of benign administration. Not only was the data collected in Newark of a commercial nature but the Princeton Radio Project itself was part of a wider movement in the emerging field of communications research and social sciences, which was beginning to examine radio's potential as a form of political and cultural control.[35] As part of the effort to examine and identify the musical tastes and preferences of audiences, the Princeton Project developed various methods to analyze the radio for the purposes of regulating and controlling the basis of "subconscious thoughts." In one study, entitled "The Psychological Analysis of Propaganda," the Princeton Project made a case for the development of what it called "technological propaganda."[36] Rather than issuing abstract pronouncements about the value of "freedom" and "democracy," technological propaganda was more effective, the study argued, if it issued specific, concrete "facts" that were conducive to producing the desired ideological effect. "Technological propaganda," according to the study, "doesn't try so hard to tell people where to go, but rather shows them the path they should choose."[37] It continues, "We should keep on remembering that propaganda is most successful when it builds up and prepares attitudes prior to the time in which they are to be effective."[38]

Yet just as much as this new mode of articulation could serve political ends, so too did it become a strategy of observation and domination of control. Researching for another Rockefeller project at the University of Chicago, Harold Lasswell described the study of radio as the objective investigation of structures of attention that regulated the "unified decision[-making] process." Lasswell saw communication as the alternative to the physical conquest of territories and dominions:

> Essential to the consolidation of the body politic and methods short of conquest is the growth of a common attention structure. The structure of attention must interact with the other principal factors. . . . In converting the current social process into a unified decision process-period, the tension pattern of a given period must impinge upon predispositions with which the period began, bringing about a change in relevant structures of demand, identification and expectation, as well as in the structures of operation. Research on communication has its direct functions to fulfill by modifying the attention structure of the non-Soviet world at strategic points, and by clarifying the factors essential to rational strategies of unification.[39]

In a similar fashion, the Princeton Radio Project was largely aimed at monitoring, deciphering, and identifying individual tastes in listening practices.

Much of the subtext of Adorno's later work can be read as a reaction to that experience. Written in 1942, Adorno and Horkheimer's *Dialectic of Enlightenment* registers the specific institutional and political predicament of the European mandarin who is confronted with the instrumentalization of precisely the forms of knowledge that Adorno had criticized at the Princeton Project. Horkheimer and Adorno's *Dialectic of Enlightenment* begins with a critique of Francis Bacon for his "substitution of belief for knowledge."[40] They describe Bacon as the "father of experimental philosophy" who propounds "vain notions" and "blind experiments."[41] Modern science, they write, renounces any claim to "meaning" by substituting "formulas" for "concepts" and "rules," and "probability" for causes and structures.[42] They decry the "triumph of the factual mentality" in which "numbers become the canon of the Enlightenment."[43] Everything that cannot be quantified for the Enlightenment thinkers is, they argue, an "illusion." "Scientific calculation" and "equivalence" drive its method.[44]

Adorno and Horkheimer thus extend the Weberian basis of Lukács's "Reification and the Consciousness of the Proletariat" to the subject of positivism. Horkheimer and Adorno were therefore not repudiating Enlightenment reason in general, but were elaborating how a specific discourse of reason had emerged out of the Enlightenment. The reification of life could be found in the very methods of "empirical" research itself. Indeed, the chapter on the concept of Enlightenment ends with a footnote attacking the Rockefeller Foundation for its funding of projects that attempt to devise "formulas" for bringing "technology under control."[45] They criticize Rockefeller sociologists who adhere to its principles in "search of an antidote."[46]

If *Dialectic of Enlightenment* challenged the prevailing way that knowledge was used as a means of control (transforming the Enlightenment into the very thing it sets out to oppose), the ideology of empiricism amplified the dislocations Adorno experienced as an exile in the America. "It is unmistakably clear to the intellectual from abroad that he will have to eradicate himself as an autonomous being if he hopes to achieve anything," Adorno later wrote in *Prisms*.[47] Positivism and empiricism had reduced reality to a prosaic and administered calculus, the effect of which was embodied in the position of the exile when confronted with modernity. In *Minima Moralia*, Adorno declared that "dwelling, in the proper sense, is now impossible. The traditional residences we have grown up in have grown intolerable: each trait of comfort in them is paid for with a betrayal of knowledge, each vestige of shelter with the musty pact of family interests."[48] The aphoristic form of *Minima Moralia* itself revealed the damaged and fragmented condition of exile, whose vicissitudes could not be narrated in the form of an essay, but rather in a series of aphoristic and parabolic observations. "The house is past," Adorno wrote. "The best mode of conduct, in the face of all this, still seems an uncommitted, suspended one. . . . It is part of reality not to be at home in one's home."[49] Empiricism had compromised the very category of experience. As he later wrote:

> [In America] I had to recognize in the form empiricism took when translated into scientific praxis that the full unregulated scope of experience is more constricted by the empiricist ground rules than it is in the concept of experience itself. It would not be the most erroneous characterization to say that what I have in mind after all that is a kind of restitution of experience against its empiricist deformation. That was not the least important reason for returning to Germany along with the possibility of pursuing my own interests in Europe without . . . contributing something toward political Enlightenment.[50]

If Adorno partially represented the experience of exile in terms of the ideology of positivism, which had damaged the very category of experience in general, in postwar Germany, his critique of positivism would face new, mostly institutional challenges.

Accommodations

The postwar Institute of Social Research was substantially different from its predecessor in New York and prewar Frankfurt. "As early as 1951, members of the Institute who remained in America noted a subtle change in its orientation," writes Martin Jay.[51] Max Horkheimer secured agreements with the same German officials who had presided over the institute's closure in the 1930s.[52] Grants from the U.S. high commissioner John McCloy,[53] who had taken a personal interest in the institute, transformed its tone and led to a systemic self-censorship of its early Marxist politics. Horkheimer placed many of the Marxist volumes of the institute's journal "in a crate in the Institute's cellar, nailed, and out of ... grasp."[54] In the 1950s, Horkheimer negotiated a contract to study the labor relations of Mannesmann, a company that had financed the Nazi Party and founded an anti-Bolshevik league during the war.[55] Furthermore, Horkheimer cultivated friendships with scholars such as Hadley Cantril, the former director of the Princeton Radio Project. By 1963, Horkheimer was even formally associated with the CCF.[56]

As a result of these ties, Adorno lost much of his ability to criticize the discourse of anticommunism, as well as critically investigate his own relationship to postwar German society and culture. He wrote a number of uncharacteristically candid political disclaimers that reiterated his and the institute's anticommunism. "We reject as strongly as possible any interpretation of our work as being an apology for Russia," Adorno wrote in a memo that he had considered publishing in Melvin Lasky's *Der Monat*, an influential Berlin magazine that was funded by the CCF.[57] Even many of Adorno's musical writings of the 1950s and early 1960s were published in the CCF's Viennese journal *Forum*, and his essay on Spengler appeared in *Der Monat*.

Der Monat provided Adorno the means to assert his anticommunist credentials. Throughout the 1950s, he wrote several essays for it, including "Remarks on the Politics of Neurosis" (1953), a review of Arthur Koestler's essay on pro-Soviet intelligentsia ("Kritik"), and most important, "Extorted Reconciliation" (1958), a polemical review of György Lukács's *Realism in Our Time*. The tone of Adorno's review was heavy-handed and conformed with *Der Monat*'s political posture. He called Lukács a "dogmatic commissar of culture," even though Lukács had expressed his disillusionment with the Soviet Union and, most critical of all, supported the Nagy regime against the Soviet invasion of his native Hungary in 1956.[58] A great deal of Adorno's critique was unwarranted. Lukács returned to Hungary after the war, where he found that his works were decried as revisionist.

Adorno's anticommunism was not simply the product of the Cold War consensus that faced West Germany; it was also reinforced by the institute's ties to the American high commissioner, John McCloy, who had an interest in assessing the attitudes of West Germans toward the American military occupation.[59] Upon returning to West Germany, Adorno's political engagement assumed the form of a sociological activism that relied on empirical methods that he criticized. In a conference sponsored by the American High Commission in 1951, Adorno delivered a talk in which he emphasized the importance of empirical methods in assessing the objective conditions of German society. "Empirical research in Germany must rigorously... bring to light the objectivity of what is socially the case, far beyond the individual or collective consciousness," he observed.[60] He suggested that the methods themselves had the aim of a critical and political activity:

> If we are confronted with the statement, based on some alleged authorities in humanist sociology, that the so-called rural population is resistant to technical and social innovations because of its essentially conservative spirit, we will not be satisfied with explanations of this sort.... We will for example send interviewers familiar with farmers into the country and encourage them to persist with further questions when farmers tell them that they stay on their farms out of love for their homeland and loyalty to the customs of their fathers.[61]

For Adorno, the sociological study of culture was thus not a neutral or objective scientific practice but one that confronted and altered the realities that the researcher was attempting to grasp. After his return to Germany, he thought it was crucial to identify the residual and latently fascist and anti-Semitic elements that remained in postwar German culture. His major collaborative project of those years grew out of *The Authoritarian Personality*.[62] Entitled "Group Experiment," the study was a sociological examination of the attitudes of the German population toward the U.S. government, the Third Reich, democracy, and the Holocaust. As he later wrote in the "Meaning of Working through the Past," he found "the survival of National Socialism within democracy to be potentially more menacing than the survival of fascist tendencies against democracy."[63] According to the results of the "Group Experiment," which attempted to gauge its subjects' predilections for authoritarianism along what was called the "A-Scale," Adorno's fears were well founded. Anti-Semitism remained a widespread phenomenon after the war. Many in Konrad Adenauer's West Germany displayed a disturbing ignorance of the realities of the Holocaust, and a sizable minority continued to express positive opinions of Nazism.[64]

In 1957, however, Adorno would reverse his course yet again. After his promotion to full professor in 1957, he no longer needed to rely as an intellectual on the legitimacy of empirical research. In several essays— "Sociology and Empirical Research" (1957), "Teamwork in Social Research" (1957), and "Opinion Delusion Society" (1961)—he systematically articulated what he clearly always thought problematic about empiricism. "Culture," he wrote, "is precisely the very condition that excludes a mentality that would wish to measure it."[65] Not only did his critique of positivism institute a major split within German sociology, which achieved its fullest expression in his debate with Karl Popper in Tübingen in 1961, but it also seems to have coincided with his realization that anticommunism undermined the democratic institutions that he was attempting to strengthen through his lectures and radio addresses. In fact, after his critique of positivism, Adorno made a more discernible effort at pointing out the ways in which anticommunism sustained the residual elements of fascism and anti-Semitism in postwar German society. In "The Meaning of Working through the Past," Adorno argued that "the resistance to the East contains its own dynamic that reawakens the German past. Not merely in terms of ideology, because the slogans of struggle against Bolshevism have always served to mask those who harbor no better intentions toward freedom than do the Bolsheviks themselves."[66] Rejecting positivism was thus not only a methodological turn for Adorno, but also a political turn. In "Sociology and Empirical Research" (1957), he repeated much of what he had already implicitly stated in the *Dialectic of Enlightenment*, but introduced an emphasis on "theory," which he variously coded as either "philosophy" or "critique," as a way in which the object and categories of analysis were to be questioned.[67]

For Adorno, the study of culture and its ideology was the reified object of empirical sociology. "Nowadays," he wrote in 1957, "in the train of disappointment with both cultural-scientific [*Geisteswissenschaftlich*] and formal sociology, there is a predominant tendency to give primacy to empirical sociology. Its immediate practicable utilizability, and its affinity to every type of administration undoubtedly play a role here."[68] Adorno's argument rests on the premise that empiricism has a reified view of its object that has been temporally and spatially fixed by empirical analysis. With its origins in market analysis, empirical sociology was yet another form of instrumental reason and identitarian thought. It imputed a status to its object that was fetishistic and avoided a questioning of the categories constituted by its method. He somewhat belatedly criticized the Princeton Project's methods, calling its research "atomistic" and "overphysical." Their interest in data was a "fetish" that concealed "from the investigator the irrelevance of his conclusions."[69]

Adorno's criticism of empiricism had the effect of emboldening his critique of instrumental reason, which he then extended to the political practices of the student movement in the 1960s. Much of his refusal to support the student and antiwar movement was the consequence of his intervention against empirical sociology, among the more dominant of the postwar academic fields in Europe as well as the United States. Adorno was not insisting that the student movement was a group of empiricists seeking to overturn the structures of existing society through an analysis of data. Rather, what motivated the thrust of his comments was the students' conflation of praxis with theory. Just as the empiricists had privileged the object of analysis, so, too, did the student movement place an unreflected emphasis on "tactics" and "action." For Adorno, this kind of thinking and activity recalled the dangers of instrumental reason. In "Critique" (1969), Adorno wrote that "the collective compulsion for positivity that allows its immediate translation into practice has in the meantime been gripped precisely by those people who believe they stand in the starkest opposition to society. This is not the least way in which actionism fits so smoothly into society's prevailing trend."[70] In "Marginalia to Theory and Practice," he concluded his attack on Weber's "de-ideologization of science" by criticizing the student movement's emphasis on priorities for action. "Actionism is regressive," he said. "Under the spell of the positivity . . . it refuses to reflect upon its own impotence."[71] For Adorno, the students' emphasis on praxis was mostly identitarian in their assumptions and based on what he and Horkheimer called "ratio." The "dogma of unity of theory and praxis . . . is undialectical," he argued. "It underhandedly appropriates simple identity where contradiction alone had the chance of becoming productive."[72] What Adorno found authoritarian and instrumental was thus no different from his excoriation of reason in the *Dialectic of Enlightenment*, ironically the same text that had inspired, and was widely distributed by, the student movement.

What resisted instrumental reason for Adorno was precisely the kind of thought that was based on its antithesis, and the refusal of a forced and reconciled identity between "means" and "ends." On a panel at Cambridge University with Lukács's former student, Lucien Goldmann, Adorno observed that "method should be a function of the object, not the inverse. This notion . . . is one which has been all too simply repressed by the positivistic spirit."[73] For Adorno, "theory" and works of art are the two practices that hold out against reification. "Works of art . . . are instructions for the praxis they refrain from: the production of life as it ought to be," he wrote.[74] The artwork, Adorno argues, expresses the antagonism inherent in society, but only as a function of art's autonomy. Were a work of art to externalize these antagonisms, Adorno suggests, it would no longer be an artwork at all.

For Adorno, the autonomy of artworks ultimately possesses a social quality insofar as the socially mediated antagonisms they represent inhere within the works themselves. These antagonisms are mediated by society, he argues, and it is the role of the critic to analyze these conflicts by emphasizing the relationship between the form and internal tensions themselves. The higher the degree of tension within the artwork, the better the art. On the one hand, Adorno makes a formalist argument, suggesting in *Aesthetic Theory* that "the unsolved antagonisms of reality return in artworks as immanent problems of form."[75] On the other hand, Adorno deprives art of its autonomy in the very act of elevating it. It is this ambivalence of which Adorno was aware: "The artwork has a double character," he told Goldmann. "It is simultaneously a social fact and also—something else in relation to reality, something which is against it and somehow autonomous. This ambiguity of art, inasmuch as it belongs to society and inasmuch as it is different from society, leads to the fact that the highest level of art, its truth content and what finally gives it its quality as a work of art, cannot be a purely aesthetic matter."[76]

Adorno's theory of critique and aesthetics grounded his relentless and intransigent independence, which was widely criticized by former students who were disappointed that he was not the least bit enthusiastic about their protests, sit-ins, and strikes. But Adorno's despair was not rooted in a blind devotion to the existing structures of society; rather, he thought that the vision of praxis that the student movement had identified in the national liberation movements of the 1960s, for example, was simply the expression of instrumental reason. Much of this critique of the movement appeared in the form of hostility to the Third World. While, like other members of the Frankfurt School, Adorno never developed a theory of imperialism or colonialism—Jürgen Habermas once expressed an active lack of interest in the developing world[77]—Adorno's Eurocentrism and dismissal of liberation movements arose out of his critique of instrumental reason. What Adorno was critical of was not the anticolonial struggles themselves but the fact that they had become unreflective calls for political action in the industrialized world—models for praxis that were unsuited to the conditions that existed in 1968.[78] In "Marginalia to Theory and Praxis," Adorno wrote:

> Barricades are ridiculous against those who administer the bomb, that is why the barricades are a game, and the lords of the manor let the gamesters go on playing for the time being. Things might be different with the guerrilla tactics of the Third World; nothing in the administered world functions wholly without disruption. This is why actionists in advanced industrial countries choose the underdeveloped ones for their models. But they are as impotent as the personality cult of leaders who are helplessly and shamefully murdered. Models that do not prove themselves even in the Bolivian bush cannot be exported.[79]

Even in his negative comments about the importation of guerrilla tactics from the "Bolivian bush," Adorno's remarks are characterized by an unshakable belief that reason should not be instrumentalized and that all identitarian thought is administrative and reified. Ultimately for Adorno, any thinking that unreflectively unified praxis with theory was nondialectical and compromised the substance of critique itself. What grounded Adorno's theory of critique was his relentless insistence on the autonomy of theory as opposed to the instrumentalization of reason and the reification of thought.

In the most explicit way, this is formulated as the irreconcilable relation between the subject and the object, idea and deed, or between the work of art and the world. In his review of Lukács's *Realism in Our Time*, Adorno argues that Lukács has "reconciled" the theory of realism to the duress of socialist practice. In Adorno's view, Lukács overlooked and expelled the antagonism and contradictions of art and subjected them to a rigid dogma that ignored the dynamic contradictions inherent in artworks. While Adorno's remarks were undoubtedly heavy-handed and not without their anticommunist bias, his argument recapitulated a current that underlies nearly all of his writing. In his review of Lukács's *Realism in Our Time*, Adorno writes, "Lukács' postulate [of the reflection between subject and object], which is the supreme criterion of his aesthetics, implies that reconciliation has been achieved, that society has been set right, that the subject has come into its own and is at home in its world."[80]

Yet in recent years, critics and intellectuals have turned to Adorno's notion of irreconcilability as a model and an unexhausted critical alternative. In many respects, Adorno's position as an intellectual who refused both the dictates of the party and the imperatives of political action has kept alive the often-embattled space of the intellectual. As Fredric Jameson remarked in 1990, Adorno "may turn out to have been the analyst of our own period."[81] For Edward Said, as well, Adorno's work—his *Negative Dialectics*, his writings on music, and his writings on late style—was a way to work through one of the central problems upon which a transformative, non-coercive, and non-dominative humanism could be established: a new humanism that is based not on the identitarian or the fixed, monolithic concepts of identity but on a negative dialectics that allowed him to develop a humanism based in philology, the study of languages, and in the realm posed by the challenges of Adorno's theory of late style.

CHAPTER 5

Humanism, Territory, and Techniques of Trouble

> What is truth? But a mobile host of metaphors, metonymies, and anthropomorphisms: in short, the sum of all human relations which have been poetically and rhetorically intensified, transferred, and embellished, and which after long usage, seem to people to be fixed, canonical and binding. Truths are illusions which we have forgotten are illusions; they are metaphors that have been worn out and have been drained of sensuous force, coins that have lost their embossing and now are considered metal and no longer as coins.
> —*Nietzsche, "On Truth and Lies in a Nonmoral Sense"*[1]

FEW TWENTIETH-CENTURY INTELLECTUALS have been the subject of such a large body of criticism in as wide an array of disciplines as Edward Said. A collection of books devoted to his oeuvre has emerged over the past several years.[2] Much of the criticism, though certainly not all of it, arises out of debates and discussions of his most internationally influential work, *Orientalism*.[3] Yet in spite of all these attempts to define and identify an overarching methodology that can be traced throughout Said's some twenty-five books, few have successfully, or at the very least convincingly, identified a method that endures from his earliest work, *Joseph Conrad and the Fiction of Autobiography*, to his later works, such as *Humanism and Democratic Criticism*.[4] That such an intellectual, who is credited with the invention of fields like postcolonial studies and who has made a decidedly transforming contribution to the reinvention of humanism in general, has proven so elusive in this respect has to do with the changing exigencies he faced as an intellectual in the context of a particular relationship to his critique of disciplines, orthodoxies, and other identitarian ways of thinking. At the same time, however, Said has exhibited a lasting affinity with a range of key figures, intellectuals, and critics, including Erich Auerbach, Giambattista Vico, Antonio Gramsci, and Theodor Adorno.[5]

What has made these critical affinities difficult to discern as a whole method of critical activity is that throughout Said's writings, as well as his interviews,[6] he has never explicitly defined a sustained method for himself. Most of the critical focus on his work has been either on his use of concepts, such as secularism and humanism, or on the introduction to *Orien-*

talism, where the theoretical contributions of Michel Foucault and Antonio Gramsci play an important, but by no means central, role in his work as a whole. In spite of the attention paid to these two theorists and their at times oblique relevance to Said's many other works, critics have generally agreed on characterizations of Said's general critical attitude—oppositional, minoritarian, or antinomian.[7] His work is often described as presenting a heightened, powerfully motivated restlessness that is executed in a variety of synthetic, yet resolutely antisystematic ways that often make unlikely connections,[8] such as, for example, between Jane Austen's *Mansfield Park* and its setting's dependence on plantation slave labor in the Antilles.[9] All of this is similarly evident in his discussion of the seemingly paradoxical representation of musical silence in the scores and performances of Ludwig von Beethoven, the operas of Wagner, the performances of Glenn Gould, and the role of silence in the works of historians as varied as E. P. Thompson and Ranajit Guha.[10]

Why Said's technique has remained so elusive is related in part to the scholarly efforts to identify a set of interpretative procedures that have overemphasized the Foucauldian dimensions of *Orientalism* to such an extent that the defining contributions of Giambattista Vico, Erich Auerbach, and Theodor Adorno have been overshadowed. Yet the importance of Foucault to *Orientalism* is unmistakable, not only in the explicit emphasis that Said places on several of Foucault's critical terms, drawn from Foucault's *Archaeology of Knowledge* and *Discipline and Punish*, but also in his elaboration of Orientalism.[11] Indeed, the dominant focus of *Orientalism*, which aimed to establish the conditions for a form of "non-dominative and non-coercive" knowledge and power in Western culture's representation of the Islamic East,[12] examined an array of nineteenth-century French and British novelists, poets, philologists, historians, travelers, and imperial administrators. Among these figures are writers such as Edward Lane, Constantine Volney, François-René de Chateaubriand, Alphonse de Lamartine, Gérard de Nerval, and Gustave Flaubert; the writings of the first modern Orientalist Sylvestre de Sacy and of the French philologist Ernest Renan; the accounts by T. E. Lawrence; the writings of Louis Massignon and H.A.R. Gibb; the lectures of Sylvain Lévi; and the records of Maurice Barrès's journey to the Near East. Drawing on the work of Foucault, Said views this ensemble of writing on the Orient as a discourse. The writings of Renan, Flaubert, T. E. Lawrence, and others comprise a discipline, a corpus of writing through which the West managed and produced the Orient, but also determined what could and could not be said about the so-called Orient. The effects of this discourse and knowledge of the Orient enabled the exercise of power and dominance over it. The writings of Orientalists expressed "a will . . . not only to understand what [was] non-European, but also to control and manipulate what was manifestly different."[13] Thus does

T. E. Lawrence "hustle" Asia "into form," all the better for Britain to be able to administer it, dominate it, and rule it.[14]

Nevertheless, Foucault's importance for Said's *Orientalism* only partly accounts for his method.[15] To read *Orientalism* in Foucauldian terms certainly helps to grasp his awareness of the inextricable relationship between the will to power and the will to knowledge, yet it is a mistake to overemphasize that Said sees Orientalism as simply an interdisciplinary mechanism that sustains itself by virtue of an economy of power. For him, Antonio Gramsci's description and conceptualization of the practice of hegemony explains how certain ideas about the so-called Orient prevail over others in democratic societies. Furthermore, what the attention lavished on Said's relation to Foucault concealed was Said's active relationship to the Romantic tradition within British Marxism: Raymond Williams's *The Country and the City*, in particular, and Said's effort to articulate an emancipatory and utopian alternative to "create objects for a new kind of knowledge."[16] Statements, such as Orientalism is an attempt to establish the conditions for non-dominative, non-coercive knowledge, and his assertion that Conrad's depiction of Africa enables one to "imagine something other than an Africa carved up into dozens of colonies," belong to the possibility of the creation of an entirely different order of knowledge.[17]

Unlike Foucault, *The Country and the City* provided Said not with a set of critical terms ("discourse," "rarity," "exteriority," "knowledge," and "power") but a theoretical problematic posed by the literary and poetic forms of the country-house poems of the eighteenth century, the nineteenth-century novels of Jane Austen, the rural accounts of the countryside by William Cobbett, and the urbanization of rural lands represented in Charles Dickens, Thomas Hardy, George Orwell, and others. Indeed, the drive of Williams's work was to emphasize the physical *absence* of the working classes, rural laborers, peasants, guest laborers, and migrant workers from Britain's colonies, whose exclusion and invisibility from representations of the city and countryside involve a contested social relationship over the geographical, territorial, and property divisions that are an inherent part of the aesthetic form.[18]

Yet, as Williams himself observed, certain kinds of methodological breakthroughs can just as easily become methodological traps.[19] Thwarting the reification of the major critical categories and insights of his work—the idea of contrapuntal criticism (which he discusses in *Culture and Imperialism*),[20] the critical concept of affiliations, and the practice of secular criticism (which he elaborates in *The World, the Text, and the Critic*)—Said's praxis would appear to rest on a negative dialectics of the secular that is very much *in* and *of* the world.[21] What makes his praxis difficult to grasp as a whole is that this critical position locates itself not simply against orthodoxies, dogmas, and systems but also in the critical space between "culture and system."[22] It is not insignificant that *The World, the Text, and the Critic* was originally titled *Criticism between Culture and System*. Thus, his work can partly be understood as negotiating a *situated* place between practice and theory. Yet where those places exactly are should not be described in terms of the simple exercise of negation or opposition; such a flattening out of his position misses the dialectical tension that Said brings to performance. It is not enough to say that "like Nietzsche, Said was oppositional to the extent that he was only attacking victorious causes."[23] Nor does Said immediately help us in these matters when he describes critical practices metaphorically as belonging to the realm of the traveler who "crosses over, traverses territory, and abandons fixed positions all the time,"[24] precisely because such statements would beg the question, from what position and how does the critic resist?

Much of the latter is rooted in Said's representations of his experience of exile from Palestine in December 1947.[25] He wrote *Orientalism*, he says, because of his "awareness of being an 'Oriental' as a child growing up in two British colonies." All of his education was colonial (first in Palestine, then in Egypt, and later in the United States). "Yet," he writes, "a deep early awareness . . . persisted." In many ways his study of Orientalism was "an attempt to inventory the traces upon [him], the Oriental subject, of a culture whose domination has been a powerful factor in the life of all Orientals."[26] Yet the conjunctures of his identity and his representation of the experience of exile have often led to a conflation of the exilic and the position of the critic's consciousness. And yet while Said does want to retain the potentialities made available by the exilic—a position defined by dislocation—such a position does not necessarily entail a dissenting standpoint, opposition, or the rejection of orthodoxy or dogma. One need only think of Henry Kissinger or Zbigniew Brzezinski, two exiles who exerted a preponderance of their energies by accommodating themselves to power, rather than someone like Theodor Adorno, who went to great lengths to resist it. Exile needs to be understood as a historical experience, yet at the same time is not *in itself* a sufficient precondition for criticism. "While it is an actual condition, exile is also for my purposes a metaphorical one," he writes. "By that I mean that my diagnosis of the intellectual in exile derives from the social and political history of dislocation and migration . . . but is not limited to it."[27]

Terrains of Philology

Of all the figures whom Said employs to articulate the basis for the praxis of a new or alternative humanism, no one has been of more importance to his work than Erich Auerbach (1892–1957). A scholar of classical and philological training and part of a defined group of German Romance scholars, including Ernest Robert Curtius (1886–1956), Leo Spitzer (1887–1960), and Karl Vossler (1872–1949),[28] Auerbach has held a lasting importance for Said as the one figure to whom he returns again and again to articulate a vision of an alternative, secular humanism.[29] Not only does Said translate his essay "Philology and *Weltliteratur*," he refers to Auerbach in multiple works: in *Orientalism* (where Auerbach's secular philology is juxtaposed to the theological philology of Orientalists); in *The World, the Text, and the Critic* (where Auerbach stands for an exemplary, situated, yet displaced critical consciousness); in *Culture and Imperialism* (where Auerbach is shown to dramatize a particular idea of history, while concealing the geographical basis of that view of history); in "History, Literature and Geography" (where he stands for a temporal, as opposed to a spatial, dialectics); and in *Humanism and Democratic Criticism* (where Auerbach enacts a secular humanism).[30]

A great deal of important work has been written about the significance of Said's affiliation with and great admiration for Auerbach, and most of the scholarship has tended to emphasize Auerbach's particular experience in writing *Mimesis: The Representation of Reality in Western Literature* (1946) while in exile in Istanbul, where he had sought refuge from Nazi Germany from 1935 to 1946.[31] The book, which Said has described "as one of the most admired and influential books of literary criticism ever written,"[32] was nothing less than an unassuming, yet monumental account of the representation of reality in Western literature in the context of the unfolding of human history over the course of three thousand years, beginning with Homer's *Odyssey* and ending with Virginia Woolf's *To the Lighthouse*. Writing in exile in wartime Istanbul in the early 1940s, Auerbach had few resources at his disposal. There were no Western libraries to consult, and he had few critical editions in his possession from which to draw. As he writes in his epilogue, the lack of access to contemporary scholarship freed him from the constraints and obligations of specialization. Writing on such an ambitious subject would have otherwise been overwhelming, if not impossible; the sheer amount of secondary sources required to study three thousand years of literary history would have made the whole project infeasible. Auerbach wrote that he had to "dispense with all periodicals, almost all recent investigations, and in some cases reliable editions of my texts . . . [but] it is quite possible," he goes on to say, "that the book owes its existence to just this lack of a rich and specialized library."[33]

The book was a product of exile in a conscious and intentional way. Auerbach was writing in the early 1940s in the midst of a European catastrophe, and though he had only a dim awareness of the contrapuntal irony that he was residing in a country that had also attempted to eliminate an entire population of its Armenian inhabitants in 1915–16, he viewed *Mimesis* as a book that was very much a part of his present. "*Mimesis* is quite consciously a book about a particular person, in a particular situation, writing at the beginning of the 1940s," he later wrote.[34] For a scholar whose main inspiration came from the Italian philologist Giambattista Vico, what those particularities meant was that *Mimesis* was a work of human will and human history. "He was performing an act of cultural, even civilizational survival," Said writes.[35] "It is an attempt," he says, "to rescue sense from the fragments of modernity with which, from his Turkish exile, Auerbach saw the downfall of Europe, and Germany in particular."[36]

On the face of it, *Mimesis* appears as Auerbach's working through his German Jewish identity by explaining the achievements of Christianity to provide an interpretative account of the way that figural interpretation explains the relation between the Old and New Testament.[37] In the semantic development of the *figura*, Auerbach did not see a technique of literary development but rather a historically specific situation that required a mode of interpretation that could grasp both the reality of the Old Testament and the New Testament without denying the veracity of either of them.[38] According to Auerbach's account of patristic interpretations, events and people narrated in the Old Testament had both a literal and a real dimension to them. They are considered real and not mere fictions, but they are also comprehended as iterations of events or people that are yet to come and that will fulfill, round out, and complete their earlier iteration promised by God. The Christian schema of the figure (the promise) and the figural (the fulfillment) served a particular rhetorical and historical function in that it allowed Saint Paul and the thinkers of early Christianity to comprehend the relationship between Judaism and Christianity as one of prolepsis and anticipation, instead of causation, while maintaining the reality of both. Thus was Adam conceived as Adam *and* Christ; Eve *as* Eve and the Church, to the extent that every event in the Old Testament is realized in Christ's Incarnation. As Hayden White remarks, this idea became central to Auerbach's *genealogical* conception of secular history:

> This notion of a real event that was complete in itself and full in meaning at the same moment of its happening but was at the same time the bearer of meaning that would be revealed only in as a different and complete event at a later time supplied Auerbach with a model for conceptualizing the relationship between historical events.[39]

The *figura* provided Auerbach with a way to not only conceptualize the relationship between historical events but also to actively connect disparate events between the past and the present and possible future. According to Said, the *figura* was the "intellectual spiritual energy that does the actual connecting of the past to present."[40] In this respect, Said goes on to say, humanism lies within the activity of interpretation because it stresses the human powers of interpretation—"a crucial element in *human* intellec-

Humanism, Territory, and Techniques • 93

tual power and will" (my emphasis).⁴¹ Auerbach, in other words, transforms an aspect of figural interpretation into a secular form of understanding in order to grasp a particular kind of relationship between the past and the present. "Basically, the way in which we view human life and society is the same whether we are concerned with things of the past or things of the present." Auerbach continues:

> A change in our manner of viewing history will of necessity soon be transferred to our manner of viewing current conditions. When people realized that epochs and societies are not to be judged in terms of the pattern concept of what is desirable absolutely speaking but rather in every case in terms of their own premises; when people reckon such premises not only natural factors like climate and soil but also the intellectual and historical factors; when, in other words, they come to develop a sense of historical dynamics, of the incompatibility of historical phenomenon and of their constant inner mobility; when they come to appreciate the vital unity of individual epochs, so that each epoch appears as a whole whose character is reflected in each of its manifestations; when finally, they accept the conviction that the meaning of events cannot be grasped in abstract and general forms of cognition and that the material needed to understand it must not be sought exclusively in the upper strata of society and in major political events but also in art, economy, material and intellectual culture, in the depths of the workaday world and its men and women, because it is only there that one can grasp what is unique, which is animated by inner forces, and what, in both a more concrete and a more profound sense, is universally valid: then it is to be expected that those insights will also be transferred to the present and that, in consequence, the present too will be seen as incomparable and unique, as animated by inner forces and in a constant state of development; in other words, as a piece of history whose everyday depths and total infrastructure lay claim to our interest both in their origins and in the direction taken by their development.⁴²

There could be no clearer expression of the aims of this historicist technique: beginning with an analysis of the particularities of the text instead of making generalizations or abstractions about it. This is what gives the plot of *Mimesis* the sense of its movement forward in time as an unfolding of literary history, one that throughout its course transmutes reality and gives it new language. *Mimesis* is experienced as a series of images of (Western) humanity remaking itself through its inventive capacity to fulfill the figures through which reality is represented as an object of human consciousness. In the chapter on Dante's *Inferno*—the crux of the book—we are presented with Auerbach's analysis of Dante's extraordinary achievement to preserve the figure of human life in the world beyond, yet at the same time maintain the earthliness, worldliness, and secularity of human life on the ground. "Dante's art," Auerbach observes, "carries the matter [of figural interpretation] so far that the effect becomes earthly." The divine order that fulfills the promise of the human figure on earth is dramatically transformed as a result. "By virtue of [Dante's] immediate and admiring sympathy of man," Auerbach writes, "the principle, rooted in the divine order, of the indestructibility of the whole historical and individual man turns *against* that [divine] order. The image of man eclipses the image of God" (my emphasis).[43] The result is that we are given the opportunity to see human life unfold out of itself anew, ontogenetically. As Said observes, Dante "produced a poem whose ambition and indeed subject were nothing less than the unification of the past with the present and the future. And this in effect becomes Auerbach's ambition in *Mimesis*, to create a historical vision of the secular world incarnated in language through an unfolding, dramatic interpretation of an entire literature, which Auerbach represents in the various readings."[44]

Said's affinity with Auerbach certainly, as Aamir Mufti has observed, lies in the way that he represents exile as contesting the stability of notions of belonging, community, home, and nation: "Auerbach's relationship to 'the Western cultural tradition' is *already* one of exile, a condition tragically dramatized by the literal displacement to Istanbul—the preeminent site of non-Europe—an exile brought about by the rise of genocidal fascism in the European home itself" (my emphasis).[45] In other words, we must understand Auerbach's perspective as *displaced* and *decentered*. Auerbach reimagines and reconstructs a Europe against the grain of an essentialized, racialized, and genocidal vision of Europe. In this way Auerbach's reinvention of the West emphasizes the sheer existence and lived reality of the human subject in opposition to the identitarian practices of Nazi Germany to remake Europe.

Nevertheless, Auerbach offered more than a way for Said to question preconceived notions of belonging and home. His circumstances provided the conditions through which Said developed the critical concepts of the secular, as well as the notions of filiation and affiliation, which were two of the terms that allowed him to analyze the relationship between culture, system, and critical consciousness. Furthermore, Auerbach's "Philology and *Weltliteratur*" established the conceptual basis through which he would rethink the coordinates for a new humanism that was addressed to the changing global realities and exigencies of the late twentieth and early twenty-first centuries. As Emily Apter has observed, "Said was taking up the challenge of using Auerbachian humanism to fashion new humanisms, not merely because of a sober conviction that great books, on the grounds of their intrinsic merit, should continue to have traction in a global, increasingly mediatized culture industry but more because of his belief that humanism provides futural parameters for defining secular criticism in a world increasingly governed by a sense of identitarian ethnic destiny and competing sacred tongues."[46] Although Auerbach's historicism was not without its limitations, his views of philology and *Weltliteratur* prepared the grounds for Said to reevaluate and reconfigure the dialectic between history and literature in the concept of humanism.

"Philology and *Weltliteratur*" (1952), an essay that Auerbach wrote and Said later cotranslated, was Auerbach's attempt to work through a methodological and cultural crisis of the Cold War that demanded he conceive *Weltliteratur* differently, within the constraints of an economic and political order that was polarized. Written five years after he left Istanbul for the United States, the essay warned of the imminent disappearance of a vast archive of human knowledge that would chill the development of an entire way of understanding the present's relationship to the past. A historical perspective introduced first by Giambattista Vico, Gottfried Johann Herder, and later expressed in the form of Goethean humanism was, he warned, rapidly being undermined by the homogenizing and standardizing forces that Adorno and Horkheimer had described nearly a decade earlier in *Dialectic of Enlightenment*. The forces of mass production and technological reproduction were eroding the foundation of "all individual traditions."[47] "Standardization dominates everywhere," Auerbach wrote. "All human activity is being concentrated into European-American or Russian-Bolshevik patterns." *Weltkultur*, he warned, was homogenizing, rationalizing, and leveling national cultures "with a greater rapidity than ever before."[48]

Auerbach perceived that the conditions for a flourishing and meaningful apprehension of *Weltliteratur* (as a mode of cultural exchange and understanding) were at risk of being dominated by the leveling spread of *Weltkultur*. The world, he warned, may have to accustom itself to uniformity, "to a single literary culture, only a few literary languages, and perhaps even a single literary language. And herewith the notion of *Weltliteratur* would be at once realized and destroyed."[49] As part of a long discourse of cultural criticism that emerged in the late eighteenth century in the context of cultural fears about the social consequences of industrialization, democratization, and revolution, Auerbach warned that an entire way of conceiving human history was on the verge of becoming a mere abstraction. He wrote:

> The inner history of the last thousand years is the history of mankind achieving self-expression: this is what philology, a historicist discipline, treats. This history contains the records of man's mighty, adventurous advance to a consciousness of his human condition and to the realization of his given potential; and this advance, whose final goal (even in its wholly fragmentary present form) was barely imaginable for a long

time, still seems to have proceeded as if according to a plan, in spite of its twisted course. All the rich tensions of which our being is capable are contained within this course. An inner dream unfolds whose scope and depth entirely animate the spectator [the philologist], enabling him at the same time to find peace in his given potential by the enrichment he gains from having witnessed the drama. The loss of such a spectacle—whose appearance is thoroughly dependent on presentation and interpretation—would be an impoverishment for which there can be no possible compensation.[50]

Faced with the prospects of such a loss, Auerbach urged philologists to collect whatever they could of the archive of human records of expression. "We are still basically capable of fulfilling this duty [as philologists]," he wrote, "not only because we have a great deal of material at our disposal, but also because we have inherited the sense of historical perspectivism." Yet the felt awareness of a concrete reality of historical multiplicity was dimming considerably, he said, even though at the very same moment the potential for a survey of human history appeared within reach.

For Auerbach, the evanescence of an entire way of viewing and experiencing the dialectical unfolding of human history meant stagnation: "Whatever we are[,] we became in history, and only in history can we remain the way we are and develop therefrom."[51] The philologist's responsibility was to present the connection between the past, present, and the future in a way that was felt, experienced, and could not possibly be forgotten. Yet the basic conditions for the transmission of *Weltliteratur* had been eroded. The manipulation and control over the modes of articulation that I described in the previous chapters had considerably undermined the foundations of historicist humanism, which essentially held that *Weltliteratur* was "the fruitful intercourse" among and between nations, as Auerbach and Goethe had seen it.[52] The consequences of a complete divorce from the components of that selective tradition meant, for Auerbach, the dissolution of a mode of scholarly investigation that had the capacity to grasp the whole of human history. The crisis was not simply the disappearance of a discipline, but the elimination of an interdisciplinary mode of secular knowledge that saw humanity "unified in its multiplicity."[53]

In Auerbach's diagnosis, economic, cultural, and political forces had obstructed the channels of mutual understanding and undermined the conditions for new forms of knowledge and understanding to emerge. Though writing a mere seven years after the signing of the UN Charter, Auerbach was prepared to place the discourse of international coexistence on perpetual hold. As a modality of mutual comprehension, Goethe's conception of *Weltliteratur* had, he lamented, become anachronistic in an era driven by its "compulsion and dependence on mass movements."[54] He argued that the crisis demanded a reconceptualization of *Weltliteratur* in terms that directly addressed the specific realities as well as the political, economic, and cultural conditions that philology faced. If Goethe saw *Weltliteratur* as a mode for mutual understanding between nations, Auerbach's conception of *Weltliteratur* was merely an aspiration turning in the direction of a mode.

Weltliteratur, in Auerbach's estimation, could only be comprehended in the limited terms of "diverse backgrounds that had come to share a common fate." He claimed that it was unrealistic to think that any new conception of *Weltliteratur* could reverse—let alone halt—the expansion of the global forces of standardization. At the very least he imagined that a different conception of the idea would be able to give historical expression to "the fateful coalescence of cultures for those people who are in the midst of a terminal phase of their fruitful multiplicity."[55] At the very most, he hoped that his notion of *Weltliteratur* would allow philology to record the human expressions of cultures at the very moment of their disappearance. The aim and overriding intention of this shift in the meaning of *Weltliteratur* was not only to establish the conditions to archive the past record of human achievements and their expressions but also to provide a philological investigation of human material that, as Vico had argued before him, was integral to the conception of a humanity "unified in its multiplicities." The loss of an element constitutive of the unity of humanity at a particular stage in time meant that knowledge of a historically contingent certainty (what Vico called *certum*) would not simply be forgotten but, more important, that the disappearance of a segment of time in which humanity had developed a particular, yet historically contingent awareness of itself would disrupt the dialectic and prevent any synthesis from emerging.

Because knowledge could only be revealed in relation to the *potential* apprehension of human history as a whole, the philologist's study of certainties (*certum*) at each stage of human development and in the wider context of its subsequent development was indispensable to grasping a truth (*verum*) only partially visible over the course of time in the form of particularities of historically contingent certainties (*certum*).[56] Unlike the historically contingent nature of *certum*, truth (*verum*), Vico claimed, was immutable and never fully revealed in its entirety at any one particular stage of human history. Because these truths could only be apprehended as the potential to know human history as a whole, the philologist's study of *certum* at each stage and in their general context contributed to the potentiality of knowledge of the whole of human history. This was why Auerbach spoke of the "rich tensions" that were advanced in the course of history.

Yet the changing circumstances and alignments in the world did mean that the methods for philological practice had to be recalibrated. To begin with, the sheer amount of material to be mastered far exceeded the capacities of any single scholar. Because of the growing dominance of specialized fields that overlapped with philology, the philologist had to acquire skills commensurable with specialists in interrelated disciplines such as religion, philosophy, and music. Pressures from disciplines such as literary criticism, sociology, and psychology had encroached on philology to the degree that specialized knowledge of those fields created additional burdens. If any kind of synthesis between literature and history was to be realized, Auerbach argued, the new historical realities facing the philologist required the adoption of different methods of analysis.

To that end, Auerbach advanced the idea that philologists begin by identifying some partially understandable phenomena (*Ansatzphänomen*) that were circumscribed and concrete. He called these points of departure (*Ansatzpunkt*). They had a specificity and particularity to them, but they also had a "radiating power." In other words, these elements that constituted the phenomenon could, through careful and patient analysis and exposition, allow the particular to become increasingly general and thus maintain a correspondence with world history so that a synthesis could be realized. Auerbach claimed that the movement from the particular to the whole was generated by a desire to realize the whole, yet each particularity had to be grasped as an essence in order for the radiating movement to be pure. The most that could be acquired even under "the most favorable circumstances is an insight into the diverse implications of the process from which we stem and in which we participate, a definition of our present situation and also perhaps the possibilities for the immediate future."[57] He presupposed that because literature corresponded to and was commensurable with history that philology could provide an account of humanity's progressive awareness of its potential. For Auerbach, no better method pertained to the exigencies of the present. "The more our earth grows closer together, the more must historical synthesis balance the contraction by expanding its activity. To make men conscious of themselves in their own history is a great task, yet the task is small—more like a renunciation—when one considers that man not only lives on earth, but that he is in the world and in the universe," he wrote.[58] In order to establish that kind of awareness, Auerbach posed an important formulation that was to become part of the genealogy of a critical cosmopolitanism that would later mostly overlook the philology that helped to define it. "Our philological home is earth; it can no longer be the nation," he wrote.[59] Against the current of hardening national identities, Auerbach viewed philology as a critical awareness and enlargement of consciousness that displaced the fixed identities of home, nation, and belonging. Quoting a passage from Hugo St. Victor, Auerbach presented these detachments to place in the form of developing self-awareness that reflected a kind of unfolding in the "renunciation" he claimed was necessary to make humans "more conscious of themselves in their own history": "The person who finds his homeland sweet is a tender beginner; he to whom every soil is as his native one is already strong; but he is perfect to whom the entire world is as a foreign place. The tender soul has fixed his love on one spot in the world; the strong person has extended his love to all places; the perfect man has extinguished his."[60]

That Auerbach did not extend his challenge to an interpretative method circumscribed by an idealism that was unable to see the disjuncture between literature and history was a task left up to Said. "Auerbach's method," Said observed, "unlocked the system of correspondences between history and literature that is the cornerstone of a whole tradition regarding temporality as both the repository of human experience, past, present, and future, as well as a mode of understanding by which historical reality can be comprehended."[61] Because history and literature were not fixed entities, Said observed, the dialectical relationship between the two were mediated by the critic. Yet because Auerbach's historicism configured the relationship between literature and history as informing each other, he presupposed that literature and history emerged out of the same element of time and together developed toward a synthesis. Though Auerbach appeared increasingly skeptical of that assumption (he remarked that history's course had been "twisted") and was able to renounce his attachments, he seemed only dimly aware that the assumptions behind historicist humanism were contingent upon his attachments to an anachronistic idealism that could not account for the rise of Nazism, which drove him into exile in Istanbul. Said would turn to Gramsci and Adorno to work this out.

Said's observation that there were obvious limitations to Auerbach's understanding that literature and history developed out of the same element in time was not to dismiss the historicist idealism out of hand. To the author of *Orientalism*, the constraints of idealist historicism were clear enough. Said valued certain aspects of that tradition and considered it the "cornerstone of a whole tradition regarding temporality as the repository of human experience past, present, and future." Yet, "as *Mimesis* immediately reveals, . . . the notion of Western literature that lies at the very core of comparative study centrally highlights, dramatizes, and celebrates a certain idea of history, and at the same time obscures the fundamental geographical and political reality empowering that idea," Said writes.[62]

The discipline of geography was by no means neutral. The earth was the space upon which power had imposed its imagination: an imaginary geography. The emergence of the discipline of comparative literature, and later iterations of it, Said argued, drew a great deal from the work of colonial geography. Figures such as Halford Mackinder, George Chisolm, Georges Hardy, Leroy-Beaulieu, and Lucien Febvre had produced a geographical vision that left the primacy of Europe unchallenged.[63] As he observed in *Culture and Imperialism*, this was precisely the horizon upon which the early practitioners of comparative literature had conceived of the discipline of comparative literature. The coincidences and convergences between these two world systems needed to be reactivated and articulated by the present, namely, in the context of the postcolonial. "We need to see that our contemporary global setting—overlapping territories and intertwined histories—was already prefigured and inscribed in the coincidence and convergences among geography, culture, and history that were so important to the pioneers of comparative literature."[64] Only then, he argued, could we critically apprehend in a "new and more dynamic way the idealistic historicist model, which fueled the map of comparative literature" and the particular, specific "imperial map of the same moment."[65]

But how, Said asked, do we provide a critical account of the relationship between the universalist aspirations of *Weltliteratur* and the synthesizing territorial ambitions of a geography upon which the claims of *Weltliteratur* were based without reducing one discourse to the other? He thought it was by no means sufficiently stimulating to suggest that both disciplines advanced the system of imperialism.[66] Such analysis gives us little understanding of how and where both practices emerged. What was necessary, Said argued, was not to analyze them as unified but as two distinct discourses that functioned together as an ensemble. But this ensemble was more than a mere conjuncture and coincidence. It was an elaboration of power—a process that needed to be accounted for from the perspectives of those who had resisted it.

The questions Said asked of Auerbach's assumptions were the same he had asked of Lukács's, who had, in *The Theory of the Novel*, placed a similar emphasis on the category of time. In a great deal of Western literary history, including Auerbach's works, Said saw a dominant tendency to embrace the "Hegelian tradition of focusing on temporality as [a way of] resolving threats to identity."[67] What struck Said was that a temporal comprehension could no longer sufficiently address the transformations and the emergence of a "new geographical consciousness":

> Hegel and Auerbach, and of course Lukács, made no secret of their predilection, not to say prejudice, for the centrality of Europe, at the same time that they argue for what they intend as a universal scheme of literary history. But what if the world has changed so drastically as to allow now for almost the first time a new geographical consciousness of a decentered or multi-centered world, a world no longer sealed within watertight compartments of art or culture or history, but mixed, mixed up, varied, complicated by the new difficult mobility of migrations, the new independent states, the newly emergent and burgeoning cultures?[68]

Against the current of a Hegelian tradition to which Auerbach and György Lukács belonged, Said saw territory as the terrain of social activity. "I do not mean to say that various interpretative modes grounded in temporality which I have ... identified with Hegel are to be discarded," he wrote. "On the contrary, as my enormous debt to Auerbach testifies, I think it is an absolutely essential thing for us. But what I do want to add is that historically the world's geography has changed so definitively as to make it impossible to attempt reconciliations between history and literature."[69] This synthesis between history and literature imposed conjunctures where there were actually disjunctures, continuities where there were discontinuities, commensurabilities where there were incommensurabilities. Auerbach's method seemed to exemplify how hegemony operated as a social process through which identities, fragments, and parts were made to *appear* as if they were whole and unified. "The basic social contest for Gramsci is one of hegemony," Said wrote, "that is control of essentially heterogeneous, discontinuous, non-identical, *unequal* geographies of human habitation and effort. There is no redemption in Gramsci's world, which is true to a remarkable Italian tradition of pessimistic materialism [and] is profoundly secular. What this all does to identity, which you recall is at the core of Hegelian temporality, is to render it unstable and extremely provisional" (my emphasis).[70] Culture and society were "productive activities occurring territorially,"[71] Said observed. The secular was the terrain of human history—a human activity that was constantly in the making. "The *secular* is the 'always, already' begun [in the earthly] realm of continuously human effort."[72] But he gave the "name 'worldliness' to ... a knowing and unafraid attitude toward exploring the world we live in." Said wrote:

> Cognate words, derived from Vico and Auerbach, have been "secular" and "secularism" as applied to "earthly" matters; in these words, which derived from the Italian materialist tradition that runs from Lucretius through to Gramsci and Lampedusa, I have found an important corrective to the German idealist tradition of *synthesizing the antithetical*, as we find it in Hegel, Marx, Lukács, and Habermas. For not only did "earthly" note the historical world made by men and women ... , but it suggested a *territorial* grounding for my argument and language, which proceeded from an attempt to understand the imaginative geographies fashioned and then imposed by power on distant lands and people.[73] (my emphasis)

Because the secular world was historical and constantly made and remade by men and women, secular criticism was the situated awareness that the world was the name for the physical terrain upon which power projected its imaginative geography. That is to say, the secular circumscribed the domain of human activity in the world, not at one particular moment but as something that was always already made and remade by human beings. If criticism required distance and detachment in order to be critical, worldliness was the particular attitude that demystified filial and affilial attachments. Secular criticism designated that distance in the form of an awareness of the critic's place in the world. Because secular human history had a territorial basis, and not simply a temporal one, the secular critic was capable of traversing boundaries as well as grasping the overlapping connections between the intertwined, discrepant experiences that comprised the realm of human activities:

> If I've insisted on the integration and connection between the past and the present, I have done so rather to convey a more urgent sense of the interdependence between things. So vast and so detailed is imperialism as an experience with crucial cultural dimensions, that we must speak of overlapping territories, intertwined histories, common to men and women, whites and nonwhites, dwellers in the metropolis and on the peripheries, past as well as present and future; these territories and histories can only be seen from the perspective of the whole of secular human history.[74]

Said's manner of retaining a particular element of historicism that understood that the past was as much a part of the present, the earthly as much a part of the future, the yet-made history of the present, echoed Auerbach's idealism in his description of a "perspective of the whole of secular human history."

The theoretical relationship between philological practice and humanism was to be elaborated upon in *Humanism and Democratic Criticism* (2004), among one of Said's last books, composed partially of three lectures he delivered at Columbia University. The complexity of the text has been often underestimated, and its importance has gone mostly unacknowledged.[75] In many ways the work aimed to establish the grounds for a humanism that was committed to philological practice and yet based on a premise that denied any reconciliation between the particularities (the novel, the work of art) to the whole (secular human history). While Said had already discerned many of the limitations of Auerbach's historicist humanism,[76] within the reading techniques established by philology, Said asked if it was possible to "develop a *modernist* theory and practice" (emphasis in the original) of interpreting the part to the whole in a dialectical way that neither concealed the specificities of the subjective experience of the aesthetic nor invalidated a possible conceptualization of the whole as the basis for humanism.[77]

Said's efforts to reactivate the resources of a particular discipline that had become one of the most antiquated, musty branches of the humanities might have appeared arcane, but it was by no means a regression for the author of *Orientalism*. After all, the distinction between theological philology (the discourse of Orientalism) and secular philology (*Geisteswissenschaften, sciences de l'homme*) was a decisive theme of *Orientalism*, and in many ways the full implications of that distinction had not been fully elaborated even in his discussions of Auerbach.[78] The return to philology was not a movement predicated on some "belief," as has been suggested; nor was it a statement that emerged out of some kind of nostalgia for a scholarly practice that depended on a kind of training and knowledge that Said had acknowledged was no longer possible; rather, it was an effort, much like Auerbach's *Mimesis*—of human will—to challenge the underlying assumptions that circumscribed the social function of the humanist in U.S. culture and society.

In his description of the changing basis of humanist practice, Said had argued that much—though not everything—that was done in the name of humanism during the Cold War had been, as I have tried to show throughout this book, administered, managed, diffused, transmitted, and organized by government organizations and other Cold War institutions. He described how, for example, the CCF funded "innumerable humanistic and academic conferences, journals like *Encounter*, *Der Monat*, and the *Partisan Review*, prizes, art exhibitions, concerts, musical competitions, and many writers and intellectuals."[79] He claimed that the activities that organizations like the CCF sponsored "had a profound effect on the kind of cultural work that was produced and the kind of activity carried out in the name of freedom and totalitarianism." Although the CCF did not "run cultural life," he said,

> much of what was done in the name of freedom and democratic values, and fighting communist totalitarianism[,] contributed significantly to humanistic practice. It provided some of the overarching carapace and numerous programs and occasions for the promotion of humanism. Even so cerebral and subtle an analyst of poetry as R. P. Blackmur . . . made an early alliance with the Rockefeller Foundation, not only to finance his remarkable series of Princeton seminars, . . . but also to take several trips to the Third World, in order, among other things, to gauge the depth of American influence there.[80]

If these Cold War activities were "part of an overall pattern in which threats to humanistic culture seemed to be ingrained in the very nature of thought and the human situation in general," Said held that the cultural divisions and distinctions belonged to a "fundamental epistemology of modern culture and the humanities."[81] The episteme seemed to demand that the situation be recast "in terms of threats to every succeeding generation."[82] He held the view, in other words, that the Cold War was not a struggle between "totalitarianism" and "democracy"; rather, it was a way of knowing, a style of thought through which power worked to create divisions, distinctions, and discriminations. Articulated through new modes of transmission, the episteme established not only "an underlying consensus . . . that aesthetic analysis was meant as a barrier against the overt politicization of art" but the conventionally held view that politics was the realm for only certain socially certified figures.[83] Cultural figures were not permitted to cross over into the political world without official sanction. At the same time, however, "culture" functioned as a realm that camouflaged certain activities. Area studies as a field of study was constituted and the teaching of languages was funded in 1958 by the National Defense Education Act, which transformed the study of foreign languages into a matter of national security. Disciplines like anthropology, history, sociology, political science, and language studies, were, he observed, "underwritten by Cold War concerns."[84]

Yet in the aftermath of 1989, the shifting political and cultural reconfigurations had transformed the landscape within U.S. universities. Not to overemphasize the role that *Orientalism* played, but Eurocentrism and many of the identitarian suppositions upon which a classical humanism had rested had apparently been defeated on many fronts within the university by the late twentieth century. *Orientalism* and much of the scholarship that the book engendered had permitted a radical rethinking of the cultural politics of representation. An enormous terrain of human history that was scarcely visible as a domain of study in the late 1970s had become many fields by the late twentieth. A dominant mode of thought that had been marginalized through various disciplinary and interdisciplinary practices had been dislodged, and what were once subjugated forms of knowledge became new forms of knowledge. Particular cultural and political victories had established the conditions for an epistemic shift, Said argued. Movements of migration had reshaped the social terrain in ways that were unimaginable in the middle of the twentieth century. He wrote, "American humanism by virtue of what was available to it and in the normal course of its own context and historical reality was in a state of civil co-existence."[85]

Precisely because there was a discrepancy between the official discourse and the multiplicity of uneven, shared experiences that constituted its civil society, he saw the United States as a realm of hybrid, shared, asymmetrically felt experiences and histories that, he claimed, provided humanism with the resources to resist official discourse. This was by no means to say that some kind of multiculturalism or levity had been achieved; or that the vast structural inequities had suddenly vanished; or that globalization had ground to a halt; or that poverty, racism, imperialism, or the death penalty had been abolished. As it turned out, many of the residual feelings that had appeared to weaken by 2000 (the very year when he delivered the *Humanism* lectures) could and *did* find their way to the surface in a country that he described as "mobile" and "restless."

A central historical fact that cannot be overlooked in any examination of *Humanism and Democratic Criticism* is that Said had delivered part of the book as a series of lectures before the tragic events of 9/11. His remarks on the "changing conditions of humanistic practice" were delivered in January 2000, well before the attacks on Washington, D.C., and New York, months before the outbreak of the first war in Afghanistan, and more than three years before the Anglo-American invasion of Iraq. In the preface, written in May 2003, he said that the book was "not a definitive statement of the world [in which] we live." But, in many ways, the book was and remains a decisive statement of a socially specific moment. It was the expression of a willed human effort. In its final words, the text reiterated Beckett's, "I can't go on, I'll go on," in its effort to establish a *"modernist* theory and practice" (emphasis in the original).[86] The domain of the intellectual was, he observed, "the place where one can first truly grasp the difficulty of what cannot be grasped and then go forth and try anyway."[87]

This is not to say that Said's view was a preparation or a simple announcement of an impending failure that posited the realm of the intellectual in the "intransigent" realm of a late style that he regarded for its difficult, antinomian relationship to society.[88] The book was much more than a stubborn Conradian conviction that the humanist mission was housed in the provisional realm of late art. The strength of *Humanism and Democratic Criticism* can be identified with the way that the text enacts its own modernist practice in its shifting metaphors of place and space—the space of words and social space. Humanism also presupposed that a fundamental irreconcilability existed between the aesthetic and the nonaesthetic. Said's historicism was not motivated by the simple negation or opposition of a dialectical synthesis; rather, *Humanism and Democratic Criticism* is more complicated because it enacts the terms of modernity in the metaphors of a space that corresponds to the humanist's consciousness of non-identity.

This was crucial for coordinating a *modernist* theory and practice of interpreting the particular to the general in terms of a negative dialectics that, unlike Hegel's, did not find reconciliation in the negation of nonidentity and identity. To reconcile the two, as Hegel ultimately did, would be, as Adorno observed in his *Lectures on Negative Dialectics*, to engage in a form of administrative thought that sees synthesis as the product of the negation of negation—the basis of Hegel's dialectic. "The negation of negation is in fact nothing other than the ... recollection, of the violence, in other words the acknowledgement that, by conjoining two opposing concepts, ... I have on the one hand bowed to a necessity implicit in them, while on the other hand I have done them a violence that has to be rectified."[89]

The strategy to relate the particular text to the potential whole of secular human history was to displace the temporal element of Auerbach's dialectic onto the "space of words." If the analysis of rhetoric and literary language was concerned with uncovering the specific lapses, silences, and distortions inherent in the process of language, Said considered philological criticism as the consciousness of a non-identity that it could "never fully grasp."[90] Only through disclosing what is concealed, hidden, and distorted by language, he argued, could the non-identical be *indirectly* revealed. *If the "space of words" was the conceptualization of the silences, lapses, and distortions of language that were always taking place*, resistance demanded "that the reader make connections that are otherwise concealed or distorted by the text." What this required then was "the ability to know the difference between what is directly given or revealed and what is withheld or concealed."[91] This resistance involved opening up the text to a wider, *general*, historically situated awareness of the "multiple worlds and complex interacting traditions."[92]

Describing the domain of the humanists' concerns in spatial and geographical terms was crucial to the way Said conceived of philology's ability to articulate what was rendered absent and silent by words. What this entailed was a refiguration of a space that resisted identitarian thought. "The movements of our time and of our country are movements in and out of territory," he wrote. "To be moved in and off it, to try to stay, to try to establish new settlements" defined an unending condition of displacing displacements. He saw an "implacable dynamic of place and displacement that, in this endlessly mobile country of ours, where the location of the frontier both metaphorical and real appears never to be settled, is still very much the issue."[93]

"Our age and our country symbolize not just what has been settled and permanently resides here," Said argued, "but always and constantly the undocumented turbulence of unsettled and unhoused exiles, immigrants, itinerant or captive populations, for whom no document, adequate expression yet exists sufficient to take account of what they go through. And in its profoundly unsettled energy, the country deserves the kind of widening awareness beyond academic specialization that a whole range of younger humanists have signaled as cosmopolitan, worldly, mobile."[94] He argued that there is no permanence to place. Exiles are unhoused and unsettled. The culture is a place of displacement as much as it is a displacing place—a displacing place of displacement. And yet, he wondered, how is it possible to give expression to the lived and historical experiences of those who undergo an "undocumented turbulence"? What language is there to describe the experiences of immigrants in a state of constant movement and in a state of captivity for which there is "no document"? How are we to understand that no "adequate expression" yet exists to sufficiently provide an account of their experience? What inventory of this experience remains? he asks. In this age of archival storage and the documentary, he argued, human experience is "being lost by homogenization."

If Said's humanism has any relevance at all in a society and culture where knowledge of itself and its own history is prohibited by little-known emergency decrees on the terrain of national security, then critics must oppose the specific dictates of an instrumentalizing reason that exercises authority in society. For secular criticism to really be secular and actually worldly, the task of the humanist, Said suggests, is to traverse the boundaries imposed by power and existing forms of dominative knowledge—whether that knowledge is produced by governments, institutions, multinational corporations, or political movements. "Humanism ... is the means, perhaps a consciousness we have for providing that kind of finally antinomian or oppositional analysis between ... [the] deployment [of words] in physical and social place, from text to actualized site of either appropriation or resistance, to transmission."[95] Humanism, in other words, mediates the particularities of language in the social space of human activity at the same time that it opposes them to the general conditions of social existence that the space of words conceal, disfigure, and silence. In a culture and a society that can assert that the "existence or nonexistence" of documents can "neither be confirmed nor denied," to what realm, Said asked, does the intellectual belong? Said located the "domain" (it is no longer the "world") of the intellectual in the challenges posed by Adorno's theory of the late style of artwork—works that were intransigent, difficult, and unresolved. Troping Auerbach's metaphor that "our philological home is earth," Said placed the intellectual's "provisional home ... in the domain of the exigent, resistant, transient art into which one can neither retreat nor search for solutions."[96]

It was from that location that the humanist "excavates the silences, the world of memory, of the itinerant, barely surviving groups, the places of exclusion and invisibility."[97] It must uncover the archives of authority, and witness in the archive's very disclosure of its impermanence the humanist's capacity to resist the ideological forms of closure, synthesis, and resolution. That is to say, the humanist never gives in to the illusion that the fissures and dislocations between literature and history are synthesized under the social compulsion to produce self-fulfilling solutions that are the abracadabras of all systematic thought and worldviews.

Notes

Introduction

1. Quoted in Frances Stonor Saunders, *Who Paid the Piper? The CIA and the Cultural Cold War* (London: Granta Books, 1999), 248–49. James Angleton graduated with a degree in English literature from Yale University, where he was the editor of the modernist journal *Furioso*. After university he joined what was to become the Central Intelligence Agency, where he was instrumental in coordinating efforts to ensure that the Italian Communist Party would not prevail in that country's elections in 1948. Angleton often referred to Eliot when representing the Soviet Union in public. That country was, he said, quoting Eliot's *Gerontion* on a television interview, "a wilderness of mirrors." See Robin Winks, *Cloak and Gown: Scholars in the Secret War, 1939–1961* (New Haven: Yale University Press, 1987).

2. Fritz Strich, *Goethe and World Literature* (London: Routledge & Kegan Paul, 1949), 349.

3. Ibid., 349–51.

4. David Damrosch, for example, asserts that world literature encompasses all literary works that circulate beyond their culture of origin. See David Damrosch, *What Is World Literature?* (Princeton: Princeton University Press, 2003), 6.

5. John Pizer, for example, has observed that a "renewed interest in Goethean *Weltliteratur* is the almost inevitable result in our day of developments that somewhat mirror, and advance, those of Goethe's time: the end of the cold war and the concomitant rise of global financial institutions and multinational corporations (including many publishing houses); the emergence of numerous authors whose political, cultural, and sometimes even linguistic allegiances transcend the bounds of individual nation-states; and technologies such as the World Wide Web. Thus Goethe's pronouncement in 1827 on the arrival of a *Weltliteratur* rendering national literatures rather insignificant is more accurate today than it was in Goethe's age." See John Pizer, "Toward a Productive Interdisciplinary Relationship: Between Comparative Literature and World Literature," *Comparatist* 31 (May 2007): 6. For an analysis of cosmopolitanism as a situation of displacement, see Bruce Robbins, "Comparative Cosmopolitanism," *Social Text*, nos. 31/32 (1992): 7.

6. For analysis of how contemporary discussions of *Weltliteratur* incapacitate a thorough critique of globalization, see Andreas Huyssen, "Geographies of Modernism in a Globalizing World," *New German Critique* 100 (2007): 196–97; and Robert E. Livingston, "Global Knowledges: Agency and Place in Literary Studies," *PMLA* 116, no. 1 (2001): 145–57.

7. According to Vilashini Cooppan, "Read through the uncanny, literature's vast life becomes in fact a kind of life-in-death, a form of haunting. The spectral haunting quality of world literature illuminates the dynamic relation of interaction,

borrowing, improvisation, and alteration that actually produce texts across time." See Vilashini Cooppan, "Ghosts in the Disciplinary Machine: The Uncanny Life of World Literature," *Comparative Literature Studies* 41, no. 1 (2004): 22.

8. See, for example, Jonathan Arac, "Commentary: Literary History in a Global Age," *New Literary History* 39, no. 3 (2009): 747–60; Walter F. Veit, "Globalization and Literary History; or, Rethinking Comparative Literary History— Globally," *New Literary History* 39, no. 3 (2009): 415–35; Emily Apter, "Untranslatables: A World System," *New Literary History* 39, no. 3 (2009): 581–98.

9. As Pheng Cheah argues "one vocational task of literature in this world of comparison is to provide an aesthetic-cognitive mapping of how the mechanisms and technologies of infrastructural comparison work in specific locations and their negative, coercive effects." See Pheng Cheah, "The Material World of Comparison," *New Literary History* 40, no. 3 (2009): 523–45. Also see Edward W. Said, "Globalizing Literary Study," *PMLA* 116, no. 1 (2001): doi:10.2307/463641; Emily Apter, "On Translation in a Global Market," *Public Culture* 13, no. 1 (2001): 1–12.

10. Sibel Irzık makes the argument that Orhan Pamuk's *The Black Book* is structured and even addressed to Western readers insofar as the story is told to a Western journalist. Sibel Irzık, "Istanbul," in *The Novel*, ed. Franco Moretti, vol. 2 (Princeton: Princeton University Press, 2006), 734–35. Orhan Pamuk, *The Black Book*, trans. Güneli Gün (New York: Farrar, Straus and Giroux, 1994). *The Black Book* was published first in Turkey in 1990.

11. Michel-Rolph Trouillot, "The Otherwise Modern: Caribbean Lessons from the Savage Slot," in *Critically Modern*, ed. B. M. Knauft (Bloomington: Indiana University Press, 2002), 220.

12. Franco Moretti, *The Modern Epic: The World-System from Goethe to García Márquez* (New York: Verso, 1996), 50. Also see Pascale Casanova, *The World Republic of Letters*, trans. M. B. DeBois (Cambridge, MA: Harvard University Press, 2004); Franco Moretti, "Conjectures on World Literature," *New Left Review* 1 (January 2000): 54–68; Franco Moretti, "More Conjectures," *New Left Review* 20 (March 2003): 73–81; Franco Moretti "The Novel: History and Theory," *New Left Review* 52 (July 2008): 111–24; Pascale Casanova, "Literature as a World," *New Left Review* 31 (2005): 71–90; Franco Moretti, *Graphs, Maps, Trees: Abstract Models for a Literary History* (New York: Verso, 2005); and Wai Chee Dimock and Laurence Buell, eds., *Shades of the Planet: American Literature as World Literature* (Princeton, NJ: Princeton University Press, 2007).

13. Casanova, *The World Republic of Letters*, 351.

14. Ibid., 354.

15. György Lukács, *The Theory of the Novel: A Historico-Philosophical Essay on the Forms of Great Epic Literature*, trans. Anna Bostock (Cambridge: M.I.T. Press, 1971).

16. Casanova, "Literature as a World," 72.

17. See, in particular, Edward Said's chapter on "Discrepant Experiences," in *Culture and Imperialism* (New York: Knopf, 1994), 31–43.

18. Critical accounts have been advanced by Aamir R. Mufti, "Orientalism and the Institution of World Literatures," *Critical Inquiry* 36, no. 3 (March 2010): 458–93; Christopher Prendergast and Benedict R. O'G. Anderson, eds., *Debating World Literature* (New York: Verso, 2004); and especially Jonathan Arac, "Anglo-

Globalism," *New Left Review* 16 (July–Aug 2002): 35–45. For an analysis of how traveling theories limit critical analysis because such theories have become deracinated from the historical situation that generated the theories in the first place, see Edward W. Said, "Traveling Theory," in *The World, the Text, and the Critic* (Cambridge, MA: Harvard University Press, 1983), 226–47.

19. Said, *Culture and Imperialism*, 56.
20. Ibid., 55.
21. See Casanova, "Literature as a World," 71. For a rebuttal of this claim, see, for example, Edward Said's discussion of Jane Austen's *Mansfield Park* in *Culture and Imperialism*, 80–97. The argument that textually based criticism and secular criticism (by which Said means a criticism that is both rooted in the world and in the idea that history is made by humans and can be remade by them as well) is not mutually exclusive is discussed by Said in *Humanism and Democratic Criticism* (New York: Columbia University Press, 2004).
22. See, for example, Montgomery McFate and Andrea Jackson, "An Organizational Solution for DOD's Cultural Knowledge Needs," *Military Review* 85, no. 4 (July–August 2005): 18; Montgomery McFate, "The Military Utility of Understanding an Adversary Culture," *Joint Forces Quarterly*, no. 38 (2005): 42–48; Montgomery McFate, "Anthropology and Counterinsurgency: The Strange Story of Their Curious Relationship," *Military Review* 27 (2005): 24–37; Montgomery McFate, "Iraq: The Social Context of IEDs," *Military Review* 85, no. 3 (2005): 37–40; Montgomery McFate and Andrea Jackson, "The Object Beyond War: Counterinsurgency and the Four Tools of Political Competition," *Military Review* 86, no. 1 (2006): 56–69; and Montgomery McFate and Steve Fondacaro, "Cultural Knowledge and Common Sense," *Anthropology Today* 24, no. 1 (2008): 27.
23. McFate, "The Military Utility of Understanding an Adversary Culture," 48.
24. "The Human Terrain System," http://humanterrainsystem.army.mil/Default.aspx.
25. Edward W. Said, *Orientalism* (New York: Vintage Books, 2003), 86.
26. Michel Foucault, *"Society Must Be Defended": Lectures at the Collège de France, 1975–1976*, trans. David Macey (London: Allen Lane, 2003), 254.
27. AAA Commission on the Engagement of Anthropology with the U.S. Security and Intelligence Communities (CEAUSSIC), "Final Report on the Army's Human Terrain System Proof of Concept Program," October 14, 2009, 21–22.
28. In 1964, the Special Operations Research Office of American University received a grant from the U.S. Army for "Operation Camelot" in an effort to recruit social scientists as part of the government's counterinsurgency efforts in Vietnam. See Immanuel Wallerstein, "The Unintended Consequences of Area Studies," in *The Cold War and the University: Toward an Intellectual History of the Postwar Years*, ed. Noam Chomsky (New York: New Press, 1997), 222.
29. Said, *Orientalism*, xix.
30. I am by no means claiming that the government ran and administered cultural life.
31. Erich Auerbach, "Philology and *Weltliteratur*," trans. Edward and Marie Said, *Centennial Review* 13 (1969): 3.
32. Ibid., 6.

33. Irene L. Gendzier, *Managing Political Change: Social Scientists and the Third World* (Boulder, CO: Westview Press Boulder, 1985).

34. Slavoj Žižek, *Living in the End Times* (New York: Verso, 2010), 474.

Chapter 1: Archives of Authority

1. John Crewdson and Joseph Treaster, "Worldwide Propaganda Network Built by the C.I.A.," *New York Times*, December 24, 1967; Saunders, *Who Paid the Piper?*, 245; Hugh Wilford, *The Mighty Wurlitzer: How the CIA Played America* (Cambridge, MA: Harvard University Press, 2008); Jason Epstein, "The CIA and the Intellectuals," *New York Review of Books* 8, no. 7 (April 20, 1967): 10; Winks, *Cloak and Gown*, 327; Richard Pells, *Not Like Us: How Europeans Have Loved, Hated, and Transformed American Culture since World War II* (New York: Basic Books, 1997); Penny Von Eschen, *Satchmo Blows Up the World: Jazz Ambassadors Play the Cold War* (Cambridge, MA: Harvard University Press, 2004), 4. Volker Berghahn, *America and the Intellectual Cold Wars in Europe* (Princeton: Princeton University Press, 2001); Edward W. Said, "Hey Mister, You Want Dirty Book?," *London Review of Books* (September 1999): 8–9; and Hugh Wilford, "'Unwitting Assets?': British Intellectuals and the Congress for Cultural Freedom," *Twentieth Century British History* 11, no. 1 (January 1, 2000): 42–60. For Said's brief criticism of Saunders, see *Humanism and Democratic Criticism*, 36.

2. Saunders, *Who Paid the Piper?*; Wilford, *The Mighty Wurlitzer*; Peter Coleman, *The Liberal Conspiracy: The Congress for Cultural Freedom and the Struggle for the Mind of Postwar Europe* (New York: Free Press, 1989), 276; Von Eschen, *Satchmo Blows Up the World*; and Said, *Humanism and Democratic Criticism*, 35, 276.

3. Serge Guilbaut, *How New York Stole the Idea of Modern Art* (Chicago: University of Chicago Press, 1985); Serge Guilbaut, ed., *Be-Bomb: The Transatlantic War of Images and All that Jazz* (Barcelona: Museu d'Art Contemporani de Barcelona, 2007); Jane de Hart Mathews, "Art and Politics in Cold War America," *American Historical Review* 81, no. 4 (October 1, 1976): 762–87, doi:10.2307/1864779; Robert Burstow, "The Limits of Modernist Art as a 'Weapon of the Cold War': Reassessing the Unknown Patron of the Monument to the Unknown Political Prisoner," *Oxford Art Journal* 20, no. 1 (January 1, 1997): 68–80. On dance, see David Caute, *The Dancer Defects: The Struggle for Cultural Supremacy during the Cold War* (New York: Oxford University Press, 2005); Naima Prevots, *Dance for Export: Cultural Diplomacy and the Cold War* (Hanover, NH: University Press of New England, 1998). On music, see Mark Carroll, *Music and Ideology in Cold War Europe* (New York: Cambridge University Press, 2003), 21; Ian Wellens, *Music on the Frontline: Nicolas Nabokov's Struggle against Communism and Middlebrow Culture* (Burlington, VT: Ashgate, 2002).

4. Hugh Wilford, *The CIA, the British Left, and the Cold War: Calling the Tune* (London: F. Cass, 2003); Liam Kennedy and Scott Lucas, "Enduring Freedom: Public Diplomacy and U.S. Foreign Policy," *American Quarterly* 57 (2005): 309–33; and Penny Von Eschen, "Enduring Public Diplomacy," *American Quarterly* 57 (2005): 335–43.

5. Von Eschen, *Satchmo Blows Up the World*, 24.

6. See Said, *Orientalism*, 275; Said, *Culture and Imperialism*, 64–65, 243; John Carlos Rowe, "Edward Said and American Studies," *American Quarterly* 56, no. 1 (2004): 33–47; Amy Kaplan, *The Anarchy of Empire in the Making of U.S. Culture* (Cambridge, MA: Harvard University Press, 2005); and Bruce Cumings, *Dominion from Sea to Sea: Pacific Ascendancy and American Power* (New Haven: Yale University Press, 2009), 389.

7. John Sutherland, *Stephen Spender: A Literary Life* (New York: Oxford University Press, 2005).

8. Kathryn Dyer, Central Intelligence Agency, Information Privacy Coordinator to the author, June 28, 2000.

9. Sol Stein, "A Short Account of International Student Politics with Particular Reference to the NSA, CIA," *Ramparts* 5, no. 9 (1967): 29–38.

10. Thomas W. Braden, "I'm Glad the CIA Is Immoral," *Saturday Evening Post*, May 20, 1967, 12. *Encounter* had two editors: one, Irving Kristol, in New York; the other, Stephen Spender, in London.

11. The National Security Act stipulates that the director of intelligence will "protect intelligence sources and methods from unauthorized disclosure." National Security Act of 1947, 50 USC § 552 (b)(1)(2010).

12. *Rubin v. Central Intelligence Agency*, 2001WL1537706 (Southern District of New York [SDNY], December 3, 2001).

13. Tim Weiner, *Legacy of Ashes: The History of the CIA* (New York: Anchor, 2008); William Blum, *Killing Hope: U.S. Military and CIA Interventions since World War II* (Monroe, ME: Common Courage Press, 1995).

14. *Central Intelligence Agency v. Sims*, 471 U.S. 159, 105 S.Ct. 1881, 85 L.Ed.2d 173 (1985).

15. 50 U.S.C. § 195 (2010) (formerly 50 USC § 195) (formally § 40) (2010). Giorgio Agamben, *State of Exception*, trans. Kevin Attell (Chicago: University of Chicago Press, 2005).

16. The National Security exemption is 5 USC § 552 (b)(1), and the statutory exemption that gives the director of intelligence the authority to protect intelligence from unauthorized disclosure is 5 USC § 552 (b)(3).

17. Executive Order 12,958; 60 Fed. Reg. 19,825 (April 17, 1995).

18. Agamben, *State of Exception*, 23.

19. Franz Kafka, *The Complete Stories*, trans. Nahum Glatzer (New York: Schocken, 1995).

20. *Rubin v. Central Intelligence Agency*, 2001WL1537706 (SDNY, December 3, 2001).

21. Ibid.

22. *Central Intelligence Agency v. Sims*, 471 U.S. 159, 105 S.Ct. 1881, 85 L.Ed.2d 173 (1985).

23. Ibid.

24. 50 USC § 552 (b)(1)(2010).

25. There is no knowledge so trivial that Sims does not consider worth "protecting from disclosure": "In exercising authority under 102 (d)(3), the Director of Intelligence has the power to withhold superficially innocuous information." We should ask what the court did not ask. Is there not a difference between protecting

from disclosure and nondisclosure? From where does this language of prophylactics derive, if from no other place than the absence of national security?

26. See Jonathan Hafetz, "Secret Evidence and the Courts in the Age of National Security: Habeas Corpus, Judicial Review, and Limits of Secrecy in Detentions at Guantanamo," *Cardozo Public Law, Policy, and Ethics Journal* (Fall 2006): 127–69.

27. Among the most interesting of these cases is John Berger's *A Painter of Our Times*, which the CCF tried, quite literally, to bury with a corpus of negative reviews. Other writers whom the CCF actively tried to marginalize included Pablo Neruda, whom it tried to discredit by rapidly duplicating his "Ode to Stalin."

28. Michael Bérubé makes the interesting point that because the CCF put forward the idea that dissidents in the arts and letters were tolerated by Western democracies, "dissent was not a position that CIA-supported artists could dissent from. Under this heading, dissent is possible but unnecessary in open societies; it follows then that for the Cold Warrior, dissent in the United States is not the index of freedom but a form of treason." Michael Bérubé, "American Studies without Exception," *PMLA* 118, no. 1 (January 2003): 106.

29. Theodor W. Adorno, *Current of Music*, trans. Robert Hullot-Kentor (Cambridge, MA: Polity, 2009), 374–78.

30. Said, *Culture and Imperialism*, 93.

31. Bruce Cumings, "Boundary Displacement: Area Studies and International Studies during and after the Cold War," in *Universities and Empire: Money and Politics in the Social Sciences during the Cold War*, ed. Christopher Simpson (New York: New Press, 1998), 159–88.

32. George Kennan, "The Sources of Soviet Conduct," *Foreign Affairs* 25, no. 4 (1947): 575; also see Nikhil Pal Singh, "Cold War Redux: On the 'New Totalitarianism,'" *Radical History Review* 85 (2003): 174.

33. Denis de Rougement, "Looking for India," *Encounter*, no. 1 (October 1953): 36–42; George Mikes, "Letter from Norway," *Encounter*, no. 7 (April 1954): 38–44; Daniel Bell, "Letter from New York: At Vecherinka," *Encounter*, no. 34 (July 1956): 65–68; Melvin Lasky, "A Sentimental Traveler in Japan," *Encounter*, no. 2 (November 1953): 5–12; and Sudhin Datta, "World Cities: Calcutta," *Encounter* 45 (June 1957): 35–45.

34. George Orwell, *The Collected Essays, Journalism, and Letters*, ed. Sonia Orwell and Ian Angus (New York: Harcourt and Brace, 1968), 1:390.

35. Vijay Prashad, *The Darker Nations: A People's History of the Third World* (New York: New Press, 2008).

36. Said, *Culture and Imperialism*, 324.

37. Casanova, *The World Republic of Letters*, 11–12.

38. At the same moment the U.S. government was exporting its modern art to Europe, Congress was eager to censor its exhibition at home. As Jane de Hart Mathews writes, "With the closely reasoned rhetoric so characteristic of conspiratorial thinking, George Dondero [Republican chairman of the House Committee on Public Works] argued that modernism had been used against the Czarist government when Trotsky's friend, Wassily Kandinsky, had released on Russians 'the black knights of the isms': cubism, futurism, dadaism, expressionism, constructionism,

surrealism, and abstractionism. Each was deadly. Cubism, according to Dondero, aimed to destroy 'by designed disorder'; futurism, 'by the machine myth'; dadaism, 'by ridicule'; expressionism, 'by aping the criminal and insane'; abstractionism, 'by the creation of brainstorms'; surrealism, 'by the denial of reason.' ... A 'horde of foreign art manglers' had descended upon this country just before World War II, spreading their pernicious doctrines. Followers of these 'international art thugs' now included Americans such as Robert Motherwell, William Baziotes, and Jackson Pollock.... In sum, a 'sinister conspiracy conceived in the black heart of Russia' had become a threat to America's cultural institutions and to those loyal American artists who sought to protect their cultural heritage from the new forms that were the symbols of a foreign ideology" ("Art and Politics in Cold War America," 772).

39. Alain Badiou, "'We Need a Popular Discipline': Contemporary Politics and the Crisis of the Negative," *Critical Inquiry* 34, no. 4 (2008): 649.

CHAPTER 2: ORWELL AND THE GLOBALIZATION OF LITERATURE

Portions of this chapter previously appeared in Andrew N. Rubin, "Orwell and Empire: Anti-Communism and Globalization of Literature," *Alif: Journal of Comparative Poetics* 28 (2008): 75–101. Printed with permission.

1. John Rodden, *The Politics of Literary Reputation: The Making and Claiming of "St. George" Orwell* (New York: Oxford University Press, 1989).

2. Lionel Trilling, introduction to *Homage to Catalonia* (New York: Harcourt Brace, 1952), x–xi; Richard Hoggart, "George Orwell and *The Road to Wigan Pier*," *Critical Quarterly* 7, no. 1 (Spring 1965): 81; and Mary McCarthy, "The Writing on the Wall," *New York Review of Books* (January 30, 1969): 5. For a critique of Orwell's consolidating and often coercive point of view, see Edward W. Said, "Tourism among the Dogs," in *Reflections on Exile* (Cambridge, MA: Harvard University Press, 2000), 97; and Simon Dentith, *A Rhetoric of the Real* (New York: St. Martin's Press, 1990), 148–73.

3. Raymond Williams, *Politics and Letters* (London: New Left Books, 1979), 384.

4. Ibid.

5. James Miller, "Is Bad Writing Necessary? George Orwell, Theodor Adorno, and the Politics of Literature," *Lingua Franca* (December/January 2000): 12–18; Judith Butler, "A 'Bad Writer' Writes Back," *New York Times*, March 20, 1999, A15; and Cleo McNelly, "On Not Teaching Orwell," *College English* 38 (1977): 553–66.

6. Ranajit Guha, "Not at Home in Empire," *Critical Inquiry* 23 (Spring 1997): 493.

7. For a discussion of the significance of Orwell's representations of totalitarianism, see Étienne Balibar, *Masses, Classes, Ideas: Studies on Politics and Philosophy Before and After Marx*, trans. James Swenson (New York: Routledge, 1994), 36; Michael Halberstam, *Totalitarianism and the Modern Conception of Politics* (New Haven: Yale University Press, 1999), 118; Irving Howe, *Politics and the Novel* (New York: Columbia University Press, 1987), 235–51; and William Pietz, "The 'Postcolonialism' of Cold War Discourse," *Social Text* 19/20 (Fall 1988): 61.

8. *George Orwell: The Critical Heritage*, ed. Jeffrey Meyers (London: Routledge & Kegan Paul, 1975), 273, 286.

9. John Rodden, *The Politics of Literary Reputation: The Making and Claiming of "St. George" Orwell* (1989), *Every Intellectual's Big Brother: George Orwell's Literary Siblings* (Austin: University of Texas Press, 2006), and *Scenes of an Afterlife: The Legacy of George Orwell* (Wilmington, DE: ISI Books, 2003).

10. Neil Genzlinger, "Bending Minds with Rats," *New York Times* online, March 25, 2009, http://theater.nytimes.com/2009/03/25/theater/reviews/25geor.html.

11. John Rodden, *Scenes from an Afterlife*, 247.

12. Ibid.

13. Darryl Campbell, "Orwell and the Tea Party," *The Millions* (blog), posted July 26, 2010, http://www.themillions.com/2010/07/orwell-and-the-tea-party.html.

14. Timothy Garton Ash, "Orwell for Our Time," *Guardian*, May 5, 2001.

15. Murray Sperber, "Gazing into the Glass Paperweight: The Structure and Psychology of Orwell's *1984*," *Modern Fiction Studies* 26, no. 2 (Summer 1980): 226.

16. Peter Davison has provided one of the best summaries in *The Complete Works of George Orwell*, vol. 20, ed. Peter Davison (London: Secker and Warburg, 1998), 323–25. Also see Perry Anderson, "A Ripple of the Polonaise," *London Review of Books* (November 1999): 7; Christopher Hitchens, letter to the editor, *London Review of Books* (January 6, 2000): 3; Perry Anderson, reply to a letter from Christopher Hitchens, *London Review of Books* (January 20, 2000): 3; Christopher Hitchens, reply to a letter from Perry Anderson, *London Review of Books* (February 3, 2000): 3; and Christopher Hitchens, "George Orwell and Raymond Williams," *Critical Quarterly* 41, no. 3 (1999): 3–22.

17. Orwell, *The Complete Works of George Orwell*, ed. Peter Davison, 18:383.

18. Quoted in Ros Wynne-Jones, "Orwell's Little List Leaves the Left Gasping for More," *Independent*, July 14, 1996, 10.

19. Gerald Kaufman, "Big Brother of the FO," *Evening Standard*, July 11, 1996, 17.

20. Quoted in Ros Wynne-Jones, "Orwell's Little List," 10.

21. Christopher Hitchens, "Was Orwell a Snitch?" *Nation* (December 14, 1998): 8.

22. Orwell, *The Complete Works*, 20:326.

23. Bernard Crick, "Why Are Radicals so Eager to Give Up One of Their Own?" *Independent*, July 14, 1996, 10.

24. Letter to the author, August 2, 2000. Also see Hitchens, "Was Orwell a Snitch?," 8; and *Why Orwell Matters* (New York: Penguin, 2002), 111–21.

25. See Dario Biocca, "Ignazio Silone e la polizia politica," *Nuova Storia Contemporanea* 2, no. 3 (May–June 1998); Mauro Canali, "Il fiduciario 'Silvestri,'" *Nuova Storia Contemporanea* 3, no. 1 (January–February 1999); and "Ignazio Silone and the Fascist Political Police," *Journal of Modern Italian Studies* 5, no. 1 (2000): 36–60.

26. Canali, "Ignazio Silone," 36–60.

27. Ibid., 60.

28. Paul Krugman, "Reign of Error: The Bush Administration Rewrites History," *Pittsburgh Post-Gazette*, July 29, 2006, B7. See, among others, Ryan Blethen, "Orwell Wrote Bush's Script," *Seattle Times*, February 17, 2006, B6.

29. Margaret Atwood writes, "The government of Airstrip One, Winston's 'country,' is brutal. The constant surveillance, the impossibility of speaking frankly to anyone, the looming, ominous figure of Big Brother, the regime's need for enemies and wars—fictitious though both may be—which are used to terrify the people and unite them in hatred, the mind-numbing slogans, the distortions of language, the destruction of what has really happened by stuffing any record of it down the Memory Hole—these made a deep impression on me. Let me re-state that: they frightened the stuffing out of me. Orwell . . . did it so well that *I could imagine such things happening anywhere*" (my emphasis). Margaret Atwood, "Orwell and Me," *Guardian*, posted June 16, 2003. http://books.guardian.co.uk/departments/generalfiction/story/0,6000,978474,00.html.

30. Andreas Huyssen, "Geographies of Modernism in a Globalizing World," 196. It is interesting to contrast Huyssen's much more compelling view of *Weltkultur* with Jameson's conceptualization of *Weltliteratur* as a process of communication that occurs between national literary forms. Jameson writes, "Our object of study is . . . the production of simulacra of national cultures; and tourism, the industry that organizes the consumption of those simulacra and those spectacles or images. This is why we by no means want to construe our discipline in terms of world culture, or of a misunderstanding of Goethe's notion of world literature as the canon or imaginary museum of all the masterpieces of history. In fact, what Goethe presciently had in mind was very much an informational or communicational concept: world literature did not mean for him Lord Byron or Rumi or the Shakuntala (all three of which he admired), but rather the *Edinburgh Review* and the *Revue des deux mondes* or *Le Globe*. World literature appears when the various national situations are able to speak to each other about the specificities of their worlds and their textual productions" (Fredric Jameson, "New Literary History after the End of the New," *New Literary History* 39, no. 3 (2009): 379–80).

31. Emily Apter, *The Translation Zone: A New Comparative Literature* (Princeton: Princeton University Press, 2006), 6.

32. Bernard Crick, *George Orwell: A Life* (London: Penguin, 1980), 556.

33. Ibid., 638.

34. Michael Shelden, *George Orwell: The Authorized Biography* (New York: HarperCollins, 1991), 429.

35. The identities of thirty-six of the individuals listed by Orwell remained concealed by the British Foreign Office until 2003.

36. Orwell, *The Complete Works*, 20:255.

37. Ibid.

38. Ibid.

39. Ibid., 249.

40. Ibid.

41. Ibid., 18:231.

42. Ibid., 18:322.

43. Letter from George Orwell to Celia Kirwan, May 2, 1949, Public Records Office (hereafter abbreviated as PRO), Kew Gardens, London, Foreign Office (hereafter abbreviated as FO) 1110/189.

44. "Outline of Communist Strategy in South-East Asia," August 15, 1949,

PRO, Kew Gardens, London, FO 1110/22; Ernest Bevin, "Top Secret Cabinet Paper on Future of Foreign Publicity Policy," FO 1110/IRD.

45. "Outline of Communist Strategy in South-East Asia," August 15, 1949, PRO, Kew Gardens, London, FO 1110/221.

46. "Progress Report: Paper on Communist Strategy in South East Asia," PRO, FO 1110/189.

47. Letter from Celia Kirwan to Ralph Murray, Adam Watson, and Lieutenant Colonel Leslie Sheridan, March 30, 1949, PRO, Kew Gardens, London, FO 1110/189.

48. Ibid.

49. Ibid.

50. Letter from George Orwell to Celia Kirwan, May 2, 1949, PRO, Kew Gardens, London, FO 1110/189.

51. Orwell, *The Complete Works*, 20:249.

52. The principle of crypto-communism itself—a neologism first used by the MP Tom Driberg and later used by Orwell against him—was characteristic of the disingenuous ambiguities that constituted the communist identity. The episteme had a logic of its own.

53. Orwell, *The Complete Works*, 20:255.

54. George Bernard Shaw, *Prefaces by George Bernard Shaw* (London: Oxford University Press, 1934), 361.

55. Ibid., 359.

56. Bill Jones, *The Russia Complex: The British Labour Party and the Soviet Union* (Manchester: Manchester University Press, 1977), 26.

57. J. B. Priestley, "The War—and After," *Horizon* 1, no. 1 (January 1941): 15.

58. Secret Letter from Chancery to Information Research Department (hereafter abbreviated as IRD), September 27, 1954, PRO, 1079/39.

59. Letter from Chancery to IRD, September 27, 1954, PRO 1079/39.

60. Martin Bauml Duberman, *Paul Robeson* (New York: Knopf, 1988), 342–50.

61. Paul Robeson Files, Home Office (hereafter abbreviated in the document location as HO), Alien Records, PRO, Kew Gardens, London, HO 382/6.

62. Geoffrey Crowther, Home Office, Ministry of Home Security, PRO, Kew Gardens, London, HO 335/40, 1949–50.

63. Orwell, *Complete Works*, 20:99.

64. Ibid., 101.

65. Raphael Samuel, *The Lost World of British Communism* (New York: Verso, 2006).

66. Leszek Kołakowski, *Main Currents of Marxism: The Founders, the Golden Age, the Breakdown* (New York: Oxford University Press, 1978), 1.

67. Perry Anderson, "Components of the National Culture," *New Left Review* 50 (1968): 3–57.

68. Ibid., 11.

69. E. P. Thompson, "Outside the Whale," in *The Poverty of Theory and Other Essays* (New York: Monthly Review Press, 1978), 213.

70. Frantz Fanon, *The Wretched of the Earth*, trans. Constance Farrington (New York: Grove Press, 2005), 79.

71. See George Kennan, "The Long Telegram," February 22, 1949, http://www.ntanet.net/KENNAN.html.
72. Anders Stephanson, *Kennan and the Art of Foreign Policy* (Cambridge, MA: Harvard University Press, 1989), 42–43.
73. "Progress Report: Paper on Communist Strategy in South East Asia," PRO, FO 1110/189.
74. R. V. Burks, "Statistical Profile of the Greek Communist," *Journal of Modern History* 27, no. 2 (1955): 153–58.
75. "Devolution," in *The Oxford English Dictionary*. See online at http://oxforddictionaries.com/definition/devolution.
76. Ibid.
77. Quoted in Vijay Prashad, *The Darker Nations: A People's History of the Third World* (New York: New Press, 2008), 38.
78. Ernest Bevin, "Top Secret Cabinet Paper on Future Foreign Publicity Policy," January 4, 1948, PRO, Kew Gardens, London, FO 1110/221.
79. See Melvyn Leffler, *A Preponderance of Power: National Security, the Truman Administration, and the Cold War* (Stanford, CA: Stanford University Press, 1992), 506–9.
80. George Kennan, "The Sources of Soviet Conduct," *Foreign Affairs* 25, no. 4 (1947): 566.
81. Ibid., 568.
82. British Foreign Office, Memorandum, "Outline of Communist Strategy in South-East Asia," August 15, 1949, PRO, Kew Gardens, London, FO 1110/221.
83. Ibid.
84. Letter from Ralph Murray to Mayhew, January 28, 1949, PRO, Kew Gardens, London, FO 1110/221.
85. See Valerie Holman, "Carefully Concealed Connections: The Ministry of Information and British Publishing, 1939–1946," *Book History* 8, no. 1 (2005): 197–226.
86. PRO, Kew Gardens, London, FO 1110/738.
87. "Progress Report: Paper on Communist Strategy in South East Asia," PRO, Kew Gardens, London, FO 1110/189.
88. Orwell, *The Complete Works*, 18:444.
89. George Orwell, *Animal Pham: Oru Palankatha*, trans. Em Pi Rosi (Kottayam: Nasanal Bukk Satal, 1956).
90. George Orwell, *O Tsiphliki Ton Zoon* (Athens: Graphikai Technai Aspiote-Elka, 1951); George Orwell, *Cuoc cách-mang trong trai súc-vât* (Saigon: Imprint d'Extrême-orient, 1951); George Orwell, *Negara Binatang*, trans. Aus Suriatna (Bandung: Penerbitan Sangkreti, 1949).
91. Letter from Ernest Main to Ralph Murray, April 4, 1949, PRO, Kew Gardens, London, FO 1110/221.
92. "Proposal to Co-operate with the Americans in Producing an Arabic Version of *Animal Farm*, by George Orwell," October 25, 1950, PRO, Kew Gardens, London, FO 1110/319.
93. Ibid.
94. Explanatory Notes, PRO, Kew Gardens, London, FO 1110/319.

95. C. F. MacLaren to Leslie Sheridan, March 3, 1951, PRO, Kew Gardens, London, FO 1110/392.

96. Letter from Ernest Main to Ralph Murray, April 4, 1949, PRO, Kew Gardens, London, FO 1110/221.

97. "Proposal to Co-operate with the Americans in Producing an Arabic Version of *Animal Farm*, by George Orwell," PRO, Kew Gardens, London, FO 1110/319.

98. "Negotiations for the Production of *Animal Farm*," August 1951, PRO, Kew Gardens, London, FO 1110/392.

99. Memorandum from Jean Sanders to Lieutenant Colonel Leslie Sheridan, June 19, 1951, PRO, Kew Gardens, London, FO 1110/392.

100. Ibid.

101. Letter from T. S. Tull to IRD officers, August 10, 1951, PRO, Kew Gardens, London, FO 1110/392.

102. The IRD's efforts to adapt Western works of art and culture took another form altogether: Jonathan Swift's *Gulliver's Travels* and Voltaire's *Candide* were produced in a work entitled "Greenhorn's Travels in Stalinovia." See "Greenhorn's Travels," PRO, Kew Gardens, n.d., FO 1110/392; Letter from T. S. Tull to John Rayner, August 3, 1951, PRO, Kew Gardens, London, FO 1110/392.

103. Masao Miyoshi, *Off Center: Power and Culture Relations between Japan and the United States* (Cambridge, MA: Harvard University Press, 1991), 103.

104. Memorandum from Labor Policy Section Chief M. Machida to Chief of Kanto Civil Affairs, August 7, 1950, National Archives Records Administration, Washington, D.C., Record Group 331.2747 (17).

105. "Reports of Distribution Reaction to *Animal Farm*, a Cartoon Blast at Communism, August 1946–1951," National Archives Records Administration, Washington, D.C., Record Group 331.2747 (17).

106. "Reactions over the Showing of *Animal Farm* throughout Ten Prefectures in the Kanto Area," n.d., National Archives Records Administration.

107. "Reports of Distribution Reaction to *Animal Farm*, a Cartoon Blast at Communism, August 1946–1951," National Archives Records Administration, Washington, D.C., Record Group 331.2747 (17).

108. Jay Rubin, "From Wholesomeness to Decadence," *Journal of Japanese Studies* 11, no. 1 (Winter 1985): 100.

109. Letter from George Orwell to Leonard Moore, August 30, 1949, in *Complete Works of George Orwell*, 20:162.

110. Memorandum from unnamed editorial advisor to IRD staff, February 21, 1955, PRO, Kew Gardens, London, FO 1110/738.

111. George Orwell, *O Porco Triunfante*, trans. Almirante Alberto Aprá (Lisbon: Livraria Popular de Francisco Franco, 1946).

112. Letter from George Orwell to Leonard Moore, November 11, 1945, Berg Archive, New York Public Library.

113. Letter from George Orwell to Leonard Moore, January 9, 1947, Berg Archive, New York Public Library, New York, New York.

114. Letter from George Orwell to Leonard Moore, July 20, 1949, in *Complete Works of George Orwell*, 20:148.

115. Letter from Celia Kirwan to Jack Brimmel, July 18, 1949, Public Records Office, FO 1110/221, PR 920.
116. George Orwell, *Skotsky Khutor*, trans. Gleb Struve (Limburg, Germany: Possev, 1950).
117. Letter from Vladimir Pugachev to George Orwell, June 24, 1949, PRO, Kew Gardens, London, FO 1110/221.
118. Letter from George Orwell to Leonard Moore, July 20, 1949, in *Complete Works of George Orwell*, 20:148.
119. PRO, FO 1110/221, PR 920.
120. Letter from George Orwell to Leonard Moore, July 20, 1949, in *Complete Works of George Orwell*, 20:143.
121. Letter from George Orwell to Leonard Moore, July 28, 1949, in *Complete Works of George Orwell*, 20:153.
122. Letter from George Orwell to Melvin Lasky, September 21, 1949, in *Complete Works of George Orwell*, 20:172.
123. See Andrew Defty, *Britain, America and Anti-Communist Propaganda, 1945–1953: The Information Research Department* (London: Routledge, 2004), 110–13.
124. Letter from Celia Kirwan to Charles Thayer, November 4, 1949, PRO, Kew Gardens London, FO 1110/221; FO 1110/738.
125. Memorandum from E. C. Miller Jr. to Bank of Japan, n.d., National Archives and Records Administration, Maryland, 290:15/34/07, Box 4079, C2-4.
126. Dean Acheson, "Participation of Books in Department's Fight against Communism," April 11, 1951, National Archives Records Administration, Maryland, 511.412/6-2851.
127. Minutes from anonymous editorial advisor to IRD staff, February 21, 1955, PRO, Kew Gardens, London, FO 1110/738.
128. Tony Shaw, *British Cinema and the Cold War: The State, Propaganda and Consensus* (London: I. B. Tauris, 2001), 95.
129. Contract for *Animal Farm* between RD-DR Corporation and Halas and Batchelor Cartoon Films Ltd., November 19, 1951, Halas and Batchelor Collections, University of Surrey; "Comment on *Animal Farm* Script," Psychological Strategy Board, January 23, 1953, Psychological Strategy Board Papers, Harry S. Truman Library, Independence, Missouri; Telegram from Louis de Rochemont to Borden Mace, August 24, 1954, Papers of Louis de Rochemont, American Heritage Center, University of Wyoming, Laramie, Wyoming.
130. Letter from H.A.H. Cortazzi to Douglas Williams, January 25, 1955, PRO, Kew Gardens, London, FO 1110/740.
131. Information Section of British Embassy to the Information Policy Department, March 9, 1955, PRO, Kew Gardens, London, FO 1110/740; Letter from H.A.H. Cortazzi to Douglas Williams, January 25, 1955, PRO, Kew Gardens, London, FO 1110/740.
132. Letter from H.A.H. Cortazzi to Douglas Williams, January 25, 1955, PRO, Kew Gardens, London, FO 1110/740.
133. Letter to the Paris Theatre from Sol Stein, July 11, 1955, American Committee for Cultural Freedom Papers, New York University, Tamiment Library.

134. Memorandum from Sol Stein, July 11, 1955, American Committee for Cultural Freedom Papers, New York University, Tamiment Library.
135. Casanova, *The World Republic of Letters*, 22–23.
136. Ibid., 22.
137. Ibid., 23.
138. For a discussion of how literature functions according to discourse systems involving the sending, receiving, feedback, and storage of literary data, see Friedrich A. Kittler, *Discourse Networks, 1800/1900* (Stanford, CA: Stanford University Press, 1990), 370. What Kittler overlooks, however, is how some literary "data" has not been "stored" or "received."
139. Said, *Culture and Imperialism*, 309.
140. Ibid., 328.
141. Walter Benjamin, "Theses on the Philosophy of History," in *Illuminations*, trans. Harry Zohn (New York: Schocken Books, 1969), 256.
142. John Guillory, *Cultural Capital* (Chicago: University of Chicago Press, 1993), 55–56.
143. Said, *Culture and Imperialism*, 306.

Chapter 3: Transnational Literary Spaces at War

1. See Odd Arne Westad, *The Global Cold War: Third World Interventions and the Making of Our Times* (New York: Cambridge University Press, 2005); William Blum, *Killing Hope: U.S. Military and CIA Interventions since World War II* (New York: Common Courage Press, 1995); Richard J. Barnet, *Intervention and Revolution* (Washington, D.C.: Institute for Policy Studies, 1968); V. G. Kiernan, *America: The New Imperialism: From White Settlement to World Hegemony* (London: Zed Press, 1978).
2. Douglas Coombs, *Spreading the Word: The Library Work of the British Council* (London: Mansell Publishing Limited, 1988), 3.
3. Bernard Lewis, *British Contributions to Arabic Studies* (London: British Council and Longmans, 1941). Stephen Spender, *Poetry since 1939* (London: Longmans, 1949); Edmund Blunden, *John Keats* (London: Published for the British Council by Longmans, Green & Co., 1950); Rex Warner, *E. M. Forster* (London: Published for the British Council by Longmans, Green & Co., 1950); Herbert Read, *Byron* (London: Published for the British Council by Longmans, Green & Co., 1951); John Lehmann, *Edith Sitwell* (New York: Published for the British Council by Longmans, Green & Co., 1951); Stephen Spender, *On "The Cocktail Party"* (London: Published for the British Council by Longmans, Green & Co., 1950); James Sutherland, *Defoe* (London: Published for the British Council and the National Book League by Longmans, Green & Co., 1954); and Oliver Warner, *Joseph Conrad* (London: Published for the British Council and the National Book League by Longmans, Green & Co., 1950).
4. Lewis, *British Contributions to Arabic Studies*. For a critical assessment of Lewis's work, see Edward W. Said, *Orientalism*, 315–20.
5. Lewis's authority as an Orientalist can certainly be located as early as 1939,

when the British Council published his pamphlet, years before works such as "The Revolt of Islam" (1964) and "The Return of Islam" (1976) established him as one of the most influential figures to discredit and impugn Islam as the religion of irrationality, zealotry, and uncontrollable passion—an unrelenting menace to the West that defined, organized, and identified itself against these putative threats to its very existence (see Said, *Orientalism*, 315–20).

6. John Hampden, "Books and the British Council," in *The Book World Today* (New York: Books for Libraries Press, 1957), 230.

7. Ibid., 226.

8. Ibid., 230.

9. T. S. Eliot, "Notes towards the Definition of Culture," in *Christianity and Culture* (New York: Harcourt, Brace, 1949), 170.

10. Michael Coyle, "'This Rather Elusory Broadcast Technique': T. S. Eliot and the Genre of Radio Talk," *ANQ* 11, no. 4 (Fall 1998): 32.

11. T. S. Eliot, "The Man of Letters and the Future of Europe," *Sewanee Review* 53, no. 3 (1945): 341.

12. R. P. Blackmur, "The Logos in the Catacomb: The Role of the Intellectual," *Kenyon Review* 21, no. 1 (1959): 8.

13. Ibid., 5.

14. Ibid., 7.

15. Jean Franco, *The Decline and Fall of the Lettered City* (Cambridge, MA: Harvard University Press, 2002), 23–24. Also see, Elizabeth Anne Cobbs, *The Rich Neighbor Policy: Rockefeller and Kaiser in Brazil* (New Haven: Yale University Press, 1992).

16. William Buxton, "John Marshall and the Humanities in Europe: Shifting Patterns of Rockefeller Foundation Support," *Minerva* 41, no. 2 (2003): 133–53.

17. Lawrence H. Schwartz, *Creating Faulkner's Reputation: The Politics of Modern Literary Criticism* (Knoxville: University of Tennessee Press, 1988), 81.

18. Robert Fitzgerald, *Enlarging the Change: The Princeton Seminars in Literary Criticism, 1949–1951* (Boston: Northeastern University Press, 1985), 10–11.

19. Ibid.

20. Williams's observations about the romantic artists' relationship to the development of the literary market are quite useful and provide a general model for my discussion here. Yet his gesture toward the unevenness of this development of the "literary market" is undermined by his claim that "it is not perhaps until our own century that it is so nearly universal as to be almost dominant." The point is precisely that the process was not universal, but thought by critics to be so. See Raymond Williams, *Culture and Society: 1780–1950* (New York: Columbia University Press, 1983), 33.

21. Congress for Cultural Freedom Papers, Regenstein Library, University of Chicago, Chicago, Illinois. Also see, Peter Coleman, *The Liberal Conspiracy*; and Franco, *The Decline and Fall of the Lettered City*.

22. See, for example, Neil Smith, *Uneven Development: Nature, Capital, and the Production of Space* (Cambridge, MA: Blackwell, 1991); and Fernando Enrique Cardoso, *Dependency and Development in Latin America* (Berkeley: University of California Press, 1979).

23. C.L.R. James, "Britain's New Monthlies," *Saturday Review* (May 22, 1954): 13.

24. B. Rajan, "Bloomsbury and the Academies: The Literary Situation in England," *Hudson Review* 2, no. 3 (1949): doi:10.2307/3847799.

25. Geoffrey Wagner, "The Minority Writer in England," *Hudson Review* 7, no. 3 (1954): 427–35.

26. T. S. Eliot and Ezra Pound, "Letters concerning *The Waste Land*," *Nine*, no. 4 (Summer 1950): 176–79.

27. Raymond Williams, "Editorial Commentary," *Essays in Criticism* 4, no. 3 (1954): 341. doi:10.1093/eic/IV.3.341.

28. Christopher Lasch, *The Agony of the American Left*; Saunders, *Who Paid the Piper?*; Coleman, *Liberal Conspiracy*.

29. Coleman, *Liberal Conspiracy*, 275–76.

30. See, for example, Arthur M. Schlesinger, *The Vital Center: The Politics of Freedom* (New York: Transaction Publishers, 1997).

31. Edward W. Said, *Humanism and Democratic Criticism*, 35–36.

32. Coleman, *Liberal Conspiracy*, 60.

33. Ibid.

34. Letter from F. J. Secker to H. Overy, June 1953, Warburg Papers, University of Reading, UK.

35. *Encounter*, no. 1 (October 1953).

36. Mary L. Dudziak, *Cold War Civil Rights: Race and the Image of American Democracy* (Princeton: Princeton University Press, 2002); Nikhil P. Singh, *Black Is a Country: Race and the Unfinished Struggle for Democracy* (Cambridge, MA: Harvard University Press, 2004); and also Penny M. Von Eschen, *Race against Empire: Black Americans and Anticolonialism, 1937–1957* (Ithaca: Cornell University Press, 1997).

37. See E. P. Thompson's "Socialist Humanism: An Epistle to the Philistines," *New Reasoner*, no. 1 (Summer 1957): 107.

38. Dwight Macdonald, "America! America!" in *Discriminations* (New York: De Capo, 1985), 49.

39. Norman Birnbaum, "Open Letter to the Congress for Cultural Freedom," *Universities and Left Review* (January 1959): 5.

40. Wagner, "The Minority Writer in England," 431. The *Hudson Review* was founded in 1947 by Frederick Morgan and Joseph Bennett, both Princeton alumni and former students of the poet Allen Tate. It ceased publication in 2007.

41. Quoted in ibid., 432.

42. Peter Bürger, *Theory of the Avant-Garde* (Minneapolis: University of Minnesota Press, 1984).

43. Congress for Cultural Freedom Papers, Regenstein Library, University of Chicago, Illinois. Also see Coleman, *Liberal Conspiracy*.

44. Michel Foucault, "What is an Author?" in *Language, Counter-Memory, Practice*, trans. Donald Bouchard (Ithaca: Cornell University Press, 1977), 137.

45. T. S. Eliot, "Dante," in *Selected Prose*, ed. Frank Kermode (New York: Farrar, Straus and Giroux, 1975), 205–30.

46. Franco, *The Decline and Fall of the Lettered City*, 35.

47. Casanova, *The World Republic of Letters*, 136.

48. *Encounter*, no. 1 (October 1953).
49. *Der Monat*, vol. 5 (September 1954).
50. *Der Monat*, vol. 3 (September 1953).
51. *Preuves*, no. 45 (November 1954).
52. See Raymond Williams's comments about the metropole becoming a site of immediate transmission in *The Politics of Modernism: Against the New Conformists* (New York: Verso, 1989), 37.
53. Witold Gombrowiscz, for example, was close with Constantin Jelenski, who became his translator. Jelenski was on the board of *Preuves*. See Casanova, *The World Republic of Letters*, 144.
54. Raymond Williams, *Culture* (London: Fontana, 1981), 197.
55. *Hiwar*, no. 1 (1963): 61–70.
56. Peter Benson, "'Border Operators': *Black Orpheus* and the Genesis of Modern African Art and Literature," *Research in African Literatures* 14, no. 4 (1983): 432.
57. Frantz Fanon, *The Wretched of the Earth*, 43.
58. Janheinz Jahn, "World Congress of Black Writers," *Black Orpheus*, no. 1 (September 1957): 40.
59. Wole Soyinka, *You Must Set Forth at Dawn: A Memoir* (New York: Random House, 2007), 74.
60. Coyle, "'This Rather Elusory Broadcast Technique,'" 32.
61. Humphrey Carpenter, *The Envy of the World: Fifty Years of the BBC Third Programme and Radio 3, 1946–1996* (London: Weidenfeld and Nicolson, 1996), 164.
62. George Orwell, *The Collected Essays, Journalism, and Letters*, 1:331.
63. Theodor W. Adorno, *Current of Music*, 376–77.
64. Stephen Spender, "We Can Win the Battle for the Minds of Europe," *New York Times*, April 25, 1948, SM15.
65. Lionel Trilling, *The Gathering of Fugitives* (New York: Harcourt, Brace, Jovanovich, 1956), 69.
66. Lionel Trilling, "The Situation of the American Intellectual at the Present Time," in *The Moral Obligation to be Intelligent: Selected Essays*, ed. Leon Wieseltier (New York: Farrar, Straus and Giroux, 2000), 282.
67. See, for example, André Visson's *As Others See Us* (New York: Doubleday, 1948).
68. Sidney Hook, "Report on the International Day of Resistance to Dictatorship and War," *Partisan Review* 16, no. 7 (Fall 1949): 43.
69. James Burnham, *What Europe Thinks of America* (New York: John Day, 1953), viii.
70. Spender, "We Can Win the Battle for the Minds of Europe," SM15.
71. Richard Wright, "What Africa Means to Me," *Encounter*, no. 12 (September 1954): 27.
72. Hugh Wilford, *The Mighty Wurlitzer*, 24. For a text of the NSC-4 directive, see "Memorandum from the Executive Secretary (Souers) to the Members of the National Security Council," December 9, 1947. Posted at http://www.fas.org/irp/offdocs/nsc-hst/nsc-4.htm.
73. NSC-4, "Memorandum from the Executive Secretary (Souers) to the Mem-

bers of the National Security Council," December 9, 1947. Posted at http://www.fas.org/irp/offdocs/nsc-hst/nsc-4.htm.

74. Quoted in Liam Kennedy and Scott Lucas, "Enduring Freedom," 312.

75. Jameson, "New Literary History after the End of the New," 379.

76. Ibid.

77. R. P. Blackmur, "The Economy of the American Writer," in *The Lion and the Honeycomb: Essays in Solicitude and Critique* (New York: Harcourt, Brace and Company, 1955), 50.

78. T. S. Eliot, "Notes towards the Definition of Culture," 202.

79. R. P. Blackmur, "Toward a Modus Vivendi," in *The Lion and the Honeycomb: Essays in Solicitude and Critique* (New York: Harcourt, Brace and Company, 1955), 152, 157.

80. James Laughlin, "The Function of This Magazine," *Perspectives USA* 1, no. 1 (Fall 1952): 5.

81. Hayden Carruth to Lionel Trilling, March 3, 1953, Lionel Trilling Papers, Butler Library, Columbia University, New York.

82. As Raymond Williams has observed, "The growth of the 'literary market' as the type of a writer's relations with his readers has been responsible for many fundamental changes in attitude. But one must add, of course, that such a growth is always uneven, both in its operations and in its effects" (*Culture and Society: 1780–1950* [New York: Columbia University Press, 1983], 330). See also Antonio Candido, "Literature and Underdevelopment," in *On Literature and Society*, trans. Howard S. Becker (Princeton: Princeton University Press, 1995), 119–41.

83. Quoted in Edward W. Said, "The Horizon of R. P. Blackmur," in *Reflections on Exile* (Cambridge, MA: Harvard University Press, 2000), 246.

84. R. P. Blackmur, "Editor's Commentary," *Perspectives USA*, no. 6 (Winter 1954): 134.

85. Ibid.

86. Blackmur, "Toward a Modus Vivendi," 4.

87. Said, "The Horizon of R. P. Blackmur," 261.

88. Ibid., 262.

89. There is an interesting comparison, of which this observation is a revision, with Said's "Note on Modernism" in *Culture and Imperialism*. For Said, "spatiality" becomes the characteristic of an aesthetic rather than of political domination. What I am suggesting is that the political aspects of the domination retain some of their modernist elements in the context of American ascendancy precisely because the interstices of the Cold War and decolonization are not contiguous. In this manner, Blackmur's description of a new modus vivendi provides an account of a modernity whose terms of dominance remain unsettled and unsedimented, while they are brought together through a new kind of literary and cultural expedition that had not been available to critics of an earlier generation, with which it is interesting to compare them. It is also further evidence of Amy Kaplan's crucial observation that American exceptionalism was an inherently unstable project. In its attempts (such as Blackmur's) to imagine full horizons, there is a disordering because of the boundlessness of the ideology. See Kaplan, *The Anarchy of Empire in the Making of U.S. Culture*.

90. Blackmur, "Editor's Commentary," 134.
91. Ibid., 134–35.
92. Ibid.
93. Ibid., 135.
94. Letter from Royce Moch, Department of State, to Lionel Trilling, March 29, 1949, Lionel Trilling Papers, Butler Library, Columbia University, New York; Letter from James L. Meader, Director of the United States Information Agency (hereafter abbreviated as USIA), to Lionel Trilling, October 24, 1956, Lionel Trilling Papers, Butler Library, Columbia University, New York.
95. Letter from John Thompson to Lionel Trilling, August 29, 1956, Lionel Trilling Papers, Butler Library, Columbia University, New York. Cf. Letter from Trilling to Thompson, September 20, 1956, Lionel Trilling Papers, Butler Library, Columbia University, New York.
96. Letter from Sol Stein to Lionel Trilling, October 27, 1954, Lionel Trilling Papers, Butler Library, Columbia University, New York. Also see letter from Pearl Kluger to Lionel Trilling, February 28, 1952, Lionel Trilling Papers, Butler Library, Columbia University, New York; Letter from Daniel James, Program and Publication Director of the American Committee for Cultural Freedom, to Lionel Trilling, April 3, 1952, Lionel Trilling Papers, Butler Library, Columbia University, New York. For CCF, see letter from Nicolas Nabokov to Lionel Trilling, June 15, 1956, Lionel Trilling Papers, Butler Library, Columbia University, New York. For U.S. Army, see letter from Royce Moch, Department of State, to Lionel Trilling, March 29, 1949, Lionel Trilling Papers, Butler Library, Columbia University, New York.
97. Letter from Lionel Trilling to James Laughlin, November 10, 1952, Lionel Trilling Papers, Butler Library, Columbia University, New York; Letter from Lionel Trilling to Irving Kristol, October 22, 1952, Lionel Trilling Papers, Butler Library, Columbia University, New York; Letter from Lionel Trilling to Melvin Lasky, December 7, 1953, Lionel Trilling Papers, Butler Library, Columbia University, New York.
98. Letter from Walter W. Wriggins to Diana Trilling, December 29, 1975; and Letter from Phillips Brooks to Lionel Trilling, March 25, 1957, Lionel Trilling Papers, Butler Library, Columbia University, New York.
99. Mark Krupnick, *Lionel Trilling and the Fate of Cultural Criticism* (Evanston, IL: Northwestern University Press, 1986), 102.
100. Letter from John A. Krout to Lionel Trilling, May 21, 1956, Lionel Trilling Papers, Butler Library, Columbia University, New York.
101. Letter from Herbert Jacobsen, Foreign Service of the United States, to Lionel Trilling, May 27, 1957, Lionel Trilling Papers, Butler Library, Columbia University, New York.
102. Letter from Harold E. Howland to Lionel Trilling, June 4, 1957, Lionel Trilling Papers, Butler Library, Columbia University, New York.
103. Letter from Royce Moch, Department of State, Magazine Liaison Section, to Lionel Trilling, June 7, 1949, Lionel Trilling Papers, Butler Library, Columbia University, New York.
104. Letter from Royce Moch, Department. of State, to Lionel Trilling, March

29, 1949, Lionel Trilling Papers. "Outlines of Psychoanalysis" was published as *Art and Neurosis* (Charlottesville: University of Virginia, 1949).

105. In August 1956, Thompson thanked Trilling for recommending and encouraging him to apply for the position at the Farfield Foundation. "The job we talked about earlier this summer developed," Thompson wrote, "and I have accepted it. It is the Farfield Foundation; I believe I recall that you mentioned the name, which then meant nothing to me.... I imagine that you are familiar with many of the things the work is concerned with, and I hope you will discuss it with me." Letter from John Thompson to Lionel Trilling, August 29, 1956. Cf. Letter from Trilling to Thompson, September 20, 1956.

106. Saunders, *Who Paid the Piper?*, 358.

107. Letter from James L. Meader, Director of USIA, to Lionel Trilling, October 24, 1956, Lionel Trilling Papers, Butler Library, Columbia University, New York.

108. Letter from Lionel Trilling to James L. Meader, Director of USIA, March 6, 1957, Lionel Trilling Papers, Butler Library, Columbia University, New York.

109. Lionel Trilling, "Editor's Commentary," 5.

110. Ibid.

111. Ibid., 8.

112. Ibid., 5.

113. Ibid., 10.

114. Letter from Hayden Carruth to Lionel Trilling, March 3, 1953, Lionel Trilling Papers, Butler Library, Columbia University, New York; and Lionel Trilling, "Editor's Commentary," 5.

115. Mary McCarthy, "America the Beautiful: The Humanist in the Bathtub," *Perspectives USA* 1, no. 2 (Winter 1953): 11.

116. Ibid., 16.

117. Ibid., 17.

118. Ibid., 17–18.

119. Ibid., 18.

120. Simone de Beauvoir, *America Day by Day* (New York: Grove, 1953).

121. James Baldwin, "Everybody's Protest Novel," *Perspectives USA* 1, no. 2 (Winter 1953): 11 and 16; Richard Gibson, "A No to Nothing," *Perspectives USA* 1, no. 2 (Winter 1953): 11.

122. See Jonathan Arac, *Critical Genealogies: Historical Situations for Postmodern Literary Studies* (New York: Columbia University Press, 1987), 310–14. Also see Russell J. Reising, "Lionel Trilling, *The Liberal Imagination*, and the Emergence of the Discourse of Anti-Stalinism," *boundary 2* 20, no. 1 (1993): 94–124.

123. "Draft of Guidelines," n.d., Lionel Trilling Papers, Butler Library, Columbia University, New York.

124. Lionel Trilling, letter to the editor, *New York Times*, November 24, 1953.

Chapter 4: Archives of Critical Theory

Portions of this chapter previously appeared in Andrew Rubin "The Adorno Files," in *Adorno: A Critical Reader*, ed. Nigel Gibson and Andrew Rubin (New York: Wiley-Blackwell, 2002), 172–90.

1. "Institute for Social Research/Columbia University," Federal Bureau of Investigation, Freedom of Information Act.
2. Alexander Stephan, *Communazis: FBI Surveillance of German Émigré Writers*, trans. Jan van Heurck (New Haven: Yale University Press, 2000), 2. For his unabridged analysis of the FBI's surveillance campaign, see the German edition of Stephan's book, *Im Visier des FBI: Deutsche Exilschriftsteller in den Akten amerikanischer Geheimdienste* (Stuttgart: Metzler, 1995).
3. Stephan, *Communazis*, 2.
4. Ibid., 231.
5. Ibid., 50.
6. J. Edgar Hoover to New York Division of the Federal Bureau of Investigation, Memorandum, October 31, 1942, Federal Bureau of Investigation, Freedom of Information Act.
7. FBI Case Report on Felix Weil, Arkadij Gurland, and Karl Wittfogel, September 9, 1942, Federal Bureau of Investigation, Freedom of Information Act.
8. Ibid.
9. Unnamed agent to J. Edgar Hoover, July 31, 1940, Federal Bureau of Investigation, Freedom of Information Act.
10. Los Angeles Bureau of the FBI, Unsigned and Undated Memorandum, Federal Bureau of Investigation, Freedom of Information Act.
11. FBI report, December 7, 1943, Federal Bureau of Investigation, Freedom of Information Act.
12. Edward A. Tamm to Ladd, Memorandum, June 25, 1943, Federal Bureau of Investigation, Freedom of Information Act.
13. In 1942, the institute retained the legal counsel of former senator King from Utah. Edward A. Tamm to Ladd, Memorandum, June 25, 1943, Federal Bureau of Investigation, Freedom of Information Act. Tamm wrote, "I told the Senator that if the Institute of Social Research were [sic] engaged in any violation of a Federal Statute, it would be indicted and prosecuted by Federal Courts."
14. Rolf Wiggershaus, *The Frankfurt School: Its History, Theories, and Political Significance*, trans. Michael Robertson (Cambridge, MA: MIT Press, 1994), 401.
15. Ibid.
16. Ibid.
17. Ibid.
18. Ibid.
19. Ibid.
20. Ibid.
21. J. Edgar Hoover to New York Special Agent in Charge (SAC), Memorandum, May 20, 1955, Federal Bureau of Investigation, Freedom of Information Act.
22. J. Edgar Hoover to Ladd, July 18, 1941, Federal Bureau of Investigation, Freedom of Information Act.
23. J. Edgar Hoover to Unnamed Special Agent in El Paso, Texas, July 18, 1941, Federal Bureau of Investigation, Freedom of Information Act.
24. "Censorship Daily Reports," vol. 6, July 22, 1942, Federal Bureau of Investigation, Freedom of Information Act.
25. Theodor Adorno, *Minima Moralia: Reflections on a Damaged Life*, trans. E.F.N. Jephcott (London: Verso, 1978), 46–47.

26. Dr. Lazarsfeld, Memorandum, n.d., Paul Lazarsfeld Papers, Butler Library, Columbia University, New York.
27. Theodor W. Adorno, *Current of Music*, 10.
28. Wiggershaus, *Frankfurt School*, 239.
29. Paul Lazarsfeld to Dr. Cantril and Dr. Stanton, Memorandum, January 1, 1938, Paul Lazarsfeld Papers, Butler Library, Columbia University, New York.
30. Adorno, *Current of Music*, 139.
31. Adorno to Lazarsfeld, n.d., Paul Lazarsfeld Papers, Butler Library, Columbia University, New York.
32. Theodor W. Adorno, "A Social Critique of Radio Music," *Kenyon Review* 8 (1945): 208–17; and "The Radio Symphony: An Experiment in Theory," *Radio Research* (New York: Harper, 1941): 110–39.
33. Lazarsfeld to Adorno, n.d., Paul Lazarsfeld Papers, Butler Library, Columbia University, New York.
34. Wiggershaus, *Frankfurt School*, 243.
35. Theodor W. Adorno, "Scientific Experiences of a European Scholar in America," in *Critical Models: Interventions and Catchwords*, trans. Henry Pickford (New York: Columbia University Press, 1998), 222.
36. "The Psychological Analysis of Propaganda," Paul Lazarsfeld Papers, Butler Library, Columbia University, New York.
37. Ibid., 16.
38. Ibid., 18.
39. Harold D. Lasswell, "Psychological Policy Research and Total Strategy," *Public Opinion Quarterly* 16, no. 4 (1952): 498.
40. Theodor W. Adorno and Max Horkheimer, *Dialectic of Enlightenment*, trans. Edmund Jephcott (Palo Alto, CA: Stanford University Press, 2007), 1.
41. Ibid., 3.
42. Ibid., 7.
43. Ibid., 4–7.
44. Ibid., 8.
45. Ibid., 41.
46. Ibid.
47. Theodor W. Adorno, *Prisms: Culture Criticism and Society*, trans. Samuel and Shierry Weber (London: Spearman, 1981), 98.
48. Adorno, *Minima Moralia*, 87.
49. Ibid.
50. Adorno, "Scientific Experiences of a European Scholar in America," 222.
51. Martin Jay, *Adorno* (Cambridge, MA: Harvard University Press, 1984), 47.
52. Wiggershaus, *Frankfurt School*, 399.
53. For a study of McCloy's role in West Germany, see Kai Bird, *The Chairman: John McCloy; the Making of the American Establishment* (New York: Simon and Schuster, 1992).
54. Jay, *Adorno*, 48.
55. Wiggershaus, *Frankfurt School*, 479.
56. Pierre Grémion, *Intelligence de l'anticommunisme: Le Congrès pour la Liberté de la culture à Paris (1950–1975)* (Paris: Fayard, 1995), 421.

57. Wiggershaus, *Frankfurt School*, 405.
58. Adorno, "Extorted Reconciliation," in *Notes to Literature*, vol. 1, trans. Shierry Weber Nicholsen, ed. Rolf Tiedemann (New York: Columbia University Press, 1991), 218.
59. Wiggershaus, *Frankfurt School*, 434.
60. Ibid., 452.
61. Ibid.
62. Theodor W. Adorno et al., *The Authoritarian Personality* (New York: Harper, 1950).
63. Theodor W. Adorno, "The Meaning of Working through the Past," in *Critical Models: Interventions and Catchwords*, trans. Henry Pickford (New York: Columbia University Press, 1998), 90.
64. Ibid., 100–103.
65. Theodor W. Adorno, "Opinion Delusion Society," in *Critical Models: Interventions and Catchwords*, trans. Henry Pickford (New York: Columbia University Press, 1998), 121.
66. Adorno, "The Meaning of Working through the Past," 94.
67. Theodor W. Adorno, "Sociology and Empirical Research," in *The Positivist Dispute in German Sociology*, trans. Glyn Adley and David Frisby (London: Heinemann, 1976).
68. Ibid., 70.
69. Theodor W. Adorno, *Sound Figures*, trans. Rodney Livingstone (Palo Alto, CA: Stanford University Press, 1999), 7.
70. Theodor W. Adorno, "Critique," in *Critical Models: Interventions and Catchwords*, trans. Henry Pickford (New York: Columbia University Press, 1998), 288.
71. Ibid., 273.
72. Theodor W. Adorno, "Marginalia to Theory and Praxis," in *Critical Models: Interventions and Catchwords*, trans. Henry Pickford (New York: Columbia University Press, 1998), 277.
73. Lucien Goldmann, "Goldmann and Adorno: To Describe, Understand and Explain," in *Cultural Creation in Modern Society* (Saint Louis, MO: Telos Press, 1976), 131.
74. Theodor W. Adorno, "Commitment," in *Notes to Literature*, vol. 2, trans. Shierry Weber Nicholsen, ed. Rolf Tiedemann (New York: Columbia University Press, 1991), 93.
75. Theodor W. Adorno, *Aesthetic Theory*, trans. Robert Hullot-Kentor (Minneapolis: University of Minnesota Press, 1997), 6.
76. Goldmann, "Goldmann and Adorno," 135–36.
77. Said, *Culture and Imperialism*, 278.
78. It should be pointed out in addition that Adorno had a similar view of the situation in Palestine and Israel. When Adorno spoke out against the killing of a student at the hands of the German police (the student had been protesting a visit to Berlin by the shah of Iran), he framed his remarks by condemning the Arab states for the 1967 Arab-Israeli war. The Arab states posed, Adorno declared, "a terrible threat to Israel." See Wolfgang Kraushaar, ed., *Frankfurter Schule und Studentenbewegung: Von der Flaschenpost zum Molotowcocktail 1946 bis 1995*, vol. 2 (Hamburg: Roger und Bernhard bei Zweitausendeins, 1998), 123.

79. Adorno, "Marginalia to Theory and Praxis," 269–70.
80. Adorno, "Extorted Reconciliation," 240.
81. Fredric Jameson, *Late Marxism: Adorno; or, The Persistence of the Dialectic* (New York: Verso, 1990), 5.

Chapter 5: Humanism, Territory, and Techniques of Trouble

1. Friedrich Nietzsche, "On Truth and Lies in a Nonmoral Sense," in *The Nietzsche Reader*, ed. Keith Ansell Pearson and Duncan Large, trans. Daniel Breazeale (Malden, MA: Blackwell, 2006), 117.

2. A by no means complete list of these works would include: Adel Iskandar and Hakem Rustom, *Edward Said: A Legacy of Emancipation and Representation* (Berkeley: University of California Press, 2010); Abdirahman A. Hussein, *Edward Said: Criticism and Society* (New York: Verso, 2004); Silvia Nagy-Zekmi, *Paradoxical Citizenship: Essays on Edward Said* (Lanham, MD: Lexington Books, 2008); William V. Spanos, *The Legacy of Edward W. Said* (Urbana: University of Illinois Press, 2009); Basak Ertur et al., *Waiting for the Barbarians: A Tribute to Edward W. Said* (New York: Verso, 2008); Ferial Ghazoul, *Edward Said and Critical Decolonization* (Cairo: American University in Cairo Press, 2007); May Telmissany and Stephanie Tara Schwartz, *Counterpoints: Edward Said's Legacy* (Newcastle upon Tyne, UK: Cambridge Scholars Publishing, 2010); Bill Ashcroft and Pal Ahluwalia, *Edward Said* (New York: Routledge, 2008); Patrick Williams, *Edward Said*, vols. 1–4 (New York: Sage Publications, 2001); Ranjan Ghosh, *Edward Said and the Literary, Social, and Political World* (New York: Routledge, 2009); Paul A. Bové et al., *Edward Said and the Work of the Critic: Speaking Truth to Power* (Durham, NC: Duke University Press Books, 2000); Mustapha Marrouchi, *Edward Said at the Limits* (Stonybrook: State University of New York Press, 2003); Michael Sprinker, ed., *Edward Said: A Critical Reader* (New York: Wiley-Blackwell, 1993); Valerie Kennedy, *Edward Said and the Work of the Critic* (Malden, MA: Blackwell, 2000); and William Hart, *Edward Said and the Religious Effects of Culture* (New York: Cambridge University Press, 2000).

3. Edward W. Said, *Orientalism*. For the numerous discussions about *Orientalism* and the controversy surrounding it, see, for example, Gyan Prakash, "Orientalism Now," *History and Theory* 34, no. 3 (1995): doi:10.2307/2505621; James Clifford, "On Orientalism," in *The Predicament of Culture: Twentieth Century Ethnography, Literature and Art* (Cambridge, MA: Harvard University Press, 1988), 255–76; Marjorie Levinson, "The Discontents of Aijaz Ahmed," *Public Culture* 6 (Fall 1993): 97–131; Moustafa Marrouchi, "Counternarrative, Recoveries, and Refusals," *boundary 2* 25, no. 2 (1998): 205–57; Bruce Robbins, "The East as Career: The Logics of Professionalism," in *Edward Said: A Critical Reader*, ed. Michael Sprinker (Cambridge, MA: Blackwell, 1992), 48–73.

4. Edward W. Said, *Joseph Conrad and the Fiction of Autobiography* (Cambridge, MA: Harvard University Press, 1966); Edward W. Said, *Reflections on Exile and Other Essays* (Cambridge, MA: Harvard University Press, 2000); Edward W. Said, *Culture and Imperialism*; and Edward W. Said, *Humanism and Democratic Criticism*.

5. See Edward W. Said, "The Horizon of R. Blackmur," in *Reflections on Exile*, 246–67.

6. See Edward W. Said, *Power, Politics, and Culture: Interviews with Edward Said*, ed. Gauri Viswanathan (New York: Pantheon, 2001).

7. See, for example, Gil Anidjar, "Secularism," *Critical Inquiry* 33 (2006): 52.

8. James Clifford, for example, writes of Said's "restless suspicion" of totality in *The Predicament of Culture: Twentieth-Century Ethnography, Literature, and Art*, 87.

9. Said, *Culture and Imperialism*, 80–97.

10. Edward W. Said, "From Silence and Sound and Back Again: Music, Literature, and History," in *Reflections on Exile and Other Essays* (Cambridge, MA: Harvard University Press, 2000). See Ranajit Guha, *Dominance without Hegemony: History and Power in Colonial India* (Cambridge, MA: Harvard University Press, 1997); Ranajit Guha, "The Prose of Counter-Insurgency," in *Selected Subaltern Studies*, ed. Ranajit Guha and Gayatri Spivak (New York: Oxford University Press, 1988), 45–86.

11. For Said, exteriority describes the process by which the Orientalist "makes the Orient speak, describes the Orient, renders its mysteries plain for and to the West ... The Orientalist [is] never concerned with the Orient except as the first cause of what he says" (*Orientalism*, 20–21). It is this idea of exteriority as an enabling structure that allows the Orientalist to objectify the Orient, with no real concern for its actuality, that Said has appropriated from Foucault. To compare Said's employment of the notion of exteriority with that of Foucault's, see Michel Foucault, *The Archaeology of Knowledge*, trans. A. M. Sheridan Smith (London: Routledge, 1972), 107–8, 118–25; Said, *Orientalism*, 20–21.

12. Said, "Orientalism Reconsidered," in *Reflections on Exile* (Cambridge, MA: Harvard University Press, 2000), 200.

13. Said, *Orientalism*, 12.

14. Ibid.

15. In *Beginnings: Intention and Method*, Said was among one of the first critics to introduce Foucault's work to an English-speaking audience in "Abecedarium Culturae," the ABC's of culture. See Edward W. Said, "Abecedarium Culturae," in *Beginnings: Intention and Method* (New York: Basic Books, 1985), 279–43. An earlier version of this work was also published as "*Abecedarium Culturae*: Structuralism, Absence, Writing," *TriQuarterly* (Winter 1971).

16. Raymond Williams, *The Country and the City* (New York: Oxford University Press, 1973). Said, "Orientalism Reconsidered," *Reflections on Exile*, 200.

17. Said, *Culture and Imperialism*, 26.

18. Edward W. Said, "Secular Criticism," in *The World, the Text, and the Critic* (Cambridge, MA: Harvard University Press, 1983), 23.

19. Raymond Williams, *Politics and Letters* (London: New Left Books, 1979), 252.

20. For Said, contrapuntal criticism entails reading a text with an understanding of what is in effect the political economy of works of art insofar as contrapuntal reading (as an interpretative procedure) emphasizes that all artists and authors maintain not only a relationship to their immediate surroundings but also to other geographical regions of the world, whose work should be read in order to make visible the overlapping experiences and interdependent histories and culture of conflict and exchange. See Said, *Culture and Imperialism*, 66–67.

21. For Said, affiliation is very much connected to the process of legitimizing the European humanistic tradition. In "Secular Criticism," Said writes, "the affilia-

tive order ... surreptitiously duplicates the closed and knit family structure that secures generational hierarchical relationships to one another." That is to say, affiliation designates the process of Eurocentrism insofar as it, by virtue of its function as a structure, reproduces and consolidates cultural relationships to works of European literature in such a way that "what is ours is good, and ... deserves incorporation and inclusion in our programs of humanistic study." See Said, "Secular Criticism," in *The World, the Text, and the Critic*, 21 and 24.

22. Ibid., 26.

23. Anidjar, "Secularism," 64.

24. Said, "Identity, Authority and Freedom: The Potentate and the Traveler," in *Reflections on Exile*, 404.

25. Edward W. Said, *Out of Place* (New York: Knopf, 1999).

26. Said, *Orientalism*, 25.

27. Edward W. Said, "Intellectual Exile: Expatriates and Marginals," *Grand Street*, no. 47 (1993): 116.

28. See Geoffrey Green, *Literary Criticism and the Structures of History: Erich Auerbach and Leo Spitzer* (Lincoln: University of Nebraska Press, 1982); Michael Holquist, "The Last European: Erich Auerbach as Precursor in the History of Cultural Criticism," *MLQ* 53, no. 3 (September 1993): 371–91; and Seth Lerer, ed., *Literary History and the Challenge of Philology* (Palo Alto, CA: Stanford University Press, 1996).

29. For an account of the tensions posed between *Orientalism* and humanism, see Emily Apter, "Saidian Humanism," *boundary 2* 31, no. 2 (2004): 35–53.

30. Auerbach, "Philology and *Weltliteratur*," 1–17; Said, *Orientalism*, 258–60; Said, *The World, the Text, and the Critic*, 16; Said, *Culture and Imperialism*, 47; and Said, "History, Literature and Geography," in *Reflections on Exile*, 457–58.

31. Emily Apter, "Saidian Humanism," *boundary 2* 31, no. 2 (2004): 35–53; Aamir R. Mufti, "Secularism and Minority: Elements of a Critique," *Social Text*, no. 45 (1995): 75–96; Aamir R. Mufti, "Auerbach in Istanbul: Edward Said, Secular Criticism, and the Question of Minority Culture," *Critical Inquiry* 25, no. 1 (1998): 95–125; Aamir R. Mufti, "Critical Secularism: A Reintroduction for Perilous Times," *boundary 2* 31, no. 2 (2004): 1–9; Bruce Robbins, "Secularism, Elitism, Progress, and Other Transgressions: On Edward Said's 'Voyage in,'" *Social Text*, no. 40 (1994): 25–37; Moustafa Bayoumi, "Our Philological Home Is the Earth," *Arab Studies Quarterly* 26, no. 4 (Fall 2004): 53–66; Stathis Gourgouris, "Transformation, Not Transcendence," *boundary 2* 31, no. 2 (2004): 55–79; W.J.T. Mitchell, "Secular Divination: Edward Said's Humanism," *Critical Inquiry* 31, no. 2 (2005): 462–71; Yumna Siddiqi, "Edward Said, Humanism, and Secular Criticism," *Alif: Journal of Comparative Poetics*, no. 25 (2005): 65–88.

32. Said, *The World, the Text, and the Critic*, 5.

33. Erich Auerbach, *Mimesis: The Representation of Reality in Western Literature*, trans. Willard R. Trask (Princeton: Princeton University Press, 2003), 557.

34. Ibid., 574.

35. Said, *The World, the Text, and the Critic*, 6.

36. Said, introduction to *Mimesis*, by Erich Auerbach, xxxi.

37. Ibid., xvii–xviii.

38. See Erich Auerbach, "Figura," in *Scenes from the Drama of European Literature: Six Essays*, trans. Ralph Mannheim (Manchester: Manchester University Press, 1984), 11–79.

39. Hayden White, *Figural Realism: Studies in the Mimesis Effect* (Baltimore: Johns Hopkins University Press, 1999), 95.

40. Said, introduction to *Mimesis*, by Erich Auerbach, xxi–xxii.

41. Ibid., xxii.

42. Auerbach, *Mimesis*, 443–44.

43. Ibid., 201–2.

44. Said, "History, Literature, Geography," in *Reflections on Exile* (Cambridge, MA: Harvard University Press, 2000), 457.

45. Mufti, "Auerbach in Istanbul," 103.

46. Apter, "Saidian Humanism," 43.

47. Auerbach, "Philology and *Weltliteratur*," 3.

48. Ibid., 2.

49. Ibid., 3.

50. Ibid., 6.

51. Ibid.

52. Ibid., 2.

53. Ibid., 4.

54. Ibid., 3.

55. Ibid., 7.

56. Erich Auerbach, *Literary Language and Its Public in Late Latin Antiquity and in the Middle Ages*, trans. Ralph Manheim (Princeton: Princeton University Press, 1993), 16.

57. Auerbach, "Philology and *Weltliteratur*," 21.

58. Ibid., 16–17.

59. Ibid., 17.

60. Said, *Culture and Imperialism*, 336.

61. Said, "History, Literature, Geography," 457.

62. Said, *Culture and Imperialism*, 47.

63. Ibid. The collaboration between Lucien Febvre and Marc Bloch established the Annales publication, *Annales d'histoire économique et sociale* in 1929. Out of their work and the work of their students, notions of *longue durée*, deep time, and world systems have become indispensable theoretical devices for Moretti, Casanova, and others. For a history of *Annales*, see Lynn Hunt, "French History in the Last Twenty Years: The Rise and Fall of the Annales Paradigm," *Journal of Contemporary History*, vol. 21, no. 2 (1986): doi:10.2307/260364. For an examination of the central assumptions, see J. H. Hexter, "Fernand Braudel and the Monde Braudellien," *Journal of Modern History* 44, no. 4 (1972): doi:10.2307/1876806. The French historian François Furet, once associated with *Annales*, offers an important critique in, "Beyond the Annales," *Journal of Modern History* 55, no. 3 (1983): doi:10.2307/1878595.

64. Said, *Culture and Imperialism*, 48.

65. Ibid.

66. Adorno diagnoses the inadequacies of this kind of thought as reproducing precisely the problems in reductive thinking. "Hegel speaks in the preface about the

vanity and vacuity of anyone who stands above the main issues because he is not inside of them. The abstract negativity involved in instantly sniffing out the defects of phenomenon, from the outside, as it were in order to be able to assert one's own superiority to them serves merely to gratify one's own intellectual narcissism and is therefore open to abuse from the outset. Resisting the temptation is surely among the primary requirements of the discipline of dialectics, one that cannot be over emphasized. We feel we are better than the swindle that has been foisted on to us. We cannot allow this to be the end of the story, and this is what is implied in the call for determinate negation." See Theodor W. Adorno, *Lectures on Negative Dialectics: Fragments of a Lecture Course, 1965/1966* (Cambridge, MA: Polity, 2008), 25–26.

67. Said, "History, Literature, Geography," 470–71.
68. Ibid.
69. Ibid., 470.
70. Said, "History, Literature, Geography," 467.
71. Ibid.
72. Said, *The World, the Text, and the Critic*, 26.
73. Said, "Between Worlds," in *Reflections on Exile*, 565.
74. Said, *Culture and Imperialism*, 61.
75. Lecia Rosenthal provides a compelling reading of the relationship between *Late Style* and *Humanism and Democratic Criticism*. But she is largely dismissive of Said's efforts; mostly, it seems, because the concept of the whole of human history is viewed as an object of mastery, whereas it is not understood as a critical category within the discourse of historicism as a potential for knowledge. In many ways the attitude is symptomatic of Rosenthal's decision to posit humanism as a question of/for the future, placing an emphasis on temporality, when, as I have been arguing, it is geography that is the terrain of activity for Said. In many respects, the spatial metaphors at work in *Humanism* define the terms of humanism and are very much part of the text's modernism. Her search for a theory of modernism overlooks the way the text is enacting a modernist practice (hence the reference to Beckett at the end). The motif of intransigence, while certainly associated with Adorno's late style, has a great deal to do with the circumstances at the time Said gave these talks, as well as Said's understanding of Benda's view of the social function of the intellectual. Humanism is not simply "force," as Rosenthal argues. Late art, as he argues, is a provisional home. But there were good grounds to locate the intellectual realm in the place of late art, and better grounds to characterize the possible positions one could occupy at the time Said was writing as "intransigent." I recall very well the atmosphere after 9/11 and the few occasions that were available for dissent. I also recall the numerous attacks on his character. Jonathan Cole has written well about the various challenges to academic freedom that were common at the time Said revised these lectures, and in recent years these tendencies have fortunately dissipated. Yet, they remain an active and residual element in the culture. Overlooking the importance of Benda's notion of opposition is understandable. Many have neglected Benda because it appears as if Said was claiming that Benda places far too much emphasis on the isolated intellectual's capacity to effectively resist the organization of the collective passions. For Said, whose own experiences seemed to confirm his argument, Benda's conception of the solitary intellectual

was not a defense of the quixotic, nor was it without reason. The isolated opposition to the political organization of the passions that threatened to undermine universal values is, after all, a form of local resistance. No matter the size or scope of the lobby, nation, party, or movement, the intellectual's job is to uphold a set of universal values. The location of that opposition might be "out of place," but is "very much *of* that place." It is a significant, local form of resistance. The alternative to quietism, conformism, or, even worse, an affirmation of the collective will is, Benda argued, the real *trahison de clercs*. "Intransigence" also captures the negativity of the late work; it adequately summarizes the conditions of the possibility of providing an imaginable alternative. The United States was on the verge of declaring yet another war on mendacious grounds, and the occupation of Palestine had continued under the leadership of Ariel Sharon. I have documented some of these activities in the introduction. "I have never seen it this bad," Said told me. "It is unimaginable." It was the last time that I saw him before he died in September 2003. Lecia Rosenthal, "Between Humanism and Late Style," *Cultural Critique* 67 (Fall 2007): doi:10.1353/cul.2007.0033. For an account of the challenges and threat to Academic Freedom since 9/11, see Jonathan R. Cole, "Defending Academic Freedom and Free Inquiry," *Social Research: An International Quarterly* 76, no. 3 (Fall 2009): 811–44; "The New McCarthyism," *Chronicle of Higher Education* 52, no. 3 (2005): B7; "Academic Freedom under Fire," *Daedalus* 135, no. 2 (Spring 2005): 1–13; and "The Patriot Act on Campus: Defending the University post-9/11," *Boston Review* 28, nos. 3–4 (Summer 2003): 13–16. For Said's discussion of Benda, see Said, "Secular Criticism," in *The World, the Text, and the Critic*, 14–15.

76. This is not to say that Said had provided the kind of full critique of historicism that he would have liked to, even if he had borrowed many of its underlying assumptions and rejected others. He still, for example, thought that there was a broader critique to be made of world historiography, which had many of same limitations as world literary historiography. In "Orientalism Reconsidered," he wrote, "What has never taken place is an epistemological critique of the connection between the development of a historicism which has expanded and developed enough to include antithetical attitudes such as ideologies of Western imperialism and critiques of imperialism, on the one hand, and, on the other, the actual practice of imperialism, by which the accumulation of territories in population, the control of economies, and the incorporation and homogenization of histories are maintained. If we keep this in mind, we will remark, for example, that in the methodological assumptions and practices of world history—which is ideologically anti-imperialist—little or no attention is given to those cultural practices, like Orientalism or ethnography, affiliated with imperialism, which in genealogical fact fathered world history itself. Hence, the emphasis in world history as a discipline has been on economic and political practices, defined by the processes of world historical writing, as in a sense separate and different from, as well as affected by, the knowledge of them which world history produces. The curious result is that the theories of accumulation on a world scale, or the capitalist world system, or lineages of absolutism depend on the same percipient and historicist observer who had been an Orientalist or colonial traveler three generations ago. They depend also on homogenizing, incorporating [a] world historical scheme that assimilates non-

synchronous developments, histories, cultures, and peoples to it." Said, "Orientalism Reconsidered," in *Reflections on Exile*, 210.

77. If Said is interested in developing a modernist theory, we could say that he does so because the study of alternative modernities provides us with a better conceptual basis for a critical understanding of globalization. As Andreas Huyssen has observed, "Modernist geographies suggest a more abstract image of spatial organization to me, very different from the more literal understanding but crucial for my argument about subliminal links between modernism and cultural globalization today. . . . We need to ask whether the market can secure new traditions, new forms of transnational communications and connectivities. But we would abandon our role as critical intellectuals if we were prematurely to exclude from such considerations the question of the complex relations between aesthetic value and political effect, which is fundamentally posed by the traditions of modernism and needs to be rescued for contemporary analyses of all culture under the spell of globalization. See Andreas Huyssen, "Geographies of Modernism in a Globalizing World," *New German Critique*, no. 100 (2007): 197, 207.

78. See, for example, Sheldon Pollock, "Future Philology? The Fate of a Soft Science in a Hard World," *Critical Inquiry* 35, no. 4 (2009): doi:10.1086/599594.

79. Said, *Humanism and Democratic Criticism*, 35.

80. Ibid., 36.

81. Ibid.

82. Ibid.

83. Ibid., 38.

84. Ibid.

85. Ibid., 49.

86. His interest in developing a "modernist" theory and practice (as opposed to a postcolonial theory and practice) was the basis through which he worked through the distinctions between attachments of filiation and affiliation in the canon of high modernism. In "Secular Criticism," Said had observed among a "large group" of late nineteenth- and early twentieth-century writers a "failure of generative impulse." Eliot's *The Waste Land*, Joyce's *Ulysses*, Mann's *Death in Venice*, even Freud's theory of the Oedipus complex—"a significant and influential aspect of which posits the potentially murderous outcome of bearing children"—in one way or another had to do with matters of regeneration. "Childless couples, orphaned children, aborted childbirths, and unregenerate celibate men and women populate the world of high modernism with remarkable insistence, all of them suggesting difficulties with filiation," he wrote (Said, "Secular Criticism," in *The World, the Text, and the Critic*, 17). While the observation led him to work out an important distinction between filiation and affiliation, and related questions of attachments, modernism and the secular were related in another way as well, apart from the title. *In saecula saeculorum* means the "generation of generation," a significant fact for an essay that exerts more energy describing the relationship of the absence of the regenerative power of filiation than it does defining the secular. All of this is to say that modernism had become a way for Said to think through questions of attachment and to develop a critical language that allowed him to work through the possible positions that could be occupied critically between culture and system. If the secular named a

history made by humans, modernism provided the conditions when forms of belonging revealed themselves as illusions that concealed the acts of displacements they presupposed.

87. Said, *Humanism and Democratic Criticism*, 144.
88. Edward Said, *On Late Style* (New York: Knopf, 2006).
89. Adorno, *Lectures on Negative Dialectics: Fragments of a Lecture Course, 1965/1966*, 30.
90. Said, *Humanism and Democratic Criticism*, 68.
91. Ibid., 75–76.
92. Ibid., 76.
93. Ibid., 82.
94. Ibid., 81.
95. Ibid., 83.
96. Ibid., 144.
97. Ibid., 81.

Bibliography

Unpublished Government Sources

Central Intelligence Agency. Freedom of Information and Privacy Acts. Langley, Virginia.
———. Congress for Cultural Freedom.
———. *Encounter* magazine.
———. Stephen Spender.
Federal Bureau of Investigation. U.S. Department of Justice. Freedom of Information and Privacy Acts. Washington, D.C.
———. Hanns Eisler.
———. Herbert Marcuse.
———. Institute for Social Research/Columbia University.
———. Max Horkheimer.
———. Theodor W. Adorno.
National Archives. National Archives Records Administration. Record Group 331. Washington, D.C.
———. Memorandum from Labor Policy Section Chief M. Machida to Chief of Kanto Civil Affairs, August 7, 1950. National Archives Records Administration, Washington, D.C., Record Group 331.2747 (17).
———. "Participation of Books in State Department's Fight against Communism," April 11, 1951, National Archives Records Administration, Record Group 511.412/6-2 851.
———. "Reactions over the Showing of *Animal Farm* throughout Ten Prefectures in the Kanto Area." National Archives Records Administration, Washington, D.C., Record Group 331.2747.
———. "Reports of Distribution Reaction to *Animal Farm*, a Cartoon Blast at Communism, August 1946–1951," National Archives Records Administration, Washington, D.C., Record Group 331.2747 (17).
Public Records Office. Papers of the Foreign Office. Kew Gardens, London.
———. *Animal Farm*: Acquisition of Cartoon Rights. Foreign and Commonwealth Office: Information Research Department. Foreign Office (hereafter FO) 1110/365.
———. *Animal Farm*. Production of Strip Cartoon and Successor. Foreign and Commonwealth Office: Information Research Department. FO 1110/392.
———. Films: "Animal Farm." Cartoon Strip for Use in Colonial Territories. Foreign and Commonwealth Office: Information Research Department. FO 1110/392.

——. Meeting with George Orwell. Foreign and Commonwealth Office: Information Research Department. Personal Correspondence. FO 1110/189.
——. Proposal to Produce Arabic Version of *Animal Farm*. Foreign and Commonwealth Office: Information Research Department. FO 1110/319.
——. Russian Language Version of *Animal Farm*. Foreign and Commonwealth Office: Information Research Department. FO 1110/221.
——. Suggestions for Book Publishing. Foreign and Commonwealth Office: Information Research Department. FO 1110/221.
——. Supply of Publication and Articles to Posts. Foreign and Commonwealth Office: Information Research Department. FO 1110/221.
Public Records Office. Papers of the Home Office. Kew Gardens, London.
——. Geoffrey Crowther Files. Home Office (hereafter abbreviated as HO) 335/40.
——. Paul Robeson Files. HO 382/6.

Manuscript Collections

American Committee for Cultural Freedom. Papers. Tamiment Collection. New York University, New York.
Congress for Cultural Freedom Papers. Regenstein Library. University of Chicago, Chicago.
Encounter Papers. University of Reading, Reading, England.
George Orwell Papers. Berg Archive. New York Public Library, New York.
George Orwell Papers. George Orwell Archive. University College London, London.
Halas and Batchelor Papers. University of Surrey, England.
Lionel Trilling Papers. Butler Library. Columbia University, New York.
Louis de Rochemont Papers. American Heritage Center, University of Wyoming, Laramie.
Paul Lazarsfeld Papers. Butler Library. Columbia University, New York.
Psychological Strategy Board Papers. Harry S. Truman Library, Independence, Missouri.

Statutes and Judicial Documents

Central Intelligence Agency Act, 1947. United States Code 50 § 403.
Central Intelligence Agency v. Sims, United States Supreme Court, April 16, 1985.
Executive Order No. 12958. 60 Fed. Reg. 19825. April 17, 1995.
Freedom of Information Act. United States Code 5 § 552.
National Security Act of 1947, 50 USC § 552 (b) (1) (2010).
Rubin v. Central Intelligence Agency, 2001WL1537706 (Southern District of New York [SDNY], December 3, 2001).

Periodicals and Newspapers

Al-Adwa
Black Orpheus
The Criterion
Cuadernos
Der Monat
Encounter
Forum
Hiwar
Hudson Review
The Independent
The London Magazine
New Reasoner
New Statesman and Society
Partisan Review
Perspectives Belgium
Perspectives Africa
Perspectives India
Perspectives Japan
Perspectives USA
Présence Africaine
Preuves
Quadrant
Solidarity
Tempo Presente
Transition
The Tribune

Selected Bibliography

Adams, Rachel. "The Worlding of American Studies." *American Quarterly* 53, no. 4 (2001): doi:10.1353/aq.2001.0034.

Adorno, Theodor W. *Aesthetic Theory*. Trans. Robert Hullot-Kentor. Minneapolis: University of Minnesota Press, 1997.

———. "Alienated Masterpiece: The *Missa Solemnis*." *Telos* 28 (1976): 113–24.

———. "Analytical Study of the NBC 'Music Appreciation Hour.'" *Musical Quarterly* 78, no. 2 (1994): 325–77.

———. "Commitment." In *Notes to Literature*. Vol. 2. Translated by Shierry Weber Nicholsen. Edited by Rolf Tiedmann. New York: Columbia University Press, 1991.

———. *Critical Models: Interventions and Catchwords*. Trans. Henry Pickford. New York: Columbia University Press, 1998.

———. "The Culture Industry Reconsidered." *Critical Theory and Society: A Reader*. Ed. Stephen Eric Bronner. New York: Routledge, 1989.

———. *The Culture Industry: Selected Essays on Mass Culture.* London: Routledge, 1991.
———. *Current of Music.* Trans. Robert Hullot-Kentor. Cambridge, MA: Polity, 2009.
———. "The Curves of the Needle." Trans. Thomas Y. Levin. *October* 55 (1990): 49–55.
———."Extorted Reconciliation." In *Notes to Literature.* Vol. 1, trans. Shierry Weber Nicholsen; ed. Rolf Tiedemann. New York: Columbia University Press, 1991.
———. "The Form of the Phonograph Record." Trans. Thomas Y. Levin. *October* 55 (1990): 56–61.
———. "Freudian Theory and the Pattern of Fascist Propaganda." *The Essential Frankfurt School Reader.* Ed. Andrew Arato and Eike Gebhardt. Oxford: Blackwell, 1978.
———. *In Search of Wagner.* Trans. Rodney Livingstone. London: New Left Books, 1981.
———. *Introduction to Sociology.* Stanford, CA: Stanford University Press, 2000.
———. *Introduction to the Sociology of Music.* New York: Continuum, 1989.
———. "Is Marx Obsolete?" *Diogenes* 64 (Winter 1968): 1–16.
———. *Lectures on Negative Dialectics: Fragments of a Lecture Course, 1965/1966.* Cambridge, MA: Polity, 2008.
———. "Marginalia to Theory and Praxis." In *Critical Models: Interventions and Catchwords,* trans. Henry Pickford. New York: Columbia University Press, 1998.
———. "The Meaning of Working through the Past." In *Critical Models: Interventions and Catchwords,* trans. Henry Pickford. New York: Columbia University Press, 1998.
———. *Minima Moralia: Reflections from Damaged Life.* Trans. E.F.N. Jephcott. London: New Left Books, 1974.
———. "Music, Language, and Composition." *Musical Quarterly* 77, no. 3 (Fall 1993): 401–14.
———. *Negative Dialectics.* Trans. E. B. Ashton. New York: Seabury Press, 1973.
———. *Notes to Literature.* Vols. 1 and 2. Trans. Shierry Nicholson Weber. New York: Columbia University Press, 1991.
———. "On the Fetish Character in Music and the Regression in Listening." In *The Essential Frankfurt School Reader,* ed. Andrew Arato and Eike Gebhardt. Oxford: Blackwell, 1978.
———. "Opera and the Long-Playing Record." Trans. Thomas Y. Levin. *October* 55 (1990): 62–66.
———. *Philosophy of Modern Music.* Trans. Anne G. Mitchell and Wesley V. Blomster. New York: Continuum, 1994.
———. *The Positivist Dispute in German Sociology.* Trans. Glyn Adley and David Frisby. London: Heinemann, 1976.
———. *Prisms.* Trans. Samuel and Shierry Weber. Cambridge, MA: MIT Press, 1981.
———. *Quasi Una Fantasia: Essays on Modern Music.* Trans. Rodney Livingstone. New York: Verso, 1992.
———. "Scientific Experiences of a European Scholar in America." In *Critical Mod-*

els: *Interventions and Catchwords*, trans. Henry Pickford. New York: Columbia University Press, 1998.

———. "A Social Critique of Radio Music." *Kenyon Review* 8 (1945): 208–17.

———. "Sociology and Empirical Research." In *The Positivist Dispute in German Sociology*, trans. Glyn Adley and David Frisby. London: Heinemann, 1976.

———. *Sound Figures*. Trans. Rodney Livingstone. Stanford, CA: Stanford University Press, 1999.

———. "Transparencies on Film." *New German Critique: An Interdisciplinary Journal of German Studies* 24–25 (1981): 186–205.

Adorno, Theodor W., Else Frenkel-Brunswik, Daniel J. Levinson, and R. Nevitt Sanford. *The Authoritarian Personality*. New York: Harper, 1950.

Adorno, Theodor W., and Hanns Eisler. *Composing for the Films*. London: Heinemann, 1994.

Adorno, Theodor W., and Max Horkheimer. *Dialectic of Enlightenment*. Trans. Edmund Jephcott. Palo Alto, CA: Stanford University Press, 2007.

Adorno, Theodor W., and Walter Benjamin. *The Complete Correspondence, 1928–1940*. Cambridge, MA: Harvard University Press, 1999.

Agamben, Giorgio. *Homo Sacer: Sovereign Power and Bare Life*. Trans. Daniel Heller-Roazen. Chicago: University of Chicago Press, 1998.

———. *Means without End: Notes on Politics*. Minneapolis: University of Minnesota Press, 2000.

———. *State of Exception*. Chicago: University of Chicago Press, 2005.

Ahmad, Eqbal. "Political Culture and Foreign Policy: Notes on American Interventions in the Third World." In *For Better or Worse: The American Influence in the World*, ed. Allen F. Davis. Westport, CT: Greenwood Press, 1981.

Alcalay, Ammiel. *Memory, Imagination, Resistance*. New York: Rest Press, 2003.

Anderson, Perry. "The Antinomies of Antonio Gramsci." *New Left Review* 100 (November 1976): 5–78.

———. "Components of the National Culture." *New Left Review* 50 (1968): 3–57.

———. *Considerations in Western Marxism*. London: Verso, 1976.

———. *English Questions*. London: Verso, 1992.

———. "Renewals." *New Left Review* 1 (January–February 2000): 1–15.

Anidjar, Gil. "Secularism." *Critical Inquiry* 33 (Autumn 2006): 52–77.

Appadurai, Arjun, ed. *Globalization*. Durham, NC: Duke University Press, 2001.

———. *Modernity at Large: Cultural Dimensions of Globalization*. Minneapolis: University of Minnesota Press, 1996.

Apter, Emily. "Global 'Translatio': The 'Invention' of Comparative Literature, Istanbul, 1933." *Critical Inquiry* 29, no. 2 (2003): doi:10.2307/1344418.

———. "The Human in the Humanities." *October* 96 (2001): doi:10.2307/779118.

———. "On Translation in a Global Market." *Public Culture* 13, no. 1 (2001): 1–12.

———. "Saidian Humanism." *boundary 2* 31, no. 2 (2004): doi:10.2307/4131870.

———. *The Translation Zone*. Princeton: Princeton University Press, 2006.

———. "Untranslatables: A World System." *New Literary History* 39, no. 3 (2008): doi:10.1353/nlh.0.0055.

Arac, Jonathan. "Commentary: Literary History in a Global Age." *New Literary History* 39, no. 3 (2008): 747–60.

———. *Critical Genealogies: Historical Situations for Postmodern Literary Studies.* New York: Columbia University Press, 1987.
———. *Postmodernism and Politics.* Minneapolis: University of Minnesota Press, 1986.
———. "What Good Can Literary History Do?" *American Literary History* 20, nos. 1–2 (2008): 1–11.
Arendt, Hannah. *The Origins of Totalitarianism.* New York: Harcourt Brace, 1951.
Arnold, Matthew. *Culture and Anarchy.* New York: Cambridge University Press, 1960.
Ashcroft, Bill, and Pal Ahluwalia. *Edward Said.* New York: Routledge, 2008.
Auerbach, Erich. "Figura." In *Scenes from the Drama of European Literature: Six Essays*, trans. Ralph Mannheim. Manchester: Manchester University Press, 1984.
———. *Literary Language and Its Public in Late Latin Antiquity and in the Middle Ages.* Trans. Ralph Manheim. Princeton: Princeton University Press, 1993.
———. *Mimesis: The Representation of Reality in Western Literature.* Princeton: Princeton University Press, 2003.
———. "Philology and *Weltliteratur*." Trans. Edward and Marie Said. *Centennial Review* 13 (1969): 1–17.
Badiou, Alain. *Being and Event.* New York: Continuum, 2005.
———. "'We Need a Popular Discipline': Contemporary Politics and the Crisis of the Negative." *Critical Inquiry* 34, no. 4 (2008): 645–79.
Baldwin, James. "Everybody's Protest Novel." *Perspectives USA* 1, no. 2 (Winter 1953): 11.
Balibar, Étienne. *Masses, Classes, Ideas: Studies on Politics and Philosophy Before and After Marx.* Trans. James Swenson. New York: Routledge, 1994.
Bardenstein, Carol. "Threads of Memory and Discourses of Rootedness: Of Trees, Oranges, and the Prickly Pear Cactus in Israel/Palestine." *Edebiyât* 8 (1998): 1–36.
Barnet, Richard J. *Intervention and Revolution.* Washington, D.C.: Institute for Policy Studies. Dublin, Ireland: Mentor Books, 1972.
———. *The Roots of War.* New York: Atheneum, 1972.
Barnhisel, Greg. "*Perspectives USA* and the Cultural Cold War: Modernism in Service of the State." *Modernism/modernity* 14, no. 4 (2007): doi:10.1353/mod.2007.0080.
Barrows, Adam. *The Cosmic Time of Empire: Modern Britain and World Literature.* Berkeley: University of California Press, 2011.
Barthes, Roland. *Writing Degree Zero.* Trans. Annette Lavers and Colin Smith. New York: Hill and Wang, 1967.
Baucom, Ian. "Globalit, Inc.; or, The Cultural Logic of Global Literary Studies." *PMLA* 116, no. 1 (2001): 158–72.
Bayoumi, Moustafa. "Our Philological Home Is the Earth." *Arab Studies Quarterly* 26, no. 4 (Fall 2004): 53–66.
Beauvoir, Simone de. *America Day by Day.* New York: Grove, 1953.
Bell, David F. "Infinite Archives." *SubStance* 33, no. 3 (2004): doi:10.1353/sub.2004.0034.
Benjamin, Walter. *Illuminations.* Trans. Harry Zohn. New York: Schocken Books, 1969.

———. *Reflections: Essays, Aphorisms, Autobiographical Writing*. Trans. Peter Demetz. New York: Schocken Books, 1986.
———. *Understanding Brecht*. New York: Verso Editions, 1998.
Bercovitch, Sacvan. "Problems in the Writing of American Literary History: The Examples of Poetry and Ethnicity." *American Literary History* 15, no. 1 (2003): 1–3.
Berghahn, Volker. *America and the Intellectual Cold Wars in Europe*. Princeton: Princeton University Press, 2001.
Berman, Russell. "Adorno's Politics." In *Adorno: A Critical Reader*, ed. Nigel Gibson and Andrew N. Rubin. Malden, MA: Blackwell, 2002.
Bernstein, Jay. "Art against Enlightenment: Adorno's Critique of Habermas." In *The Problems of Modernity: Adorno and Benjamin*, ed. Andrew Benjamin, 49–66. London: Routledge, 1989.
———. *The Fate of Art: Aesthetic Alienation from Kant to Derrida and Adorno*. University Park: Pennsylvania State University Press, 1992.
Bérubé, Michael. "American Studies without Exception." *PMLA* 118, no. 1 (January 2003): 106.
Biocca, Dario. "Ignazio Silone e la polizia politica." *Nuova Storia Contemporanea* 2, no. 3 (May–June 1998).
Biocca, Frank A. "The Pursuit of Sound: Radio, Perception and Utopia in the Early Twentieth Century." *Media, Culture & Society* 10, no. 1 (1988): doi:10.1177/016344388010001005.
Bird, Kai. *The Chairman: John McCloy; The Making of the American Establishment*. New York: Simon and Schuster, 1992.
Birnbaum, Norman. "The End of Anti-Communism." *Partisan Review* 29, no. 3 (1962): 386–94.
———. "Open Letter to the Congress for Cultural Freedom." *Universities and Left Review* (January 1959): 5.
Blackmur, Richard P. "Editor's Commentary." *Perspectives USA* 6 (Winter 1954): 134–36.
———. "Henry Adams: Three Late Moments." *Kenyon Review* 2, no. 1 (1940): doi:10.2307/4332122.
———. *The Lion and the Honeycomb: Essays in Solicitude and Critique*. New York: Harcourt, Brace, and Company, 1955.
———. "The Logos in the Catacomb: The Role of the Intellectual." *Kenyon Review* (1959): 1–22.
———. "The Politics of Human Power." *Kenyon Review* (1950): 663–73.
———. "Reflections of Toynbee." *Kenyon Review* 17, no. 3 (1955): doi:10.2307/4333585.
———. "The Substance that Prevails." *Kenyon Review* (1955): 94–110.
———. "Toward a Modus Vivendi." *Kenyon Review* (1954): 507–35.
Bloom, Alexander. *Prodigal Sons: The New York Intellectuals*. New York: Oxford University Press, 1986.
Bloom, Harold. *George Orwell*. New York: Chelsea House, 1987.
Blum, William. *Killing Hope: U.S. Military and C.I.A. Interventions since World War II*. Monroe, ME: Common Courage Press, 1995.
Bourdieu, Pierre. *Distinction: A Social Critique of the Judgement of Taste*. Cambridge, MA: Harvard University Press, 1984.

———. *The Field of Cultural Production: Essays on Art and Literature*. New York: Columbia University Press, 1993.
———. *The Logic of Practice*. Boston: Blackwell, 1990.
———. *Practical Reason: On the Theory of Action*. Cambridge: Polity Press, 1998.
———. *The Rules of Art: Genesis and Structure of the Literary Field*. Cambridge: Polity Press, 1996.
Bové, Paul A., ed. *Edward Said and the Work of the Critic: Speaking Truth to Power*. Durham, NC: Duke University Press Books, 2000.
Braden, Thomas W. "I'm Glad the CIA Is Immoral." *Saturday Evening Post*, May 20, 1967.
Brennan, Timothy. *At Home in the World: Cosmopolitanism Now*. Cambridge, MA: Harvard University Press, 1997.
———. "The Illusion of a Future: *Orientalism* as Traveling Theory." *Critical Inquiry* 26 (Spring 2000): 558–83.
Buck-Morss, Susan. *The Origin of Negative Dialectics: Theodor W. Adorno's Debt to Walter Benjamin*. New York: Free Press, 1977.
Bürger, Peter. *Theory of the Avant-Garde*. Minneapolis: University of Minnesota Press, 1984.
Burnham, James. *What Europe Thinks of America*. New York: John Day Co., 1953.
Burstow, Robert. "The Limits of Modernist Art as a 'Weapon of the Cold War': Reassessing the Unknown Patron of the Monument to the Unknown Political Prisoner." *Oxford Art Journal* 20, no. 1 (January 1, 1997): 68–80.
Butler, Judith. "A 'Bad Writer' Writes Back." *New York Times*, March 20, 1999, A15.
Buxton, William. "John Marshall and the Humanities in Europe: Shifting Patterns of Rockefeller Foundation Support." *Minerva* 41, no. 2 (2003): 133–53.
Calder, Jenni. *Chronicles of Conscience: A Study of George Orwell and Arthur Koestler*. Pittsburgh: University of Pittsburgh Press, 1968.
Canali, Mauro. "Ignazio Silone and the Fascist Political Police." *Journal of Modern Italian Studies* 5, no. 1 (2000): 36–60.
———. "Il fiduciario 'Silvestri.'" *Nuova Storia Contemporanea* 3, no. 1 (January–February 1999).
Candido, Antonio. *On Literature and Society*. Trans. Howard Saul Becker. Princeton: Princeton University Press, 1995.
Cantril, Hadley. "Causes and Control of Riot and Panic." *Public Opinion Quarterly* 7, no. 4 (1943): doi:10.2307/2745636.
———. "Concerning the Nature of Perception." *Proceedings of the American Philosophical Society* 104, no. 5 (1960): doi:10.2307/985231.
———. "The Effect of Modern Technology and Organization upon Social Behavior." *Social Forces* 15, no. 4 (1937): doi:10.2307/2571419.
———. "Propaganda Analysis." *English Journal* 27, no. 3 (1938): doi:10.2307/806063.
———. "A Psychological Reason for the Lag of 'Non-Material' Culture Traits." *Social Forces* 13, no. 3 (1935): doi:10.2307/2570400.
———. "The Qualities of Being Human." *American Quarterly* 6, no. 1 (1954): doi:10.2307/3031431.
———. "The Role of the Radio Commentator." *Public Opinion Quarterly* 3, no. 4 (1939): doi:10.2307/2744999.

———. "The Roles of the Situation and Adrenalin in the Induction of Emotion." *American Journal of Psychology* 46, no. 4 (1934): doi:10.2307/1415495.
———. *Soviet Leaders and Mastery over Man*. New Brunswick: Rutgers University Press, 1960.
Cantril, Hadley, and William A. Hunt. "Emotional Effects Produced by the Injection of Adrenalin." *American Journal of Psychology* 44, no. 2 (1932): doi:10.2307/1414829.
Cardoso, Fernando Enrique. *Dependency and Development in Latin America*. Berkeley: University of California Press, 1979.
Carpenter, Humphrey. *The Envy of the World: Fifty Years of the BBC Third Programme and Radio 3, 1946–1996*. London: Weidenfeld and Nicolson, 1996.
Carroll, Mark. *Music and Ideology in Cold War Europe*. New York: Cambridge University Press, 2003.
Casanova, Pascale. "Literature as a World." *New Left Review*, no. 31 (2005): 71–90.
———. *La République mondiale des letters*. Paris: Éditions du Seuil, 1999.
———. *The World Republic of Letters*. Trans. M. B. DeBois. Cambridge, MA: Harvard University Press, 2004.
Caute, David. *The Dancer Defects: The Struggle for Cultural Supremacy during the Cold War*. New York: Oxford University Press, 2005.
Cheah, Pheng. "The Material World of Comparison." *New Literary History* 40, no. 3 (2009): doi:10.1353/nlh.0.0105.
Cheah, Pheng, and Bruce Robbins. *Cosmopolitics: Thinking and Feeling beyond the Nation*. Minneapolis: University of Minnesota Press, 1998.
Chomsky, Noam. *Deterring Democracy*. New York: Verso, 1991.
———. "Intellectuals and the State." *Towards a New Cold War*. New York: Pantheon, 1982.
———. "The Politicization of the University." In *Radical Priorities*, ed. Carlos P. Otero. Montreal: Black Rose Books, 1984.
———. "The Responsibility of the Intellectuals." In *The Noam Chomsky Reader*, ed. James Peck. New York: Pantheon, 1987.
Clifford, James. "On Orientalism." In *The Predicament of Culture: Twentieth Century Ethnography, Literature and Art*. Cambridge, MA: Harvard University Press, 1988.
———. *The Predicament of Culture: Twentieth-Century Ethnography, Literature, and Art*. Cambridge, MA: Harvard University Press, 1988.
Cohen, Debra Rae. "Radio Modernism: Literature, Ethics, and the BBC, 1922–1938 (Review)." *Modernism/modernity* 14, no. 3 (2007): doi:10.1353/mod.2007.0057.
Colby, Gerard, and Charlotte Dennett. *Thy Will Be Done: The Conquest of the Amazon; Nelson Rockefeller and Evangelism in the Age of Oil*. New York: HarperCollins, 1995.
Cole, David. *Enemy Aliens: Double Standards and Constitutional Freedoms in the War on Terrorism*. New York: New Press, 2003.
Coleman, Peter. *The Liberal Conspiracy*. New York: Free Press, 1989.
Collini, Stefan. *Absent Minds: Intellectuals in Britain*. New York: Oxford University Press, 2006.

———. *Common Reading: Critics, Historians, Publics*. New York: Oxford University Press, 2008.

Combe, Sonia. *Archives interdites: L'histoire confisquée*. Paris: La Découverte, 2001.

Coombs, Douglas. *Spreading the Word: The Library Work of the British Council*. London: Mansell Publishing Limited, 1988.

Cooppan, Vilashini. "Ghosts in the Disciplinary Machine: The Uncanny Life of World Literature." *Comparative Literature Studies* 41, no. 1 (2004): 10–36.

Coyle, Michael. "'This Rather Elusory Broadcast Technique': T. S. Eliot and the Genre of Radio Talk." *ANQ* 11, no. 4 (Fall 1998): 32–42.

Crewdson, John, and Joseph Treaster. "Worldwide Propaganda Network Built by the C.I.A." *New York Times*, December 24, 1967.

Crick, Bernard R. *George Orwell: A Life*. London: Penguin, 1980.

Crossman, Richard, ed. *The God that Failed: Six Studies in Communism*. London: Hamish Hamilton, 1950.

Cumings, Bruce. "Boundary Displacement: Area Studies and International Studies during and after the Cold War." In *Universities and Empire: Money and Politics in the Social Sciences during the Cold War*, ed. Christopher Simpson. New York: New Press, 1998.

———. *Dominion from Sea to Sea: Pacific Ascendancy and American Power*. New Haven: Yale University Press, 2009.

Damrosch, David. *What Is World Literature?* Princeton: Princeton University Press, 2003.

Davison, Peter, ed. *The Complete Works of George Orwell*. Vol. 20. London: Secker and Warburg, 1998.

———. *George Orwell: A Literary Life*. New York: St. Martin's Press, 1996.

Defty, Andrew. *Britain, America and Anti-Communist Propaganda, 1945–1953: The Information Research Department*. London: Routledge, 2004.

Dentith, Simon. *A Rhetoric of the Real*. London: Hemel Hempstead, 1990.

Dimock, Wai Chee. "Deep Time: American Literature and World History." *American Literary History* 13, no. 4 (2001): doi:10.2307/3054595.

———. "Literature for the Planet." *PMLA* 116, no. 1 (2001): 173–88.

———. *Through Other Continents: American Literature aross Deep Time*. Princeton: Princeton University Press, 2008.

Dimock, Wai Chee, and Laurence Buell, eds. *Shades of the Planet: American Literature as World Literature*. Princeton: Princeton University Press, 2007.

Donoghue, Denis. "*Nineteen Eighty-Four*: Politics and Fable." In *George Orwell and "Nineteen Eighty-Four": The Man and the Book*. Washington, D.C.: Library of Congress, 1985.

Douglas, Ann. "The Failure of the New York Intellectuals." *Raritan* 17, no. 4 (Spring 1998): 1–23.

———. "Periodizing the American Century: Modernism, Postmodernism, and Postcolonialism in the Cold War Context." *Modernism/modernity* 5, no. 3 (Sept. 1998): 71–98.

Duberman, Martin Bauml. *Paul Robeson*. New York: Knopf, 1988.

Dudziak, Mary L. *Cold War Civil Rights: Race and the Image of American Democracy*. Princeton: Princeton University Press, 2002.

Eagleton, Terry. *Against the Grain: Essays, 1975–1985*. London: Verso, 1986.
———. *Exiles and Émigrés: Studies in Modern Literature*. London: Chatto & Windus, 1970.
———. *The Function of Criticism: From the Spectator to Post-Structuralism*. London: Verso, 1984.
———. *The Idea of Culture*. Malden, MA: Blackwell, 2000.
———. *The Ideology of the Aesthetic*. Cambridge, MA: Basil Blackwell, 1990.
Eliot, T. S. "The Man of Letters and the Future of Europe." *Sewanee Review* 53, no. 3 (1945): 333–42.
———. "Notes towards the Definition of Culture." In *Christianity and Culture*. New York: Harcourt, Brace, 1949.
———. *Selected Prose*. Ed. Frank Kermode. New York: Farrar, Straus and Giroux, 1975.
Eliot, T. S., and Ezra Pound, "Letters concerning *The Waste Land*." *Nine*, no. 4 (Summer 1950): 176–79.
Engelhardt, Tom. *The End of Victory Culture: Cold War America and the Disillusioning of a Generation*. New York: Basic Books, 1995.
Engerman, David C. "Rethinking Cold War Universities: Some Recent Histories." *Journal of Cold War Studies* 5, no. 3 (2003): 80–95.
Epstein, Jason. "The CIA and the Intellectuals." *New York Review of Books* (April 20, 1967): 2–9.
Ertur, Basak, et al., eds. *Waiting for the Barbarians: A Tribute to Edward W. Said*. New York: Verso, 2008.
Fanon, Frantz. *Black Skin, White Masks*. New York: Grove Press, 1967.
———. *A Dying Colonialism*. New York: Grove Press, 1967.
———. *The Wretched of the Earth*. Trans. Constance Farrington. New York: Grove Press, 1963.
Fekete, John. *The Critical Twilight: Explorations in the Ideology of Anglo-American Literary Theory from Eliot to McLuhan*. London: Routledge & Kegan Paul, 1977.
Ferguson, Frances. "Planetary Literary History: The Place of the Text." *New Literary History* 39, nos. 3–4 (2009): doi:10.1353/nlh.0.0042.
Fergusson, Francis. "The Human Image." *Kenyon Review* 19 (1957): 1–14.
Fitzgerald, Robert. *Enlarging the Change: The Princeton Seminar in Literary Criticism, 1949–1951*. Boston: Northeastern University Press, 1985.
Foner, Eric. *The Story of American Freedom*. New York: W. W. Norton, 1998.
Foucault, Michel. *The Archaeology of Knowledge*. New York: Pantheon Books, 1972.
———. *Discipline and Punish: The Birth of the Prison*. New York: Pantheon Books, 1977.
———. *The History of Sexuality*. New York: Vintage Books, 1990.
———. *Madness and Civilization: A History of Insanity in the Age of Reason*. New York: Pantheon Books, 1965.
———. *The Order of Things: An Archaeology of the Human Sciences*. New York: Pantheon Books, 1971.
———. *Politics, Philosophy, Culture: Interviews and Other Writings, 1977–1984*. New York: Routledge, 1990.
———. *Power*. Trans. James D. Faubion. New York: New Press, 2000.

———. *Power/Knowledge: Selected Interviews and Other Writings, 1972–1977.* New York: Pantheon Books, 1980.

———. *Security, Territory, Population: Lectures at the Collège de France, 1977–1978.* Edited by Michel Senellart, François Ewald, and Alessandro Fontana. New York: Palgrave Macmillan, 2007.

———. *"Society Must Be Defended": Lectures at the Collège de France, 1975–1976.* Trans. David Macey. London: Allen Lane, 2003.

Fowler, Roger. *The Language of George Orwell.* New York: St. Martin's Press, 1995.

Franco, Jean. *The Decline and Fall of the Lettered City: Latin America in the Cold War.* Cambridge, MA: Harvard University Press, 2002.

Furlough, Ellen. "Selling the American Way in Interwar France: 'Prix Uniques' and the Salons des Arts Ménagers." *Journal of Social History* 26, no. 3 (1993): doi:10.2307/3788624.

Fyvel, T. R. *George Orwell: A Personal Memoir.* London: Weidenfeld and Nicolson, 1982.

Gaonkar, Dilip, ed. *Alternative Modernities.* Durham, NC: Duke University Press, 2001.

Gendzier, Irene L. *Managing Political Change: Social Scientists and the Third World.* Boulder, CO: Westview Press, 1985.

Ghazoul, Ferial. *Edward Said and Critical Decolonization.* Cairo: American University in Cairo Press, 2007.

Ghosh, Ranjan. *Edward Said and the Literary, Social, and Political World.* New York: Routledge, 2009.

Goldknopf, David. "The New Ambassadors." *Antioch Review* 12, no. 1 (1952): doi:10.2307/4609538.

Goldmann, Lucien. "Goldmann and Adorno: To Describe, Understand and Explain." In *Cultural Creation in Modern Society.* Saint Louis, MO: Telos Press, 1976.

Golffing, F. "Review: Humanist in the Enemy Camp." *Kenyon Review* (1959): 164–68.

Gourgouris, Stathis. "Transformation, Not Transcendence." *boundary 2* 31, no. 2 (2004): doi:10.2307/4131871.

Graff, Gerald. *Professing Literature: An Institutional History.* Chicago: University of Chicago Press, 1997.

Gramsci, Antonio. *Selections from the Prison Notebooks of Antonio Gramsci.* Trans. Quintin Hoare and Geoffrey Nowell-Smith. London: Lawrence & Wishart, 1971.

Green, Geoffrey. *Literary Criticism and the Structures of History: Erich Auerbach and Leo Spitzer.* Lincoln: University of Nebraska Press, 1982.

Grémion, Pierre. *Intelligence de l'anticommunisme: Le Congrès pour la liberté de la culture à Paris (1950–1975).* Paris: Fayard, 1995.

Guha, Ranajit. *Dominance without Hegemony: History and Power in Colonial India.* Cambridge, MA: Harvard University Press, 1997.

———. "Not at Home in Empire." *Critical Inquiry* 23 (Spring 1997): 482–93.

———. "The Prose of Counter-Insurgency." In *Selected Subaltern Studies,* ed. Ranajit Guha and Gayatri Spivak. New York: Oxford, 1988.

Guilbaut, Serge. *How New York Stole the Idea of Modern Art: Abstract Expressionism,*

Freedom, and the Cold War. Trans. Arthur Goldhammer. Chicago: University of Chicago Press, 1985.

———. *Reconstructing Modernism: Art in New York, Paris, and Montreal, 1945–1964*. Cambridge: MIT Press, 1992.

Guilbaut, Serge, and Manuel J. Borja-Villel. *Be-Bomb: The Transatlantic War of Images and All that Jazz*. Barcelona: Museu d'Art Contemporani de Barcelona, 2007.

Guillory, John. *Cultural Capital: The Problem of Literary Canon Formation*. Chicago: University of Chicago Press, 1993.

Gunn, Giles. "Introduction: Globalizing Literary Studies." *PMLA* 116, no. 1 (2001): 16–31.

Habermas, Jürgen. *The Philosophical Discourse of Modernity*. Trans. Frederick G. Lawrence. Cambridge, MA: MIT Press, 1987.

———. *The Structural Transformation of the Public Sphere: An Inquiry into a Category of Bourgeois Society*. Trans. Thomas Burger. Cambridge, MA: M.I.T Press, 1991.

Hafetz, Jonathan. "Secret Evidence and the Courts in the Age of National Security: Habeas Corpus, Judicial Review, and Limits of Secrecy in Detentions at Guantanamo." *Cardozo Public Law, Policy, and Ethics Journal* (Fall 2006): 127–69.

Halberstam, Michael. *Totalitarianism and the Modern Conception of Politics*. New Haven: Yale University Press, 1999.

Halliday, Denis. *The Second Cold War*. New York: Verso, 1984.

Hampden, John. "Books and the British Council." In *The Book World Today*. New York: Books for Libraries Press, 1957.

Harding, James Martin. *Adorno and "A Writing of the Ruins."* Albany: State University of New York Press, 1997.

———. "Adorno, Ellison, and the Critique of Jazz." *Cultural Critique* 31 (1995): 129–58.

Hardt, Michael, and Antonio Negri. *Empire*. Cambridge, MA: Harvard University Press, 2000.

Hart, William. *Edward Said and the Religious Effects of Culture*. New York: Cambridge University Press, 2000.

Hitchens, Christopher. *Blood, Class, and Nostalgia*. New York: Farrar, Straus and Giroux, 1990.

———. "George Orwell and Raymond Williams." *Critical Quarterly* 41, no. 3 (1999): 3–22.

———. *Orwell's Victory*. London: Penguin, 2002.

———. "Was Orwell a Snitch?" *Nation*, December 14, 1998, 8.

Hofstadter, Richard. *Anti-Intellectualism in American Life*. New York: Vintage, 1962.

———. *The Paranoid Style in American Politics and Other Essays*. New York: Knopf, 1965.

Hohendahl, Peter. "The Displaced Intellectual? Adorno's American Years Revisited." *New German Critique* 56 (1992): 76–100.

———. *Prismatic Thought: Theodor W. Adorno*. Lincoln: University of Nebraska Press, 1995.

Holman, Valerie. "Carefully Concealed Connections: The Ministry of Information and British Publishing, 1939–1946." *Book History* 8, no. 1 (2005): 197–226.

Holquist, Michael. "The Last European: Erich Auerbach as Precursor in the History of Cultural Criticism." *MLQ* 53, no. 3 (September 1993): 371–91.
Horkheimer, Max, and Theodor W. Adorno. *Dialectic of Enlightenment*. London: Allen Lane, 1973.
Horsman, Reginald. *Race and Manifest Destiny: The Origin of American Racial Anglo-Saxonism*. Cambridge, MA: Harvard University Press, 1981.
Howe, Irving. *Politics and the Novel*. New York: Columbia University Press, 1987.
Hullot-Kentor, Robert. "Notes on Dialectic of Enlightenment: Translating the Odysseus Essay." *New German Critique* 56 (1992): 101–8.
———. "Odysseus or Myth and Enlightenment." *New German Critique* 56 (1992): 109–41.
Hussein, Abdirahman A. *Edward Said: Criticism and Society*. New York: Verso, 2004.
Huyssen, Andreas. "Adorno in Reverse: From Hollywood to Richard Wagner." In *Adorno: A Critical Reader*, ed. Nigel Gibson and Andrew Rubin. Malden, MA: Blackwell, 2002.
———. *After the Great Divide: Modernism, Mass Culture, Postmodernism*. Bloomington: Indiana University Press, 1986.
———. "Geographies of Modernism in a Globalizing World." *New German Critique* 100 (2007): 189–207.
———. "Introduction: Modernism after Postmodernity." *New German Critique* 99 (2006): 1–5.
———. "Postscript 2000." In *Adorno: A Critical Reader*, ed. Nigel Gibson and Andrew Rubin. Malden, MA: Blackwell, 2002.
Irzık, Sibel. "Istanbul." In *The Novel*, ed. Franco Moretti. Vol. 2. Princeton: Princeton University Press, 2006.
Iskandar, Adel, and Hakem Rustom. *Edward Said: A Legacy of Emancipation and Representation. Berkeley:* University of California Press, 2010.
Israel, Nico. "Damage Control: Adorno, Los Angeles, and Dislocation of Culture." *Yale Journal of Criticism* 10, no. 1 (1997): 95–121.
———. *Outlandish: Writing between Exile and Diaspora*. Palo Alto, CA: Stanford University Press, 2000.
James, C.L.R. "Britain's New Monthlies." *Saturday Review* (May 22, 1954): 13.
Jameson, Fredric. *Late Marxism: Adorno; or, The Persistence of the Dialectic*. New York: Verso, 1990.
———. *Marxism and Form*. Princeton: Princeton University Press, 1971.
———. "New Literary History after the End of the New." *New Literary History* 39, no. 3 (July 2008): 375–87.
———. *The Political Unconscious: Narrative as a Socially Symbolic Act*. Ithaca: Cornell University Press, 1981.
———. *A Singular Modernity: Essay on the Ontology of the Present*. New York: Verso, 2002.
———. "T. W. Adorno; or, Historical Tropes." *Salmagundi* 2, no. 1 (1967): 3–43.
Jay, Martin. *Adorno*. Cambridge, MA: Harvard University Press, 1984.
———. "Adorno in America." *New German Critique* 31 (Winter 1984): 157–82.

———. *The Dialectical Imagination: A History of the Frankfurt School and the Institute of Social Research, 1923–1950*. London: Heinemann, 1973.
Kadir, Djelal. "To World, to Globalize—Comparative Literature's Crossroads." *Comparative Literature Studies* 41, no. 1 (2004): doi:10.2307/40468099.
Kafka, Franz. *The Complete Stories*. Trans. Nahum Glatzer. New York: Schocken, 1995.
Kaplan, Amy. *The Anarchy of Empire in the Making of U.S. Culture*. Cambridge, MA: Harvard University Press, 2005.
Katz, B. M. "The Criticism of Arms: The Frankfurt School Goes to War." *Journal of Modern History* (1987): 439–78.
Keddie, Nikki. *Roots of Revolution: An Interpretive History of Modern Iran*. New Haven, CT: Yale University Press, 1981.
Kennan, George. "The Sources of Soviet Conduct." *Foreign Affairs* 25, no. 4 (1947): 566–82.
———. "The Long Telegram." February 22, 1949, http://www.ntanet.net/KENNAN.html.
Kennedy, Liam, and Scott Lucas. "Enduring Freedom: Public Diplomacy and U.S. Foreign Policy." *American Quarterly* 57 (2005): 309–33.
Kennedy, Valerie. *Edward Said and the Work of the Critic*. Malden, MA: Blackwell, 2000.
Khoury, Elias. *Gate of the Sun*. Trans. Humphrey Davis. New York: Vintage, 2006.
Kiberd, Declan. *Inventing Ireland*. Cambridge, MA: Harvard University Press, 1996.
Kiernan, V. G. *America: the New Imperialism; From White Settlement to World Hegemony*. London: Zed Press, 1978.
———. *European Empires from Conquest to Collapse, 1815–1960*. Leicestershire: Leicester University Press, 1982.
———. *The Lords of Human Kind: Black Man, Yellow Man, and White Man in an Age of Empire*. New York: Columbia University Press, 1986.
Kirkpatrick, B. J. "E. M. Forster's Broadcast Talks." *Twentieth Century Literature* 31, nos. 2/3 (1985): doi:10.2307/441300.
Kittler, Friedrich A. *Discourse Networks, 1800/1900*. Stanford, CA: Stanford University Press, 1990.
Koestler, Arthur. *Darkness at Noon*. Trans. Daphne Hardy. New York, Bantam, 1968.
———. *The Spanish Testament*. London: Victor Gollancz, 1937.
Kołakowski, Leszek. *Main Currents of Marxism: The Founders, the Golden Age, the Breakdown*. New York: Oxford University Press.
Kraushaar, Wolfgang, ed. *Frankfurter Schule und Studentenbewegung: Von der Flaschenpost zum Molotowcocktail 1946 bis 1995*. Vols. 1 and 2. Hamburg: Roger und Bernhard bei Zweitausendeins, 1998.
Krupnick, Mark. *Lionel Trilling and the Fate of Cultural Criticism*. Evanston, IL: Northwestern University Press, 1986.
Kurzweil, Edith, and Jon Westling. "Our Country, Our Culture Conference." *Partisan Review* 69, no. 4 (2002): 501–8.
Lasch, Christopher. *The Agony of the American Left*. London: Andre Deutsch, 1968.

Lashmar, Paul, and James Oliver. *Britain's Secret Propaganda War*. London: Sutton Publishing, 1998.
Lasswell, Harold D. "The Contribution of Freud's Insight Interview to the Social Sciences." *American Journal of Sociology* 45, no. 3 (1939): doi:10.2307/2769853.
———. "The Function of the Propagandist." *International Journal of Ethics* 38, no. 3 (1928): doi:10.2307/2378152.
———. "Psychological Policy Research and Total Strategy." *Public Opinion Quarterly* 16, no. 4 (1952): 491–500.
———. "Review: Personality, Prejudice, and Politics." *World Politics: A Quarterly Journal of International Relations* (1951): 399–407.
———. "The Strategy of Soviet Propaganda." *Proceedings of the Academy of Political Science* 24, no. 2 (1951): doi:10.2307/1173235.
———. "The Study of the Ill as a Method of Research into Political Personalities." *American Political Science Review* 23, no. 4 (1929): doi:10.2307/1946501.
Latham, Sean. "New Age Scholarship: The Work of Criticism in the Age of Digital Reproduction." *New Literary History* 35, no. 3 (2004): doi:10.1353/nlh.2004.0043.
Lazarsfeld, Paul Felix. *Radio Listening in America: The People Look at Radio—Again*. New York: Prentice-Hall, 1948.
Leavis, F. R., ed. *A Selection from Scrutiny*. Vols. 1–2. London: Cambridge University Press, 1968.
Leffler, Melvyn P. *A Preponderance of Power: National Security, the Truman Administration, and the Cold War*. Stanford, CA: Stanford University Press, 1992.
Lerer, Seth, ed. *Literary History and the Challenge of Philology*. Palo Alto, CA: Stanford University Press, 1996.
Levin, Thomas Y. "For the Record: Adorno on Music in the Age of Its Technological Reproducibility." *October* 55 (1990): 23–47.
Levinson, Marjorie. "The Discontents of Aijaz Ahmed." *Public Culture* 6 (Fall 1993): 97–131.
Lewis, Bernard. *British Contribution to Arabic Studies*. London: British Council and Longmans, 1941.
Livingston, Robert E. "Global Knowledges: Agency and Place in Literary Studies." *PMLA* (2001): 145–57.
Logue, Christopher. "To My Fellow Artists." *Universities and Left Review* 4 (Summer 1958): 1.
Louis, William Roger. *Imperialism at Bay: The United States and the Decolonization of the British Empire, 1941–1945*. London: Oxford University Press, 1977.
Lowenthal, Leo. "Introduction." *Public Opinion Quarterly* 16, no. 4 (1952): v–x.
Lukács, György. *A Defence of History and Class Consciousness: Tailism and the Dialectic*. Trans. Esther Leslie. New York: Verso, 2000.
———. *Essays on Realism*. Trans. Rodney Livingstone. Cambridge, MA: MIT Press, 1981.
———. *History and Class Consciousness: Studies in Marxist Dialectics*. Trans. Rodney Livingstone. Cambridge, MA: MIT Press, 1972.
———. *The Theory of the Novel: A Historico-Philosophical Essay on the Forms of Great Epic Literature*. Trans. Ann Bostock. Cambridge, MA: MIT Press, 1971.

Macdonald, Dwight. *Against the American Grain*. New York: Random House, 1962.
———. "America! America!" In *Discriminations*. New York: De Capo, 1985.
———. *The Ford Foundation: The Men and the Millions*. New York: Reynal, 1956.
Marrouchi, Moustafa. "Counternarrative, Recoveries, and Refusals." boundary 2 25, no. 2 (1998): 205–57.
———. *Edward Said at the Limits*. Stonybrook: State University of New York Press, 2003.
Masuji, Ibusé. "The Crazy Iris." *Encounter* 6, no. 5 (May 1956): 10–19.
Mathews, Jane de Hart. "Art and Politics in Cold War America." *American Historical Review* 81, no. 4 (October 1, 1976): 762–87, doi:10.2307/1864779.
Mattelart, A. "An Archaelogy of the Global Era: Constructing a Belief." *Media, Culture & Society* 24, no. 5 (2002): 591.
May, Ernest R., ed. *American Cold War Strategy: Interpreting NSC 68*. Boston: Bedford, 1993.
McCarthy, Mary. "America the Beautiful: The Humanist in the Bathtub." *Perspectives USA* 1, no. 2 (Winter 1953): 11.
———. "The Writing on the Wall." *New York Review of Books*, January 30, 1969.
McFate, Montgomery. "Anthropology and Counterinsurgency: The Strange Story of Their Curious Relationship." *Military Review* 85, no. 2 (2005): 24–37.
———. "Iraq: The Social Context of IEDs." *Military Review* 85, no. 3 (2005): 37–40.
———. "The Military Utility of Understanding Adversary Culture." *Joint Forces Quarterly*, no. 38 (2005): 42–48.
McFate, Montgomery, and Andrea Jackson. "The Object Beyond War." *Military Review* 86 (January–February 2006): 13–26.
———. "An Organizational Solution for the DOD's Cultural Knowledge Needs." *Military Review* 85 (July–August 2005): 18–21.
McFate, Montgomery, and Steve Fondacaro. "Cultural Knowledge and Common Sense." *Anthropology Today* 24, no. 1 (2008): 27.
McNelly, Cleo. "On Not Teaching Orwell." *College English* 38 (1977): 553–66.
Menocal, Rosa. *The Ornament of the World*. New York: Little, Brown and Company, 2002.
Miller, James. "Is Bad Writing Necessary? George Orwell, Theodor Adorno, and the Politics of Literature." *Lingua Franca* (December/January 2000): 12–18.
Mitchell, W.J.T. "Postcolonial Culture, Postimperial Criticism." *Transition* 56 (1992): 11–24.
———. "Secular Divination: Edward Said's Humanism." *Critical Inquiry* 31, no. 2 (2005).
Miyoshi, Masao. "'Globalization' and the University." In *The Cultures of Globalization*, ed. Fredric Jameson and Masao Miyoshi. Durham, NC: Duke University Press, 1998.
———. "Ivory Tower in Escrow." boundary 2 27, no. 1 (Spring 2000): 7–50.
———. *Off Center: Power and Culture Relations between Japan and the United States*. Cambridge, MA: Harvard University Press, 1991.
Modisane, Bloke. "African Writers' Summit." *Transition* 5 (July 30, 1962): 5–6.
Moreiras, Alberto. "Global Fragments: A Second Latinamericanism." In *The Cul-

tures of Globalization, ed. Fredric Jameson and Masao Miyoshi. Durham, NC: Duke University Press, 1998.

Moretti, Franco. "Conjectures on World Literature." *New Left Review* 1 (January 2000): 54–68.

———. *Graphs, Maps, Trees: Abstract Models for a Literary History*. New York: Verso, 2005.

———. *The Modern Epic: The World-System from Goethe to García Márquez*. New York: Verso, 1996.

———. "More Conjectures." *New Left Review* 20 (March 2003): 73–81.

———. "The Novel: History and Theory." *New Left Review* 52 (July 2008): 111–24.

Mufti, Aamir R. "Auerbach in Istanbul: Edward Said, Secular Criticism, and the Question of Minority Culture." *Critical Inquiry* 25, no. 1 (1998): doi:10.2307/1344135.

———. "Critical Secularism: A Reintroduction for Perilous Times." *boundary 2* 31, no. 2 (2004): 1–9.

———. "Global Comparativism." *Critical Inquiry* 31, no. 2 (2005): doi:10.2307/3651499.

———. "Orientalism and the Institution of World Literatures." *Critical Inquiry* 36, no. 3 (March 2010): 458–93.

———. "Secularism and Minority: Elements of a Critique." *Social Text* no. 45 (1995): 75–96.

Mulhern, Francis. *Culture/Metaculture*. London: Routledge, 2000.

Nagy-Zekmi, Silvia. *Paradoxical Citizenship: Essays on Edward Said*. Lanham, MD: Lexington Books, 2008.

Ngugi, J. T. "A Kenyan at the Conference." *Transition* 5 (July 30, 1962): 5.

Nietzsche, Friedrich. "On Truth and Lies in a Nonmoral Sense." In *The Nietzsche Reader*, ed. Keith Ansell Pearson and Duncan Large; trans. Daniel Breazeale. Malden, MA: Blackwell, 2006.

Nixon, Rob. *London Calling*. New York: Oxford University Press, 1989.

Nye, Joseph S. *Soft Power: The Means to Success in World Politics*. New York: Public Affairs, 2004.

O'Hara, Daniel T. *Lionel Trilling: The Work of Liberation*. Madison: Wisconsin University Press, 1988.

Ohmann, Richard M. "English and the Cold War." In *The Cold War and the University*, ed. Noam Chomsky. New York: New Press, 1997.

———. *English in America: A Radical View of the Profession*. Middleton, CT: Wesleyan University Press, 1996.

———. *Politics of Letters*. Middletown, CT: Wesleyan University Press, 1987.

Orwell, George. *All Propaganda Is Lies, 1941–1942*. London: Secker & Warburg, 1998.

———. *Animal Pham: Oru Palankatha*. Trans. Em Pi Rosi. Kottayam: Nasanal Bukk Satal, 1956.

———. *Collected Essays*. London: Secker and Warburg, 1961.

———. *The Collected Essays, Journalism, and Letters*. Ed. Sonia Orwell and Ian Angus. New York: Harcourt and Brace, 1968.

———. *The Complete Works of George Orwell*. Vols. 1–20. Ed. Peter Davison. London: Secker and Warburg, 1998.

———. *Cuoc cách-mang trong trai súc-vât*. Saigon: Imprint d'Extrême-orient, 1951.
———. *Facing Unpleasant Facts, 1937–1939*. London: Secker & Warburg, 1998.
———. *Homage to Catalonia*. New York: Harcourt Brace, 1952.
———. *I Belong to the Left, 1945*. London: Secker & Warburg, 1998.
———. *I Have Tried to Tell the Truth, 1943–1944*. Complete ed. London: Secker & Warburg, 1998.
———. *It Is What I Think, 1947–1948*. Complete ed. London: Secker & Warburg, 1998.
———. *Keeping Our Little Corner Clean, 1941–1942*. London: Secker & Warburg, 1998.
———. *A Kind of Compulsion, 1903–1936*. Complete ed. London: Secker & Warburg, 1998.
———. *The Lion and the Unicorn: Socialism and the English Genius*. London: Secker & Warburg, 1941.
———. *Negara Binatang*. Trans. Aus Suriatna. Bandung: Penerbitan Sangkreti, 1949.
———. *O Porco Triunfante*. Trans. Almirante Alberto Aprá. Lisbon: Livraria Popular de Francisco Franco, 1946.
———. *O Tsiphliki Ton Zoon*. Athens: Graphikai Technai Aspiote-Elka, 1951.
———. *Our Job Is to Make Life Worth Living, 1949–1950*. Complete ed. London: Secker & Warburg, 1998.
———. *A Patriot after All, 1940–1941*. London: Secker & Warburg, 1998.
———. *Rebelión en la granja*. Buenos Aires: G. Kraft, 1948.
———. *Skotsky Khutor*. Trans. Gleb Struve. Limburg, Germany: Possev, 1950.
———. *Smothered under Journalism, 1946*. London: Secker & Warburg, 1998.
———. *Talking to India*. London: G. Allen & Unwin, 1943.
Osborne, Peter. "A Marxism for the Postmodern? Jameson's Adorno." *New German Critique* 56 (1992): 171–92.
Padmore, George. "Behind the Mau Mau." *Phylon* 14, no. 4 (1953): doi:10.2307/272073.
Pamuk, Orhan. *The Black Book*. Trans. Güneli Gün. New York: Farrar, Straus and Giroux, 1994.
Pease, Donald E., and Robyn Wiegman. *The Futures of American Studies*. Durham, NC: Duke University Press, 2002.
Pells, Richard. *Not Like Us: How Europeans Have Loved, Hated, and Transformed American Culture since World War II*. New York: Basic Books, 1997.
Pickford, Henry. "Critical Models: Adorno's Theory and Practice of Cultural Criticism." *Yale Journal of Criticism* 10, no. 2 (1997): 247–70.
Pietz, William. "The 'Postcolonialism' of Cold War Discourse." *Social Text* 19/20 (Fall 1988).
Pizer, John. "Goethe's 'World Literature' Paradigm and Contemporary Cultural Globalization." *Comparative Literature* 52, no. 3 (2000): 213–27.
———. "Toward a Productive Interdisciplinary Relationship: Between Comparative Literature and World Literature." *Comparatist* 31 (May 2007): 6–28.
Pletsch, Carl E. "The Three Worlds; or, The Division of Social Scientific Labor, circa 1950–1975." *Comparative Studies in Society and History* 23, no. 4 (October 1981): 565–90.

Poulantzas, Nicos, and Patrick Camiller. *State, Power, Socialism*. New York: Verso, 2001.
Prakash, Gyan. "Orientalism Now." *History and Theory* 34, no. 3 (1995): doi:10.2307/2505621.
Prashad, Vijay. *The Darker Nations: A People's History of the Third World*. New York: New Press, 2008.
Prendergast, Christopher. "Making the Difference: Paul de Man, Fascism, and Deconstruction." In *Intellectuals: Aesthetics, Politics, and Academics*, ed. Bruce Robbins. Minneapolis: University of Minnesota Press, 1990.
Prendergast, Christopher, and Benedict R. O'G. Anderson, eds. *Debating World Literature*. New York: Verso, 2004.
Prevots, Naima. *Dance for Export: Cultural Diplomacy and the Cold War*. Hanover, NH: University Press of New England, 1998.
Rajan, Balachandra. "Bloomsbury and the Academies: The Literary Situation in England." *Hudson Review* 2, no. 3 (1949): doi:10.2307/3847799.
Ratner, Michael. *Guantanamo: What the World Should Know*. New York: Chelsea Green, 2004.
Rees, Richard. *George Orwell, Fugitive from the Camp of Victory*. London: Secker and Warburg, 1961.
Reising, Russell J. "Lionel Trilling, *The Liberal Imagination*, and the Emergence of the Discourse of Anti-Stalinism." *boundary 2*, 20, no. 1 (1993): 94–124.
Robbins, Bruce. "Comparative Cosmopolitanism." *Social Text*, nos. 31/32 (1992): 169–86.
———. "The East as Career: The Logics of Professionalism." In *Edward Said: A Critical Reader*, ed. Michael Sprinker. Cambridge, MA: Blackwell, 1992.
———. *Feeling Global: Internationalism in Distress*. New York: New York University Press, 1999.
———. *Intellectuals: Aesthetics, Politics, Academics*. Minneapolis: University of Minnesota Press, 1990.
———. *The Phantom Public Sphere*. Minneapolis: University of Minnesota Press, 1993.
———. "Secularism, Elitism, Progress, and Other Transgressions: On Edward Said's 'Voyage in.'" *Social Text*, no. 40 (1994): 25–37.
———. *Secular Vocations: Intellectuals, Professionalism, Culture*. New York: Verso, 1993.
Robbins, Louise S. "Publishing American Values: The Franklin Book Programs as Cold War Cultural Diplomacy." *Library Trends* 55, no. 3 (2007): 638–50.
Rodden, John. *Every Intellectual's Big Brother: George Orwell's Literary Siblings*. Austin: University of Texas Press, 2006.
———, ed. *Lionel Trilling and the Critics: Opposing Selves*. Nebraska: University of Nebraska Press, 1999.
———. *The Politics of Literary Reputation: The Making and Claiming of "St. George" Orwell*. New York: Oxford University Press, 1989.
———. *Scenes of an Afterlife: The Legacy of George Orwell* (Wilmington, DE: ISI Books, 2003).
Rougé, Jean-Robert. *L'anticommunisme aux États-Unis de 1946 à 1954*. Paris: Presses de l'Université de Paris-Sorbonne, 1995.

Rowe, John Carlos. "Edward Said and American Studies." *American Quarterly* 56, no. 1 (2004): 33–47.

Rubin, Jay. "From Wholesomeness to Decadence: The Censorship of Literature under the Allied Occupation." *Journal of Japanese Studies* 11, no. 1 (Winter 1985).

Said, Edward W. "Abecedarium Culturae." In *Beginnings: Intention and Method*. New York: Basic Books, 1985.

———. "Adorno as Lateness Itself." In *Adorno: A Critical Reader*, ed. Nigel Gibson and Andrew N. Rubin. Malden, MA: Blackwell, 2002.

———. *Beginnings: Intention and Method*. New York: Columbia University Press, 1985.

———. *Culture and Imperialism*. New York: Knopf, 1993.

———. *The Edward Said Reader*. Ed. Moustafa Bayoumi and Andrew Rubin. New York: Vintage Books, 2000.

———. "From Silence and Sound and Back Again: Music, Literature, and History." In *Reflections on Exile and Other Essays*. Cambridge, MA: Harvard University Press, 2000.

———. "Globalizing Literary Study." *PMLA* 116, no. 1 (2001): 64–68.

———. "Hey Mister, You Want Dirty Book?" *London Review of Books* (September 1999): 8–9.

———. "History, Literature, Geography." In *Reflections on Exile*. Cambridge, MA: Harvard University Press, 2000.

———. "The Horizon of R. P. Blackmur." In *Reflections on Exile*. Cambridge, MA: Harvard University Press, 2000.

———. *Humanism and Democratic Criticism*. New York: Columbia University Press, 2004.

———. *Joseph Conrad and the Fiction of Autobiography*. Cambridge, MA: Harvard University Press, 1966.

———. *Musical Elaborations*. New York: Columbia University Press, 1991.

———. *On Late Style*. London: Bloomsbury, 2006.

———. *Orientalism*. New York: Vintage Books, 2003.

———. "Orientalism Reconsidered." In *Reflections on Exile*. Cambridge, MA: Harvard University Press, 2000.

———. *Power, Politics, and Culture: Interviews with Edward W. Said*. Ed. Gauri Viswanathan. New York: Pantheon Books, 2001.

———. *The Question of Palestine*. New York: Vintage Books, 1992.

———. *Reflections on Exile and Other Essays*. Cambridge, MA: Harvard University Press, 2000.

———. *Representations of the Intellectual: The Reith Lectures*. New York: Pantheon Books, 1994.

———. "Secular Criticism." In *The World, the Text, and the Critic*. Cambridge, MA: Harvard University Press, 1983.

———. "Tourism among the Dogs." In *Reflections on Exile*. Cambridge, MA: Harvard University Press, 2000.

———. "Traveling Theory." In *The World, the Text, and the Critic*. Cambridge, MA: Harvard University Press, 1983.

———. "Traveling Theory Reconsidered." In *Critical Reconstructions: The Relationship of Fiction and Life*, ed. Robert M. Polhemus and Roger B. Henkle. Stanford, CA: Stanford University Press, 1994.

———. "An Unresolved Paradox." *MLA Newsletter* (Summer 1999): 3.

———. *The World, the Text, and the Critic*. Cambridge, MA: Harvard University Press, 1983.

Samuel, Raphael. *The Lost World of British Communism*. New York: Verso, 2006.

Samuels, Stuart. "English Intellectuals and Politics in the 1930s." In *On Intellectuals: Theoretical Case Studies*, ed. Philip Rieff. New York: Doubleday and Company, 1969.

Saunders, Frances Stonor. *Who Paid the Piper? The CIA and the Cultural Cold War*. London: Granta Books, 1999.

Schlesinger, Arthur M. *The Vital Center: The Politics of Freedom*. Transaction Publishers, 1997.

Schrecker, Ellen W. *No Ivory Tower: McCarthyism and the Universities*. New York: Oxford University Press, 1986.

Schwartz, Lawrence H. *Creating Faulkner's Reputation: The Politics of Modern Literary Criticism*. Knoxville: University of Tennessee Press, 1987.

Shaw, George Bernard. *Prefaces by George Bernard Shaw*. London: Oxford University Press, 1934.

Shaw, Tony. *British Cinema and the Cold War: The State, Propaganda and Consensus*. London: I. B. Tauris, 2001.

———. "The Politics of Cold War Culture." *Journal of Cold War Studies* 3, no. 3 (2001): 59–76.

Shelden, Michael. *Orwell: The Authorized Biography*. London: Heinemann, 1991.

Siddiqi, Yumna. "Edward Said, Humanism, and Secular Criticism." *Alif: Journal of Comparative Poetics* no. 25 (2005): 65–88.

Siebers, Tobin. *Cold War Criticism and the Politics of Skepticism*. New York: Oxford University Press, 1993.

Simpson, Christopher. *Science of Coercion: Communication Research and Psychological Warfare*. New York: Oxford University Press, 1994.

Singh, Nikhil Pal. *Black Is a Country: Race and the Unfinished Struggle for Democracy*. Cambridge, MA: Harvard University Press, 2004.

———. "Retracing the Black-Red Thread." *American Literary History* 15, no. 4 (2003): doi:10.2307/3567939.

Smith, Barbara Herrnstein. *Contingencies of Value: Alternative Perspectives for Critical Theory*. Cambridge, MA: Harvard University Press, 1988.

Smith, Neil. *Uneven Development: Nature, Capital, and the Production of Space*. Cambridge, MA: B. Blackwell, 1991.

Soyinka, Wole. *You Must Set Forth at Dawn: A Memoir*. New York: Random House, 2007.

Spanos, William V. *The Legacy of Edward W. Said*. Urbana: University of Illinois Press, 2009.

Spender, Stephen. "The English Intellectuals and the World Today." *Twentieth Century* 149 (1951): 470–76.

———. "The New Orthodoxies." *New Republic* 129, no. 1 (1953): 15–17.

———. "One Man's Conscience." *New Republic* 128, no. 11 (1953): 18.

———. *Poems for Spain*. London, 1939.

———. "The Predatory Jailer." *New Republic* 128, no. 25 (1953): 18.
———. "Speaking for Spain." *New Republic* 128, no. 5 (1953): 18–19.
———. *The Still Centre*. London: Faber and Faber, 1939.
———. "We Can Win the Battle for the Minds of Europe." *New York Times*, April 25, 1948, SM15.
———. *What I Believe*. London: F. Muller, 1937.
———. *World within World: The Autobiography of Stephen Spender*. London: Hamish Hamilton, 1951.
Spender, Stephen, and Melvin J. Lasky. *Encounters: An Anthology from the First Ten Years of "Encounter" Magazine*. New York: Basic Books, 1963.
Sperber, Murray. "Gazing into the Glass Paperweight: The Structure and Psychology of Orwell's *1984*." *Modern Fiction Studies* 26, no. 2 (Summer 1980).
Spivak, Gayatri Chakravorty. "Rethinking Comparativism." *New Literary History* 40, no. 3 (2009): doi:10.1353/nlh.0.0095.
Sprinker, Michael, ed. *Edward Said: A Critical Reader*. New York: Wiley-Blackwell, 1993.
Stansky, Peter, and William Miller Abrahams. *Orwell: The Transformation*. New York: Knopf, 1980.
———. *The Unknown Orwell*. New York: Knopf, 1972.
Stephan, Alexander. *Communazis: FBI Surveillance of German Émigré Writers*. Trans. Jan van Heurck. New Haven: Yale University Press, 2000.
———. *Im Visier des FBI: Deutsche Exilschriftsteller in den Akten amerikanischer Geheimdienste*. Stuttgart; Weimar: Metzler, 1995.
Stephanson, Anders. *Kennan and the Art of Foreign Policy*. Cambridge, MA: Harvard University Press, 1989.
———. *Manifest Destiny: American Expansion and the Empire of Right*. New York: Hill and Wang, 1995.
Stoler, Ann Laura. *Along the Archival Grain: Epistemic Anxieties and Colonial Common Sense*. Princeton: Princeton University Press, 2008.
Strachey, John. *The End of Empire*. New York: Random House, 1960.
Strich, Fritz. *Goethe and World Literature*. London: Routledge & Kegan Paul, 1949.
Sutherland, James. *Stephen Spender: A Literary Life*. New York: Oxford University Press, 2005.
Telmissany, May, and Stephanie Tara Schwartz. *Counterpoints: Edward Said's Legacy*. Newcastle upon Tyne, UK: Cambridge Scholars Publishing, 2010.
Thiong'o, Ngugi wa. "The Commitment of the Intellectual." *Review of African Political Economy*, no. 32 (1985): doi:10.2307/4005703.
———. *Penpoints, Gunpoints, and Dreams: Towards a Critical Theory of the Arts and the State in Africa*. New York: Oxford University Press, 1998.
Thompson, E. P. *The Poverty of Theory and Other Essays*. London: Monthly Review Press, 1978.
———. "Socialist Humanism: An Epistle to the Philistines." *New Reasoner*, no. 1 (Summer 1957): 107.
Trilling, Lionel. "Editor's Commentary." *Perspectives USA* 1, no. 2 (Winter 1953): 4–6.
———. *E. M. Forster*. Norfolk, CT: New Directions Books, 1943.

———. *The Gathering of Fugitives*. New York: Harcourt, Brace, Jovanovich, 1956.
———. Introduction to *Homage to Catalonia*. New York: Harcourt Brace, 1952.
———. *The Liberal Imagination: Essays on Literature and Society*. New York: Viking Press, 1950.
———. *Matthew Arnold*. New York: Columbia University Press, 1949.
———. *The Middle of the Journey*. New York: Viking Press, 1947.
———. *The Moral Obligation to Be Intelligent: Selected Essays*. New York: Farrar, Straus and Giroux, 2000.
———. *The Opposing Self: Nine Essays in Criticism*. New York: Viking Press, 1955.
———. "Outlines of Psychoanalysis." Published as *Art and Neurosis*. Charlottesville: University of Virginia, 1949.
———. "The Situation of the American Intellectual at the Present Time." In *The Moral Obligation to be Intelligent: Selected Essays*, ed. Leon Wieseltier. New York: Farrar, Straus and Giroux, 2000.
———. "La valeur des idées augmente en Amérique." *Preuves* 18 (Winter 1955): 54–66.
Trouillot, Michel-Rolph. *Silencing the Past: Power and the Production of History*. Boston: Beacon Press, 1995.
Varadharajan, Asha. *Exotic Parodies: Subjectivity in Adorno, Said, and Spivak*. Minneapolis: University of Minnesota Press, 1995.
Veit, Walter F. "Globalization and Literary History; or, Rethinking Comparative Literary History—Globally." *New Literary History* 39, no. 3 (2008): doi:10.1353/nlh.0.0037.
Visson, André. *As Others See Us*. Garden City, NY: Doubleday, 1948.
Viswanathan, Gauri. *Masks of Conquest: Literary Study and British Rule in Colonial India*. New York: Columbia University Press, 1989.
Von Eschen, Penny M. "Enduring Public Diplomacy." *American Quarterly* 57, no. 2 (2005): 335–43.
———. *Race against Empire: Black Americans and Anticolonialism, 1937–1957*. Ithaca: Cornell University Press, 1997.
———. *Satchmo Blows Up the World: Jazz Ambassadors Play the Cold War*. Cambridge, MA: Harvard University Press, 2004.
Voorhees, Richard J. *The Paradox of George Orwell*. Lafayette, IN: Purdue University, 1961.
Wagner, Geoffrey. "The Minority Writer in England." *Hudson Review* 7, no. 3 (1954): 427–35.
Walcott, Derek. "A Far Cry from Africa." *Universities and Left Review* 7 (Autumn 1959): 4.
Wald, Alan M. *The New York Intellectuals: The Rise and Decline of the Anti-Stalinist Left from the 1930s to the 1980s*. Chapel Hill: University of North Carolina Press, 1987.
Wang, Ban. "The Cold War, Imperial Aesthetics, and Area Studies." *Social Text* 72, no. 3 (Fall 2002): 45–65.
Weinberg, Albert K. *Manifest Destiny: A Study of Nationalist Expansionism in American History*. Gloucester, MA: Smith, 1958.
Weiner, Tim. *Legacy of Ashes: The History of the CIA*. New York: Anchor, 2008.

Wellens, Ian. *Music on the Frontline: Nicolas Nabokov's Struggle against Communism and Middlebrow Culture*. Burlington, VT: Ashgate, 2002.
Westad, Odd Arne. *The Global Cold War: Third World Interventions and the Making of Our Times*. New York: Cambridge University Press, 2005.
White, Hayden V. *The Content of the Form: Narrative Discourse and Historical Representation*. Baltimore: Johns Hopkins University Press, 1987.
———. *Figural Realism: Studies in the Mimesis Effect*. Baltimore: Johns Hopkins University Press, 1999.
———. "Historicism, History, and the Figurative Imagination." *History and Theory* 14, no. 4 (1975): 48–67.
Whittemore, Reed. *Little Magazines*. Minneapolis: University of Minnesota Press, 1963.
Wiggershaus, Rolf. *The Frankfurt School: Its History, Theories, and Political Significance*. Cambridge, MA: MIT Press, 1994.
Wilford, Hugh. *The CIA, the British Left, and the Cold War: Calling the Tune*. London: F. Cass, 2003.
———. *The Mighty Wurlitzer: How the CIA Played America*. Cambridge, MA: Harvard University Press, 2008.
———. *The New York Intellectuals: From Vanguard to Institution*. Manchester: Manchester University Press, 1995.
———. "'Unwitting Assets?': British Intellectuals and the Congress for Cultural Freedom." *Twentieth Century British History* 11, no. 1 (January 1, 2000): 42–60.
Williams, Patrick. *Edward Said*. Vols. 1–4. New York: Sage Publications, 2001.
Williams, Raymond. "Base and Superstructure in Marxist Cultural Theory." *New Left Review* 82 (1973): 3–16.
———. *The Country and the City*. London: Chatto and Windus, 1973.
———. *Culture*. London: Fontana, 1981.
———. *Culture and Materialism: Selected Essays*. London: Verso, 2005.
———. *Culture and Society, 1780–1950*. New York: Columbia University Press, 1983.
———. *The English Novel from Dickens to Lawrence*. London: Hogarth Press, 1984.
———. *George Orwell*. New York: Columbia University Press, 1984.
———. *The Long Revolution*. Orchard Park, NY: Broadview Press, 2001.
———. *Marxism and Literature*. New York: Oxford University Press, 1977.
———. *Politics and Letters: Interviews with "New Left Review."* New York: New Left Books, 1979.
———. *The Politics of Modernism: Against the New Conformists*. London: Verso, 1989.
———. *Problems in Materialism and Culture: Selected Essays*. London: Verso, 1980.
———. *Writing in Society*. New York: Verso, 1991.
Winks, Robin W. *Cloak and Gown: Scholars in the Secret War, 1939–1961*. New Haven: Yale University Press, 1987.
Wood, Neal. *Communism and British Intellectuals*. New York: Columbia University Press, 1959.
Woodcock, George. *The Crystal Spirit: A Study of George Orwell*. New York: Schocken Books, 1984.

Wynne-Jones, Ros. "Orwell's Little List Leaves the Left Gasping for More." *Independent*, July 14, 1996, 10.
Young, Robert J. C. *Colonial Desire: Hybridity in Theory, Culture and Race.* New York: Routledge, 1995.
———. *Postcolonialism: A Historical Introduction.* Malden, MA: Blackwell Publishers, 2001.
Žižek, Slavoj. *Did Somebody Say Totalitarianism?* New York: Verso, 2001.
———. "Georg Lukács as the Philosopher of Leninism." In *A Defence of History and Class Consciousness: Tailism and the Dialectic.* New York: Verso, 2000.
———. *Living in the End Times.* New York: Verso, 2011.
Zwerdling, Alex. *Orwell and the Left.* New Haven: Yale University Press, 1974.

Index

abstractionism, 114n38
Abu's Pointed Well (Halas and Batchelor), 43
Achebe, Chinua, 65
Acheson, Dean, 43
Adamic, Louis, 29
The Addams Family (Halas and Batchelor), 43
Adelphi, 54
Adenauer, Konrad, 82
Adorno, Theodor, 22, 61, 74–75; aesthetic theory of, 84, 85; anticommunism of, 81, 82, 83; on anti-war movement, 83, 85; and Congress for Cultural Freedom, 81; on empiricism, 82–83; employed by American High Commission, 81–82; exile of, 76, 80, 90; FBI's surveillance of, 75–76; on Hegel, 105; and the intellectual, 85–86, 105–7; and Lazarsfeld, 77; and Lukács, 81, 86; on negative dialectics, 86, 105, 136n66; and Popper, 82; on positivism, 80, 82–83; on radio broadcasting, 18, 61; on radio music, 77–78; representation of America, 76; research at Princeton Radio Research Project, 22, 76–79; and Rockefeller Foundation, 78–79; Said's use of, 86–88, 99, 107; theory of late style, 86, 107; and Zionism, 131n78
Adorno, Theodor, works: *Aesthetic Theory*, 84, 85; *Authoritarian Personality*, 82; Critical Models, 82–85; "Critique," 84; *Currents of Music*, 18, 61; *Dialectic of Enlightenment*, 79–80, 83–84, 94; "On Extorted Reconciliation," 81, 86; *Lectures on Negative Dialectics*, 105; "Marginalia to Theory and Praxis," 84–85; "The Meaning of Working through the Past," 83; *Minima Moralia*, 76, 80; *Negative Dialectics*, 86; *Notes to Literature*, 81; "Opinion Delusion Society," 82; *Prisms*, 80; "Sociology and Empirical Research," 83; *Sound Figures*, 83
Aesthetic Theory (Adorno), 84, 85
aesthetic: autonomy of, 84, 85, 86, 89, 102–103, 105–107; as conventional barrier to political activity, 56, 66, 67, 84, 103; and empire, 68; humanism contingent on distinction between the non-aesthetic and the, 105; irreconcilable with history, 102; as provisional domain of the oppositional intellectual provided by, 107; value of, 46, 66. *See also* literature
affiliation: 17–18, 57–58, 65, 89, 94, 133n21, 138n86
Afghanistan: Anglo-American invasion of 5; as zone of cultural translation, 5–8
Africa, 10, 20, 43, 53, 57, 59
African Congress of Writers and Intellectuals, 60
African Voices (BBC), 9
Agamben, Giorgio, 14–15, 113n15
Alexandria, 48
Algeria, 65
Allen Lane, 37
America: An Orwellian Tale (Blair), 25
America, Day by Day (Beauvoir), 71–72
American Anthropology Association, 6
American Committee for Cultural Freedom, 44, 69
American exceptionalism, 68, 73, 125n89
Amis, Kingsley, 18
The Anarchy of Empire (Kaplan), 126n89
Anderson, Perry, 33
Angleton, James, 1, 109n1
Anglo-Iranian Oil Company, 34
Anidjar, Gil, 90, 133n7, 134n23
Animal Farm (Orwell), 37–43; adaptations of, 24–25; Arabic translation of, 38; British government's dissemination of, 38; CIA's adaptation of, 43–44; Dutch translation of, 41; Japanese-American production of, 43; Malayalam translation of, 37; Portuguese translation of, 40; Russian translation of, 40–42; Telugu translation of, 40; Ukrainian translation of, 41; U.S. Army's adaptation of, 39–40. *See also* Information Research Department (IRD)
Anna Livia Plurabelle (Joyce), 51
Annales School, 3. See *longue durée*

168 • Index

Annan, Noel, 62
Ansatzphänomen, 98. *See also* philology
Ansatzpunkt, 98. *See also* philology
anticommunism: as antidemocratic force, 83; and anti-Semitism, 83; conformity of, 62; constitutive powers of, 34, 36–39; and decolonization, 34, 50; discourse of, 8, 34–35, 50, 64, 81; as episteme, 8, 10, 13, 18, 103; hegemony of, 53, 62, 75; institutions of, 8, 9, 11, 17, 18, 19, 20, 22, 45, 50–51, 81; as new civilizing mission, 34, 36, 50; Orientalist roots of, 36; philology and, 8; political failure of, 64, 81; as rearticulation of British colonialism, 8, 31, 34, 35, 36; rhetoric of, 34–38; and Stalinism, 36, 62, 64, 71, 73; and transfer of imperial authority, 34, 45–46; and U.S. hegemony, 36, 46–47. *See also* Cold War
anti-Semitism, 82–83
Aprá, Almirante Alberto, *O Porco Triunfante*, 40
Apter, Emily, 28, 94, 110n8, 119n9, 134n29, 134n31, 135n46
Arabic (language), 17, 37, 38, 59, 68, 69
Arac, Jonathan, 110n8, 110n118, 128n122
Aragon, Louis, 52
Archaeology of Knowledge (Foucault), 88
archive: authority of, 15; as disciplinary mechanism, 13; as indeterminate place of power, 15; investigative criticism of, 11, 12, 13–17, 22, 23, 105, 106; and literary historiography, 3, 22, 105–106, 137n76; modes for cultural transmission, of 9, 10; resistance as a form of elaboration of, 9–10; as structures for cultural domination, 8; U.S. government's manipulation of, 16–17; as zone of indifference, 15. *See also* Freedom of Information Act
Area Studies, 18, 20, 104
Arena, 52
Arendt, Hannah, 17
Argentina, 57, 74
Armenian genocide, 91
Arnold, Matthew, 33
Aron, Raymond, 17, 58
art exhibitions, government sponsorship of, 11–12, 18, 103, 112n3, 114n38
Ash, Timothy Garton, 25
Así veían a Stalin (Neruda), 12
Asia and Western Dominance (Panikkar), 53
Atlantic Charter, 46

Atlee, Clement, 29
Atwood, Margaret, 27
Auden, W. H., 9, 17, 21, 33, 54, 58
Auerbach, Erich: and the Cold War, 51, 95; cosmopolitanism of, 98–99; on dialectic between history and literature, 95, 97, 99; and doctrine of incarnation, 92; Eurocentrism of, 99; exile of, 91–92, 94; *figura* conceived by, 92–93; on Goethe, 8, 95; historicism of, 93–94, 96–97, 99; Jewishness of, 92; on nationalism, 92, 94, 99; and philology, 91, 95–98; reconceptualization of *Weltliteratur* by, 8, 95–97; and Saidian humanism, 90–91, 94, 101–102, 105; secularism of, 91, 94, 101; on Vico, 95, 97
Auerbach, Erich, works: *Literary Language and Its Public in Late Latin Antiquity and in the Middle Ages*, 97; *Mimesis: Representation of Reality in Western Literature*, 91–94; "Philology and *Weltliteratur*," 8, 91, 94–95; *Scenes from the Drama of European Literature*, 92–93
Austen, Jane, 73, 111n21
Australia, 12, 57
The Authoritarian Personality (Adorno, et al.), 82
avant-garde, 33, 51, 56
Azerbaijan, 36

Bacon, Francis, 79
Badiou, Alain, 23
Bagram, Afghanistan, 27
Bahrain, 38
Baldwin, James, 72
Balibar, Étienne, 115n7
Bandung Conference, 35, 53, 65
Barrès, Maurice, 88
Barzun, Jacques, 67
Basic English, 50
Batchelor, Joy, 43–44
Baziotes, Williams, 114n38
BBC (British Broadcasting Corporation), 9, 20, 49, 61–62
Beauvoir, Simone de, 71–72
Beckett, Samuel, 51, 105, 136n75
Beethoven, Ludwig von, 77, 88
Beethoven (Adorno), 107
"Before the Law" (Kafka), 15
Beginnings (Said), 89
Beirut, 9, 21, 38, 51, 59

Belinsky, Vissarion, 54
Bell, Daniel, 17, 44
Bellow, Saul, 72
Benda, Julien, 136n75
Bengal, 42
Benghazi, 38
Benjamin, Walter, 46, 76
Bentham, Jeremy, 33
Berger, John, 12, 54, 114n27
Berlin, Isaiah, 9, 18, 21, 54, 58, 61–62
Berlin Wall, 13
Bernal, J. D., 29, 32
Bérubé, Michael, 114n28
Bevin, Ernest, 29
biopower, 6–7
Birnbaum, Norman, 55
The Black Book (Pamuk), 3
Black Orpheus: as a disciplinary mechanism, 12, 59; importance to Cold War of, 9; as a new mode of articulation, 21; origins of, 59; regulatory powers of, 59–60; replicating powers of, 21; silences of, 65; translations in, 60; transnationalism of, 60
Blackett, P.M.S., 30
Blackmur, R. P.: on aesthetics and the culture industry, 66; on American exceptionalism, 67–68; on the changing structures of national experience, 68; on the consequences of "Americanization" abroad, 67; criticism and incorporation of the foreign, 68; as editor of *Perspectives*, 67, 70; imperial anxieties of, 73, 126n89; on imperial responsibility of U.S., 68, 103; on intellectuals and the state, 50; on modernity, empire, and the imagination, 68; representations of America, 68; representations of transnational experience, 67
Blackmur, R. P., works: "The Economy of the American Writer," 66; "Editor's Commentary," 68; *The Lion and the Unicorn*, 49–50; "The Logos in the Catacomb," 49–50; "Toward a Modus Vivendi," 67–68
Bloch, Marc, 3. See also *longue durée*
Bloomsbury group, 53
Blunden, Edmund, 48
Bolshevism, 35, 42, 64, 81
Borges, Jorge Luis, 21, 56–57
Borkenau, Franz, 30, 57
Boston Symphony Orchestra, 13
Bowie, David, 24
Braden, Tom, 13

Braudel, Fernand, 3. See also *longue durée*
Brazil, 9, 12, 38
Bread and Wine (Silone), 26–27, 62
Brecht, Bertolt, 76
British Contributions to Arabic Studies (Lewis), 48
British Council, 9; and changing function of public writer, 9; as a conjuncture for cultural domination, 48; consecrating powers of, 21; coordinated movements of writers, 19–20; establishment of, 47; and Information Research Department, 20, 37; as new modes for domination, 20; silences of, 20; as strategy of control and cultural domination, 47–48; transnationalism of, 19, 47–48
British empire, 20, 21, 29–35, 37, 41–42, 44–46, 60, 62, 88–89; the adaptation of *Animal Farm* by, 37–40; anticommunist anxieties of, 37; changing basis of imperial practices of, 8, 12, 34; colonial policies of, 30, 34; contrasted with American, 47; language of decolonization used by, 35; postwar alignment with American empire 8, 12; rhetoric of, 31, 34, 46; strategies of domination redeveloped by, 29–31. See also imperialism
British Foreign Office. See Information Research Department (IRD)
British Guiana, 44
British Honduras, 44
British Marxism, 33, 89
Brown, Ivor, 48
Brzezinski, Zbigniew, 70
Burke, Edmund, 38
Burma, 36, 38, 44
Burmese Days (Orwell), 24
Burnham, James, 64
Butler, Judith, 115n5
Byron, George Gordon, 48, 177n39

Cadernos Brasileiros, 9, 12
Caillois, Roger, 57
Cairo, 37, 43, 48
Cambridge University, 84
Camus, Albert, 17–18, 35, 52–54
Cantril, Hadley, 77
The Captive Mind (Miłosz), 24
Cardoso, Fernando, 123n22
Caribbean Voices (BBC), 9
Carruth, Hayden, 67, 70

170 • Index

Casanova, Pascale: on the consecration of Borges, 56; critique of postcolonial criticism, 4–5, 111n12; definition of "world literary space," 4, 45; on function of *littérisation*, 56–57; on the role of translator, 45; unified theory of literary evolution advanced by, 4, 21, 135n63
Castro, Fidel, 14
Caudwell, Christopher, 33
CBS (Central Broadcasting Corporation), 77
CCF. *See* Congress for Cultural Freedom
Central Intelligence Agency: Allende government overthrown by, 14; animation of *Animal Farm* produced and revised by, 43–45; assassination attempts against Castro by, 25; Congress for Culture Freedom operated by, 1, 11, 13, 17 43, 51–53; 60; covert activities sponsored in the Congo by, 14; discourse of national security invoked by, 15; extrajudicial attempts to assassinate Nehru, 14; extrajudicial efforts to murder Sukarno, 14; and Farfield Foundation, 69; and intellectuals, 18, 21–22; manipulation of Italian elections by, 14; and National Security Act of 1947, 13, 16; ouster of government in Guatemala carried out by, 14; pathologies of power embodied in, 13, 14, 15; power expressed in the juridical discourse employed by, 15; suspension of the law by, 13–15; void of power expressed in concealment of suspension of law, 15. *See also* Freedom of Information Act
Césaire, Aimé, 60, 65
Ceylon, 38
Chaplin, Charlie, 30
Chateaubriand, François-René de, 88
Chiaromonte, Nicola, 57–58
Childe, V. Gordon, 30
Chile, 14
China, 8, 36, 38 40, 43
Chinese (language), 38, 40
Chisholm, George, 99
Chomsky, Noam, 7, 22, 7728
Church Committee Hearings, 24
Churchill, Winston, 38
CIA. *See* Central Intelligence Agency
CIA v. Sims, 16, 113n25
circulation: changes spaces of, 51; as form of domination 3, 9, 48; persistence and repetition of, 48; power of, 3; public writer as object of, 10; as spatial redistribution, 51; as structural domain of transnational culture, 56; velocity of, 9, 57
A Clergyman's Daughter (Orwell), 24
Clifford, James, 133n8
Clinton, Bill, 15
Cloak and Gown (Winks), 1, 11
Cobbett, William, 89
Coetzee, J. M., 3
Cold War: and anticommunism, 8; and area studies, 18; and Bandung Conference, 35, 53, 65; and decolonization, 9, 13, 23; discourse of, 8, 52, 103; education and, 18; epistemology of, 8, 18, 103; and humanistic practice, 18, 52; and imaginary geographies, 20; importance of *Nineteen Eight-Four* to, 24, 46, 52; proliferation institutions of, 8; intellectuals in, 10, 52; language study in, 10; and mobilization of writers by, 9; rhetoric during, 20, 52; and Third World, 20, 52; and totalitarian imaginary, 8, 18, 24–25, 28, 46, 52, 115n7; and *Weltliteratur*, 8–9, 28, 52–54, 56–58, 59–60, 64, 95, 103
The Cold War and the University (Chomsky), 111n28
Cold War Civil Rights (Dudziak), 53
Cole, Jonathan, 136n75
Colombia, 38
Colombo, 38
colonialism, 8, 20, 24, 32, 35, 36, 38, 39, 45, 47, 85, 90, 99, 137n76; and anticolonial discourse, 31, 32, 34
Columbia University, 69, 73, 74, 102
Cominform. *See* Communist Information Bureau
Coming Up for Air (Orwell), 24
Comintern. *See* Communist International
Communazis (Stephan), 74
Communist Information Bureau (Cominform), 11, 53, 64
Communist International (Comintern), 36, 74
Communist Party of Great Britain (CPGB), 28, 33
comparative literature: as a discourse distinct from geography, 100; origins in imperial geography, 99; 100; overlapping histories concealed by, 100; and *Weltliteratur*, 2

confession, and discourse of ex-communism, 64
Congress for Cultural Freedom (CCF): artistic and cultural practices advanced by, 11; attitudes reinforced by, 53–54; 12; CIA's funding of, 1, 11, 13, 17 43, 51–53; consecrating powers of, 17, 53, 58; dissent marginalized by, 17; divide between aesthetics and politics sanctioned by, 17; dominant mode of *Weltliteratur* occupied by, 8–10, 17–21, 51–51–60; emergence of, 11; and humanism, 12, 58, 103; mobilization of public writers by, 9, 12, 17, 22, 56; modes of articulation of, 10, 12, 18, 56, 59; restriction of discourse by, 54, 58; sources of funding concealed by, 17; tactics of subjugation of, 57–58; techniques of cultural replication exploited by, 17–19, 21, 59, translation practices of, 10, 20–22; 56–59, transnational imagination upheld by, 9, 19–22, 45, 51, 52, 56–58, 63
Congress for Cultural Freedom, works: *Black Orpheus*: 9, 12, 21, 59–60, 65; *Cadernos Brasileiros*, 9, 12; *Cuadernos*, 9, 11, 19, 20, 51, 56, 57–59; *Encounter*, 1, 9, 11–12, 13, 19, 20, 21, 42, 51–58, 59, 60, 61, 65, 69, 72, 103; *Forum*, 9, 12, 81; *Hiwar*, 21, 51, 59; *Jiyu*, 21, 51, 59; *Der Monat*, 9, 12, 19, 20, 21, 42, 51, 52, 57–59, 69; *Preuves*, 9, 12, 19, 21, 42, 51,52, 57, 58, 59, 69; *Quadrant*, 9, 12; *Quest*, 9, 12, 21, 51; *Sasangge*, 59; *Solidarity*, 51, *Tempo Presente*, 9, 12, 19, 20, 21, 42, 51, 52, 58, 59; *Transition*, 9, 12, 20, 21, 51, 59, 60, 65
conjunctures: definition of, 100; as elaboration of power, 100, epistemological effects of, 18; of imperial powers after World War II, 8, 12, 17, 34, 45, 46, 47; as reinforcing of structures of attitude and reference, 13, 18, 49, 59; between the *Third Programme* and Congress for Cultural Freedom, 6; between writers and modes of articulation in Cold War, 9, 18
Connolly, Cyril, 17, 19, 51, 55, 56, 58
Conrad, Joseph, 47, 89, 105
contrapuntal criticism: apprehension of overlapping histories and experiences, 98, 99,100; definition, 4, 89; as mode of interpretation grounded in geographical awareness, 100; *Weltliteratur* as an Eurocentric mode of, 2; world literature and contrapuntal criticism, 2
Convegno (Rome), 51
Coombs, Douglas, 47
cosmopolitanism, 2, 9, 34, 98, 99, 106, 109n5; American exceptionalism as obstacle to, 68; Auerbach on, 94, 98; challenges posed by study of "world" literature to, 4, 10; as contrapuntal criticism, 4; misappropriations of, 3; and neoliberalism, 3; roots in philology, 99; as situated displacement, 3, 94. *See also* discrepant experiences
Council for Democratic Germany, 74
counterinsurgency, 5–7
Counterinsurgency Guidance Source, 5
The Country and the City (Williams), 89
CPGB. *See* Communist Party of Great Britain
Crick, Bernard, 26, 28
Criterion, 51
criticism, 12–17, 22–23, 67, 90, 101. *See* secular criticism
Croce, Benedetto, 56–57
Crossman, Richard, 29, 37; *The God that Failed*, 62, 64
Crowther, J. G., 32
Cruz, Juana Inés de la, 54
Cuadernos: changing conditions of cultural transmission, 19; CIA's sponsorship of, 11; consecrating powers of, 58; as disciplinary mechanism, 12; importance to the Cold War of, 9; regulatory powers of, 58; replicating powers of, 19; as a structure of cultural domination, 51; translations in, 56; transnationalism of, 56–58
Cuba, 14, 47
cubism, 114n38
Culture and Imperialism (Said), 4, 89, 91,99, 111n21, 126n89, 133n20,
Culture and Society (Williams), 51
Cultural and Scientific Conference for World Peace, 32
Cultural Capital (Guillory), 4
culture industry, 66–67, 94
culture: as camouflage for power, 4, 17–18, 32, 50, 54, 56, 64, 104; circulation of power in, 2, 3 9; definition of, 57; determinants of, 8, 18, 61–62; disciplinary mechanisms of, 13, 57, 60–61; as displacing place, 106; heterogeneity of, 4, 57; interpellation of empire by, 4, 12, 17, 45,

culture (cont)
  46, 47, 48, 49, 52; intertwining of power with, 12, 49; as modes of transmission, 45, 49, 58, 59, 60, 61, 62; national, 45; overlapping aspects of, 2, 4, 100, 102, 104, 133n20; power and the objectification of, 5, 7, 8; structures for domination of, 68; and system, 138n86
Curtius, Ernest Robert, 91
Cyprus, 44

dada, 114n38
Damas, Léon, 60
Damrosch, David, 109n4
The Dance of the Forest (Soyinka), 59
Dante, Alighieri, 51; Auerbach on, 93–94; figural approach in, 93–94
The Darker Nations (Prashad), 20
Darkness at Noon (Koestler), 62
Darlington, C. D., 30
Davison, Peter, 26, 116n16
Day-Lewis, Cecil, 17, 29, 53, 62
De l'Allemagne (Paris), 2
Dean, Vera, 29
Dear Parent and Ogre (Soyinka), 59
Death in Venice (Mann), 138n86
The Decline and Fall of the Lettered City (Franco), 50
decolonization: defined as devolution, 35; and independence without liberation, 50, 60; and interstices with Cold War, 1, 9, 10, 11, 12, 21, 23, 46, 126n89; modes articulation of, 18, 46, 50, 60, 126n89. *See also* colonialism
democratic criticism, 17, 23
Description de l'Égypte, 6
Deutscher, Isaac, 29, 30
Dialectic of Enlightenment (Adorno and Horkheimer), 22, 75, 79, 80, 83, 95
dialectics, Adorno's critique of, 86; Eurocentrism of, 100; Said's negation of Hegel's model of, 100–101; temporal basis of, 100
Dimock, Wai Chee, 110n12
Diop, Alioune, 85
Discipline and Punish (Foucault), 88
discourse, 59, 88–89, 100, 102
discrepant experiences, 2, 4, 9, 94, 98–99, 102
displacement, 94, 106, 109n5
Dissent, 55

dissenting practices: marginalization of, 8, 20–21, 32, 54, 90, 114n28, 136n75; *Nineteen Eighty-Four* and the incapacitation of, 28; opportunities for, 107; social prerequisites for, 28, 32
The Divine Comedy (Dante), 41, 93–94
Dōbutsu nōjō, (Keisuke), 43
Doctor Faustus (Mann), 51
Dominance without Hegemony (Guha), 88
Dominican Republic, 47
Dover, Cedric, 29–30
Driberg, Tom, 30, 188n52
DuBois, W.E.B., 53–54
Dudziak, Mary, 53
Dulles, John Foster, 13, 54
Durkheim, Émile, 33
Duthuit, Georges, 51
Dylan, Bob, 24

East Germany, 53
East Indian Division of the BBC, 61
Eastern Europe, 36, 48, 53
Eckermann, Johann Peter, 1
Eco, 2
Edinburgh Review, 2
Egypt, 43, 67, 90; distribution of *Animal Farm* in, 38; Napoleon's conquest of, 6
Eisenhower, Dwight D., 13
Eliot, T. S.: on British Council 48–49; and CIA, 1, 109n1; and Congress for Cultural Freedom, 1; on cultural planning, 49, radio broadcasts of, 49; Rockefeller Foundation's arrangements with, 50–51, 66; *Third Programme* broadcasts by, 49, 61
Éluard, Paul, 52
empiricism, 76, 78, 80, 81, 82, 83
Empson, William, 62
Encounter (London): anticommunism of, 52, 53; and Bloomsbury, 53, 54, 55; and changing conditions of humanistic practice, 52; CIA's sponsorship of, 11, 13, 17 43, 51–53; consecrating powers of, 9; as a disciplinary mechanism, 13, 54; importance to Cold War of, 9, 12; as new mode of articulation, 19–20; origins of, 52; regulatory powers of, 53, 54, 57; replicating powers of, 19, 21; silences of, 12, 53, 54; translations in, 9, 20; transnationalism of, 56
Enlarging the Change (Fitzgerald), 51
Enlightenment, 79–80

Eritrea, 38
Essays in Criticism (Cambridge), 52
ethnography, 5–7
eurocentricism, 12, 73, 85, 99–100. *See also* imperialism; orientalism
Europe, 2, 10, 12, 13, 29, 36, 49, 63–64, 68, 69, 80, 92, 94
Executive Order 12958 (Clinton), 14–15; as concealment of state of exception, 15; and indeterminacy of power, 15; as a power over the non-existent, 15; power of state contingent upon void, 15; as state of exception, 15; and zone of indeterminacy, 15; as zone of indifference, 15
exile: Adorno's experience of, 73, 76, 80; Auerbach's experience of, 91–93; Brecht's experience of, 76; condition of, 90, 106; cosmopolitanism and, 94, 98–99, 106; Eisler's experience of, 76; Heinrich Mann's experience of, 76; Said's conceptualization of, 90, 94; Said's experience of, 90; Wright's experience of, 65
La experiencia de Guatemala (Gorkin), 57

Fabian Society. *See* Fabianism
Fabianism, 31, 33
Faith, Reason, and Civilization (Laski), 37
Fanon, Frantz, 12, 54, 60, 118n70, 125n57
Faulkner, William, 17, 18, 45, 49, 57, 63, 64, 66
FBI. *See* Federal Bureau of Investigation
Febvre, Lucien: 99, 135n63. *See* also *longue durée*
Federal Bureau of Investigation: anticommunism of, 74; provincialism of, 74; surveillance of Frankfurt School, 74–76
Federal Republic of Germany. *See* West Germany
Fergusson, Francis, 51
Fiedler, Leslie, 17, 53, 55, 58
figura, 92–93. *See also* Auerbach, Erich
Figural Realism (White), 92
Finland, 29
Fischer, Ruth, 37
Fitzgerald, Robert, 51
Flaubert, Gustave, 73
Ford Foundation, 9, 20, 50, 67
Forster, E. M., 48
Forum (Vienna), 12, 81
Foucault, Michel: *Archaeology of Knowledge*, 88; on biopower, 5–6; *Discipline and Punish*, 88; on discourse of Orientalism, 89; on exteriority of Orientalism, 89; on modes of circulation, 56; on Orientalism as a will to knowledge and power, 88; rarity of Orientalism, 89; Said's differences with, 89, 133n11; theoretical limitations of, 89
Four Quartets (Eliot), 59
France, 9, 12, 13, 19, 21, 27, 42, 51, 52, 61, 64, 65, 67, 71
Franco, Francisco, 36
Franco, Jean, *The Decline and Fall of the Lettered City*, 50
Frankfurter Schule und Studentenbewegung (Kraushaar), 131n79
Franklin Press, 67
Free Germany Movement, 74
Freedom of Information Act: history of, 14; illusions implied by, 15; as instrument of archival investigation, 12–13; juridical interpretation of, 16; limits imposed by Clinton's Executive Order 12958 on, 14; limits imposed by National Security Act on, 16; as state of exception, 13, 14, 15, 16; symbolic power of, 17; and void of power, 15, 23
Freud, Sigmund, 73
Furet, François, 135n63
furioso, 1, 109n1
futurism, 114n38
Fyvel, Tosco, 54, 58

Galsworthy, John, 47
García Márquez, Gabriel, 3, 49
Geisteswissenschaften, as secular philology, 102
Geneva Conventions, 28
geography: absence of unity in, 106; as academic discipline, 99; conjunctures with comparative literature, 99, as displacement, 106; and historicism, 99, 100; imperial vision of, 99–100; lack of permanence to, 101; projection of power on, 99; as terrain for human social activity, 100, 104; transformations in, 101; worldliness as awareness of, 102
German Democratic Republic. *See* East Germany
German Romanticism, 2
Germany, 33, 83, 91–92, 94
The Ghost of Stalin (Sartre), 12

Gibb, H.A.R., 88
Gibson, Richard, 72
Gide, André, 73
Ginsberg, Allen, 1
globalization, 3, 10, 66, 104, 109n6, 138n77
Globe, Le, 2, 117n30
The God that Failed (Crossman), 37, 62, 64
Goethe, Johann Wolfgang, 1, 2, 8, 95, 96, 97, 109n5, 117n30. See also *Weltliteratur*
Goethe and World Literature (Strich), 1–3
Gold Coast, 44
Golding, Louis, 32
Goldmann, Lucien, 84–85
Gollancz, Victor, 30
Gombrowiscz, Witold, 125n53
Gorkin, Julián, 57
Gould, Glenn, 88
Gramsci, Antonio, 33, 87, 88, 89, 99, 101
Graphs, Maps, and Trees (Moretti), 4, 135n63
Graves, Robert, 54
Greece, 35–36
Greenberg, Clement, 51
Grisewood, Herman, 61
Grossman, Henryk, 74
Guantánamo Bay Detention Camp, 27
Guha, Ranajit, 88
Guillén, Nicholás, 54, 60
Guillory, John, 46
Gurland, Arkadij, 75

Habermas, Jürgen, 85, 101
habeas corpus, 27
Hafez, Abbas, 37
Halas, John, 43, 44
Halberstam, David, 115n7
Hardy, Thomas, 89
Heaney, Seamus, 3
Hegel, G.W.F., 100–101, 105, 135n66
hegemony, 36, 46, 89, 101. See also Gramsci, Antonio
Herder, Johann Gottfried von, 95
Hikmet, Nâzım, 54
Hill, Christopher, 26
historicism: Auerbach on, 95; as dialectical mode of understanding, 99; dynamics of, 93; oversights of, 99; possible end of, 95; premises of, 93; scope of, 93; secular basis for, 96, 98; temporal aspects of, 97; territorial blindness of, 96; unity of epochs in, 93; universalist claims of, 93; Vico on, 97

history: asymmetries with literature, 101; and contrapuntal criticism, 4; deterritorialization of, 4; and dislocation of place, 90; displacement of, 106; epistemological problems with world, 137n76; essentialist and Eurocentric visions of, 2, 95, 100; *figura* and genealogical conception of, 92; geopolitical awareness of, 99; as human-made, 10, 92, 101; implicated in modernity, 106; investigation of archives of, 22; irreconcilable with literature, 101; literary, 45, 57, 58, 91, 100; as multiple, interacting worlds, 106; Orientalism as world, 137n76; overlapping aspects of, 4, 9, 100, 102, 104; as revealed by philologist, 106; as secular terrain for human activity, 101; silences as condition of possibility for, 13–17; state archives exempt from record of, 14, 106–107; temporal assumptions of, 93; unified accounts of literary, 4, 85, 97. See also historicism; philology
History and Class Consciousness (Lukács), 79
Hitchens, Christopher, 26, 116n20, 116n21, 116n24
Hitler–Stalin Pact. See Molotov–Ribbentrop Pact
Hiwar (Beirut), 21, 51; affiliations with T. S. Eliot, 59; changing conditions of humanistic practice, 52; CIA's sponsorship of, 51; consecrating powers of, 21; and powers of circulation, 59; and powers of redistribution, 59; as structure for cultural domination, 51; transnationalism of, 59
Hobsbawm, Eric, 54
Hoggart, Richard, 115n2
Holocaust, 82, 92, 94
Homage to Catalonia (Orwell), 24
Homer, 6, 91
homogenization, 51–54, 58–59, 61–62, 71, 95, 97
Hook, Sidney, 44, 63–64
Hoover, J. Edgar, 74–76
Horizon (London), 19, 51
Horkheimer, Max: connections to CCF, 81; critique of student and anti-war movement, 84; dedication of *Minima Moralia* to, 76; *Dialectic of Enlightenment*, 79–81; experience of exile in America, 74; FBI's inability to comprehend, 75–76; FBI's surveillance of, 74–75; postwar compromises of, 80; self-censorship, 81

Hourani, Albert, 59
How New York Stole the Idea of Modern Art (Guilbaut), 11
Hudson Review, 51, 55
Hugo of St. Victor, 98–99
Hulme, T. E., 33
Human Terrain System Project, 5–7
humanism: aesthetics and, 107; and Cold War, 22, 103–4; and democracy, 103; and negative dialectics, 22, 86, 95, 105–7; oppositional analysis in, 104–106; orthodox, 103–104; philological basis of, 86, 106; possibility of a modernist, 102–105; as resistance, 86, 102, 104, 106–7; as secular, 86–87, 91; and view of history, 92–93, 96, 106–7. *See also* late style; philology
Humanism and Democratic Criticism (Said), 22, 91, 102–107, 111n21, 137n75, 138n77
Hussein, Taha, 59
Huyssen, Andreas, 109n6, 117n30, 138n77
hybridity, 2, 4, 102, 104

Illuminations (Benjamin), 46
imaginary geographies, 20, 99
immigrants, in America, 106
imperial sublime, 73
imperialism, 2, 4, 34, 35, 36, 47, 47, 48, 53, 85, 100–105; British contrasted with American, 34, 47; and conjunctures with culture 5, 7, 8, 17–20; and deterritorialization, 45, 46; and discourse of anticommunism, 34; languages of, 50; and modes of transfer, 12, 17, 34, 49; neo- vs. classical, 34; and NGOs, 50; as occupation of cultural space, 20; as projection of power, 52; as strategies for domination, 47, 48, 49; as structures of cultural domination, 51; United States and, 47, 50–58
India, 19, 37–38, 44, 48, 53, 57
Indochina, 37, 44
Indonesia, 14, 37, 44, 65
Information Research Department (IRD): anticommunism of, 34; arrangements with CIA, 43; and changing function of public writer, 20; as a colonial disciplinary mechanism, 40; diffusive powers of, 38; imperial ambitions articulated by, 29, 31; imperial authority transferred by, 34, 36, 37; incorporative powers of, 37, 38; intervention in Iran refashioned by, 34; localization of *Animal Farm*, 38, 39; rapid translations of *Animal Farm* by, 37; recoding of anticolonial resistance by, 34; strategies of domination practiced by, 34; as translation zone, 37, 42; as zones of cultural (mis)translations, 34, 36
intellectuals: censorship of, 54; challenges facing, 18, 45, 50, 86, 104–7; changing public role of, 9, 12, 20, 45, 47, 49, 51, 57; and Cold War, 20, 22, 50; conformity of, 56–65; and democratic criticism, 23, 49, 51; the domain of, 105; and empire, 45–50, 56–58; and exile, 80; globalization of literature and, 45–48; humanistic praxis of, 22; and isolated acts of resistance performed by, 136n75; positions occupied by, 20, 47–48, 51, 58; responsibility of, 23, 50, 136n75; silencing of, 11, 20–21, 50, 53–54, 58; subjugation by the state, 11–12, 20, 22, 25, 26, 27, 48, 49, 50, 52, 58; technology and power of, 10–18, 21, 57, 58; transmission of, 47, 49, 53, 57; transnational basis of, 56, 57, 58
international literary domain, 3, 9, 18, 57, 58
investigational criticism, 10, 22, 23, 27
Iran, 34, 37, 42–43, 131n78
Iraq, 5, 6, 7, 43, 105
Ireland, 29, 35
Isherwood, Christopher, 17, 53
Ishiguro, Kazuo, 3
Islam, 8, 36, 38, 46, 88, 123n5
Israel, 131n78
Istanbul, 91, 94, 95, 99
Italian Communist Party, 26–27, 109n1
Italy, 14, 19, 33, 36, 57, 65, 67

The Jackson Five (Halas and Batchelor), 43
Jahn, Janheinz, 60
Jamaica, 44, 48, 60
James, C.L.R., 51, 54, 76,
Jameson, Fredric, 66, 86, 117n30
Japan, 19, 39, 43, 50, 57
Jarrell, Randall, 51
Jaspers, Karl, 17
Javaherkalam, Ali, 37
Jelenski, Constantin, 125n53
Jiyu (Tokyo), 21, 51, 59
Jolas, Eugene, 51
Jones, Daniel, 48
Joseph Conrad and the Fiction of Autobiography (Said), 87

Josselson, Michael, 52
Joyce, James, 51, 138n86

Kafka, Franz, 15, 73
kamishibai, 39
Kandinsky, Wassily, 114n38
Keep the Aspidistra Flying (Orwell), 24
Keisuke Nagashima, 43
Kennan, George, 19, 24, 34, 36
Kenya, 44, 48, 57
Keynes, John Maynard, 33
Kiernan, Victor, 36, 54
Kirwan, Celia. *See* Information Research Department (IRD)
Kîs, Danilo, 56
Kissinger, Henry, 90
Kittler, Friedrich, 122n138
Koestler, Arthur: Adorno's critique of, 81; as central to postwar literary formation, 17, 21, 58; conformity of, 21; and Congress for Cultural Freedom, 9, 17; *Darkness at Noon*, 62; embattled by contradictions of ex–communism, 62, 64; experience contrasted with Spender's, 62; *The God that Failed*, 64; international recognition of, 21, 58; in *Der Monat*, 57, and persistence of discourse of anticommunism, 64; regularity of translations of, 58; rise to dominance in the 1950s of, 58, 62, 64; translation as worlding of, 17; transnationalization of, 9, 17, 21, 58
Kołakowski, Leszek, 33
Kolhosp tvaryn (Ševčenko), 41
Korea, 42
Koteliansky, Samuel, 54
Kristol, Irving, 12, 52, 55
Krout, John, 69
Krugman, Paul, 27

Labour Party (British), 32–33, 37
Lacerda, Alberto de, 38
Lamartine, Alphonse de, 88
Lampedusa, Giuseppe Tomasi de, 101
Lane, Edward William, 88
Larbaud, Valery, 45, 59
Laski, Harold, 30, 37
Lasky, Melvin, 42, 58, 81
Lasswell, Harold, 78–79
Late Marxism (Jameson), 86
late style: constitutive of oppositional humanism, 106; difficulties posed by, 105; as domain of negation, 107; futility of grasping works of, 105; humanism as awareness of exigencies of, 106, 107, 136n75; incompleteness of works of, 106; realm of philology circumscribed by, 107; unity of belonging negated by, 105; unresolved struggle in, 105. *See also* humanism; philology
On Late Style (Said), 105
Laughlin, James, 67, 70
Lawrence, D. H., 34
Lawrence, T. E, 88–89
Leavis, F. R., 51, 54
Lebanon, 57
Lectures on Negative Dialectics (Adorno), 105
Leeper, R. A., 47
Left Book Club, 30
Lessing, Doris, 54
Lévi, Sylvain, 88
Lewis, Bernard, 48, 122n5
Lewis, Sinclair, 63
Lewis, Wyndham, 33
The Liberal Imagination (Trilling), 69
liberalism, 73
Libya, 42
Lindsay, Jack, 52
The Lion and the Unicorn (Blackmur), 67–68
Litauer, Stefan, 30
literature: aesthetics and, 4–5, 27, 69; audiences of, 3–4, 28; changes in, 45, 51, 122n138; as domain of liberalism, 73; and empire, 66; globalization of, 2, 3, 40, 48, 59; localities of, 60; and negative dialectic with history, 95, 97–98. *See also* Weltliteratur
literary historiography. *See* history
literary prizes, 11, 58
little magazines, 51–52
Living in the End of Times (Žižek), 10
"The Logos in the Catacomb" (Blackmur), 50
Logue, Christopher, 54
London Magazine, 52, 56
The Lone Ranger (Halas and Batchelor), 43
longue durée, 4, 135n63
Lowell, Robert, 17, 66
Lowenthal, Richard, 57
Lukács, György: Adorno's polemic with, 81; conception of totality of, 79; discovery by Williams of, 89; influence on *Dialectic of Enlightenment*, 79; resistance to Soviet

Union's invasion of Hungary, 80–81; Said's critique of, 100; and temporal basis of dialectics in, 100; on universal scheme of literary history of, 8

Lukács, György, works: *History and Class Consciousness* 79; *Realism in our Times*, 81; *The Theory of the Novel*, 100

Lüthy, Herbert, 58

Lycurgus, 6

MacDiarmid, Hugh, 29–30, 52

Macdonald, Dwight: attack on American popular culture, 54; attempts to silence, 54; on board of American Committee for Cultural Freedom, 44; and CCF's censorship of "America! America!" 55; criticism of American empire, 55; Orwell and, 29; support for, 55; as temporary editor of *Encounter*, 54

Mace, Borden, 44

Mackinder, Halford, 99

MacNeice, Louis, 56, 62

Madariaga, Salvador de, 58

Major, John, 25

The Making of the English Working Class (Thompson), 33, 54, 88

Malaya, 34, 37–38

Mann, Golo, 57–58

Mann, Heinrich, 74

Mann, Thomas: American postwar interest in, 50–51; and *Doctor Faustus*, 51; exile in U.S. of, 74, 76; involvement with Congress for Cultural Freedom, 18; as a modernist, 138n86; multiple public positions occupied by, 9; repeated translations of, 17; as subject of "cultural renewal" at Princeton Seminar in Literary Criticism, 51; transnational replication of, 58; "worlding" of, 56, 57–58

The March of Time (Halas and Batchelor), 43

Marcuse, Herbert, 74

Mariners, Renegades, and Castaways (James), 54

Maritain, Jacques, 51

Marshall, John, 50, 66, 7

Martin, Kingsley, 30

Masses, Classes, Ideas (Balibar), 115n7

Massignon, Louis, 88

Mbari Writers Club, 59

McCarthy, Mary, 21, 53; "American the Beautiful," 71; on American indifference to nuclear war; 71; on commodity fetishism in US, 72; contributor to *Perspectives*, and *Encounter*, 53; response to Beauvoir's *America Day by Day*, 72; Trilling's manipulation of, 71

McCarthyism, 70

McCloy, John, 81

McFate, Montgomery, 111n22, 111n23

Menzel, Wolfgang, 2

Mikardo, Ian, 29

Mill, John Stuart, 33

Miller, Perry, 67

Mills, C. Wright, 54

Miłosz, Czesław, 18, 21, 24, 57

Mimesis: The Representation of Reality in Western Literature (Auerbach), 91–94, 99, 103

Minima Moralia (Adorno), 22, 76, 80

Miyoshi, Masao, 39

modalities of articulation, 47, 56–57, 96; and the changing function of the public writer, 18; definition of, 45; emergence of, 18; profusion of, 18; transnationalism of, 22

The Modern Epic (Moretti), 4

modernism, 19, 45, 51, 102, 105, 109n1, 112n3, 114n38, 126n89, 136n75, 138n77, 138n86

modernity, 10, 22, 67–68, 80, 92, 105–106, 126n89

modernization, 19

modes of literary replication: definition of, 21

Molotov–Ribbentrop Pact, 31, 62

Monat, Der: Adorno's contribution to, 81; anticommunism of, 52, 53; and changing conditions of humanistic practice, 52; CIA's sponsorship of, 12, 51; consecrating powers of, 9; coordinated and regulatory powers of, 53, 54, 57; as a disciplinary mechanism, 13, 54; importance to Cold War of, 9, 12; as mode of articulation, 19–20; multiple transnational positions provided by, 58; as platform to discredit Lukács, 81; power of multiple distributions, 59; replicating powers of, 19, 21; serialization of *Nineteen Eighty-Four*, 42; translations in, 9, 20, 42; transnationalism of, 56; U.S. Army's sponsorship of, 42; "worlding" of writers, 57; as zone of occupation, 42; as zone of translation, 42

Moore, Leonard, 40–42

Moretti, Franco, 4, 135n63
Morley, Iris, 30
Morocco, 19
Moscow Trials, 31, 62
Mossadegh, Mohammad, 34
Motherwell, Robert, 114n38
Mounier, Emmanuel, 29
Mufti, Aamir, 94
Murdoch, Rupert, 25
"Murti-Bing" (Miłosz), 57
Murray, John Middleton, 54
Mussolini, Benito, 26

Nabokov, Nicolas, 52, 127n96
Napoleon Bonaparte, 6
National Defense Education Act, 18, 104
National Security Act of 1947, 13–16
National Security Directive (NSC-4), 65, 125n72
National Security Directive (NSC-10), 1, 52
Native Son (Wright), 72
Nazism, 82–83, 91–92, 96, 99
Negara Binatang (Suriatna), 37, 119n90
negative dialectics: absence of reconciliation in, 86, 105; art work as, 85; as awareness of non-identity, 105; contrasted with the negation of negation in Hegel, 103; Saidian humanism rooted in the practice of, 86; secular foundations of, 89
Negative Dialectics (Adorno), 86
négritude, 60, 65
Nehru, Jawaharlal, 14
Neogy, Rajat, 59–60
neoliberalism, 3
Neruda, Pablo, 12, 52, 114n27
Nerval, Gérard de, 88
Neue Rundschau (Berlin), 51
Neumann, Franz, 74
Neumann, Robert, 30
New Criticism, 50
New Directions, 67
New Folio, 51
New Reasoner, 54
New Signatures, 48
New Statesman, 30
New Writing and Daylight, 51
Nietzsche, Friedrich Wilhelm, 75–76, 87, 90
Nigeria, 44, 48, 57, 59, 60
Nine, 52
9/11, 27, 104, 136n75, 137n75

Nineteen Eighty-Four (Orwell) 45–46, 57; Acheson on the significance of, 43; adaptations of, 24–25, 27; British government investment in translation rights to, 42; changing conditions of textual encounters with, 45; collective imagination of totalitarianism popularized by, 24; determinants of transmission of, 28, 45; epistemic deformations sustained by, 26, 46; Kennan on, 24; and the mechanisms of world literature; Miłosz on, 24; *Der Monat*'s serialization of, 42; new demands on literary historiography entailed by translations of, 45; theoretical constraints culturally imposed by, 26–28
The Non-Jewish Jew (Deutscher), 30
Norway, 19, 40, 42
Nouvelle Revue Française (Paris), 51

O'Casey, Sean, 29
Odierno, General, 5
Odyssey (Homer), 91
Office of Special Projects (OSP). *See* Central Intelligence Agency
O'Flaherty, Liam, 29
Ogden, C. K., 33
Ondaatje, Michael, 3
Open Government Act, 25
"Operation Camelot," 111n26
The Opposing Self (Trilling), 69
orientalism: discourse of, 19, 102; exteriority of, 89; as interdisciplinary mechanism, 6, 88, 89; militarization of, 6–8; rarity of, 89
Orientalism (Said), 4, 6, 87–91, 99, 102, 104, 133n11
Orwell, George: affiliation with British Foreign Office, 29, 30; affiliation with *Der Monat*, 42; anticommunism of, 29, 32, 33; apparent intentions behind list, 30; arrangement with IRD to translate works of, 37–38, 40, 41; as asset to the IRD, 40; attitude of British intellectual's toward the Soviet Union represented by, 33; collaboration with IRD alleged against, 26; contemporary adaptation of works of, 24–25; controversy over IRD's correspondence with, 26; cultural determinants of "world" writer exemplified by, 25, 40; enthusiasm over Russian translation of *Animal Farm*

expressed by, 41–42; essentialism of, 29; illness of, 40; on Irish writers, 29; on Isaac Deutscher, 30; on J. B. Priestly, 30; limitations of, 27–28; list of "crypto-communist and fellow-travelers," 28–30; notebook of "crypto-communists and fellow-travelers" written by, 28; political alignments of foreign translators expressed concern of, 21, 40; retention of influence by, 24–25; Russian émigrés' affiliation with, 41–42; totalitarianism as abstract vision of, 24
As Others See Us (Visson), 63
Out of Place (Said), 90
Oxford University Press, 37

Padmore, George, 30–32
A Painter of Our Times (Berger), 12
Pakistan, 38, 44, 48
Palestine, 43, 59, 90
Pamuk, Orhan, 3
Panama, 47
Panikkar, K. M., 53
Pareto, Vilfredo, 33
Parker, Ralph, 30
Partisan Review (New York), 63
peace, 11, 20, 32
Perspectives (New York), 9, 20, 67, 69–72
Peru, 38
The Phenomenology of the Spirit (Hegel), 100–103
Phillips, Morgan, 32
philology: Auerbach's conception of, 91, 93, 95, 97–98; changing conditions of practice of, 96, 98; classical tradition of, 91; common enterprise of, 96; as compulsion to grasp the non-identical, 105; cosmopolitanism as condition of, 98; excavation of linguistic silences, 106; historicism of, 95–96; imperatives and exigencies of, 96; late style as realm of practice of, 107; linguistic silences obliquely presented by, 106; non-identity of words indirectly revealed in the practice of, 106; postwar crisis of, 96; role of in humanism, 22, 86, 94. *See also* humanism; late style
"Philology and *Weltliteratur*" (Auerbach), 8, 91, 94, 95–100
Pletsch, Carl, 38

Podhoretz, Norman, 25
Poland, 42, 69
Politics and Letters (Williams), 24
Pollock, Frederick, 74
Pollock, Jackson, 114n38
Popper, Karl, 82
Portugal, 42, 69
positivism, 22, 76, 78–79, 80, 82–83
Possev (Limburg), 41–42
postcolonial criticism, 4–5, 100, 138n86
postcolonial studies, 2, 87
Potsdam Accords, 39
Pound, Ezra, 52
power: circulation of, 2, 3, 9, 10, 48, 51, 56, 57; consistency of, 57; and disciplinary techniques of articulation of, 2, 10, 13, 18, 45, 46, 47, 50, 56, 59, 63, 78, 96; dispersion of, 57; distributive character of, 7; domination as reterritorialization of, 50, 57; general economy of, 28, 89; governmentality as exercise in, 35; hierarchies of circulation of, 9; of incorporation, 2, 45, 137n76; intense circulation of, 48, 57; knowledge in service of, 6; linguistic exchange as site of, 57; redisposal of, 50, 64; redisposition of, 57; regimes of consecrated by, 9, 21, 45, 56; regularity of, 17, 31, 57, 58; repetition of, 17, 32, 58; spatial redistribution as reterritorialization of, 37, 50, 57; transmitting mechanisms of, 9, 64
The Predicament of Culture (Clifford), 133n8
Prensa, La (Mexico City), 38
Présence Africaine (Paris), 60, 65
Preuves (Paris): anticommunism of, 52;; and changing conditions of humanistic practice, 12, 52; CIA's sponsorship of, 12, 51; consecrating powers of, 21; coordinated and regulatory powers of, 53, 54, 57; as a disciplinary mechanism, 13, 54; importance to Cold War of, 9, 12; and manipulation of Richard Wright, 57; as mode of articulation, 19–20; multiple transnational positions provided by, 58; replicating powers of, 19, 21; translations in, 9, 20, 42; transnationalism of, 56, 59; "worlding" of writers by, 57, 58, 59
Priestley, J. B., 29, 30, 31
Princeton Radio Research Project, 76, 78, 81, 83; imperial aspects of, 79

Princeton Seminar in Literary Criticism, 51, 103
Prison Notebooks (Gramsci), 99
Pritchett, V. S., 48
Pritt, D. N., 31. *See also* Fabianism
propaganda, 20, 25, 37, 38, 41, 43, 78
Prose Literature since 1939 (Spender), 48
psychological warfare, 43. *See also* Congress for Cultural Freedom
public writers: changing conditioned experienced by, 10, 12, 18, 20, 47, 56; institutional mobilization of, 20; marginalization of, 12, 54–56; radio broadcasting of, 18, 21–22; transnationalism of, 9, 18–21; unexpected site of reception, 57

Quadrant (Sidney), 9, 12, 21, 51
Quest (Mumbai), 12, 51

Rabearivelo, Jean-Joseph, 60
radio: Adorno on, 18, 61, 77; attraction of writers to, 62 cognitive structures shaped by, 78–79; consecrating powers of, 21–22; expansion of, 18; generic modes developed by, 60; George Orwell on, 61; intellectuals domesticated by access to, 79; Isaiah Berlin on, 61; listening habits structured by, 61; literary practices shaped by, 62; new modes of subjectivity created by, 60; political control exercised by, 78; position of intellectuals redefined by, 22, 62; retrogressive listening structured by, 77; specific features of production of, 18, 77; T. S. Eliot on, 61; *Third Programme* as new phase of, 20; transnationalism of, 20, 62; World War II's legitimation of, 62
Rahv, Philip, 24
Ramakrishna, Janamanci, 37
Ramparts, 12
Ranaïvo, Flavien, 60
Rao, Raja, 57
Read, Herbert, 17, 48, 51, 58
Realism in Our Time (Lukács), 81, 86
reconciliation, 84, 86, 103, 105
Reflections on Exile (Said), 91, 99–101
Renan, Ernst, 88
Retour de l'U.S.S.R (Gide), 64
Revista de Occidente (Madrid), 51
Richards, I. A., 33
The Road to Wigan Pier (Orwell), 30, 33

Robbins, Bruce, 109n5, 132n3, 134n31
Robeson, Paul, 29, 32
Rochemont, Louis de, 43–44
Rockefeller Foundation, 20, 50–51, 66, 76, 78–79, 103
Rodden, John, 24
Romulo, Carlos, 35
Rosenberg Trial, 53
Rosenthal, Lecia, 136n75
Rougement, Denis de, 53, 114n33
Rubin v. CIA: 12, 14–16
Rulfo, Juan, 9, 17, 57
Rushdie, Salman, 3
Russell, Bertrand, 33, 37, 57, 58
Russian Repatriation Commission, 41

Sackville-West, Edward, 61
Sacy, Sylvestre de, 88
Said, Edward: and Adorno, 90, 105; aesthetics and politics, 105; anti-systematic criticism of, 88; on Auerbach, 90–91, 94, 95, 99; on Benda's conception of the intellectual, 136n75; on the changing condition of the United States, 104–106; on Conrad's *Heart of Darkness*, 89; on contrapuntal criticism, 4, 89, 91; critique of historicism, 99, 102; on Dante, 94; definition of secular criticism, 95, 101–2; on discrepant experiences, 9, 102; on displacing place as non-identity, 106; on elaboration of power as resistance, 100; emancipatory project, 88, 89; on epistemic deformations, 45; exile of, 90; on Foucault's contribution to *Orientalism*, 88–89; on the foundations of *Orientalism*, 87–89; geographical consciousness of, 90–91, 99–101, 106; on Gramsci's geographical consciousness, 101; on hegemony's importance to durability of Orientalism, 88; on humanism and secular philology, 102; on humanist's activation of silences, 107; on imaginary geographies, 101; on late style as domain of resistance, 107; on Lukács and time, 100; on modernity of U.S., 100; negative dialectics as philological practice, 106; on non-dominative knowledge, 86, 89; on Orientalism as an interdisciplinary mechanism of domination, 89; Orientalism as theological philology, 102; on overlapping histories, 4, 100, 102, 104, 133n20; on resistance,

90, 100, 104, 106; on secular criticism, 89, 94–95, 101–102, 107, 111n21, 133n21; on secular history, 94, 101–102, 105, 138n86; on silence, 88, 105, 106, 107

Said, Edward, works: *Culture and Imperialism*, 4, 89, 91, 99–100, 102; *Humanism and Democratic Criticism*, 87, 92, 102–107; *Joseph Conrad and the Fiction of Autobiography*, 87; *Orientalism*, 4, 87, 89, 90, 102, 104; *Reflections on Exile*, 91–93, 99–101; *The World, the Text, and the Critic*, 89–91, 94

Salazar, António de Oliveira, 40

Sartre, Jean-Paul, 12, 54

Sasangge (Seoul), 59

Satchmo Blows Up the World (Von Eschen), 11

Saudi Arabia, 38

Saunders, Frances Stonor, 1, 11, 12

Saville, John, 54

Sayigh, Tawfiq, 59

Schlesinger, Arthur, 52

Schwartz, Delmore, 51

Scotland, 29, 35

Scrutiny, 52

secular criticism, 87, 89, 91–97, 101–2 105, 107, 111n21, 133n21, 138n86

secular history, 94; awareness of shared, discrepant experiences entailed by, 102; displacement of place condition as condition of knowledge of, 105; *figura* as conception of, 92; human activity as terrain of, 101; interconnections between past, present, and future visible in understanding of, 101; potential knowledge of whole of, 102

secular world, 4, 92, 94, 96, 101–102, 105

Senghor, Léopold Sédar, 60, 65

Seton-Watson, Hugh 53–54, 57–58

Ševčenko's, Ihor, 41

Shaw, George Bernard, 29, 31, 47

Shelden, Michael, 28

Sierra Leone, 44

Silone, Ignazio: *Bread and Wine*, 27; central to postwar literary formations, 17, 58, comparison to Orwell, 26–28; conformity of, 21; and Congress for Cultural Freedom, 17, 53; consecration of, 21, 45; excommunism of, 62, 64; experience contrasted with Spender's, 62; and *The God that Failed*, 64; and persistence of discourse of anticommunism, 64; as a police informant, 26; rise to dominance in the 1950s, 62, 64; transnationalization of, 9, 21,45, 58, 62, 64–65

Silone Prize, 26

Sinclair, Upton, 56

Sinhalese, 38

Sitwell, Edith, 48, 53–54

Skotsky Khutor (Struve), 41, 121n116

Smith, Neil, 123n22

Smith-Mundt Act, 66

Smollett, Peter, 38

Socialist Asia (Rangoon), 3

Society Must be Defended (Foucault), 6

Solidarity (Manila), 51

Solon, 6

Soueif, Ahdaf, 3

South Korea, 39

The Southern Question (Gramsci), 101

Soviet Union: attempts to distribute *Animal Farm* in, 41: British intellectuals' sympathies with, 33: East German strike suppressed by, 53: intellectuals' disillusionment with, 62: invasion of Hungary by, 54: invented perceptions of, 34, 42, 44, 114n38; IRD's deployment of Orwell in contest against, 37–43: Kennan's representations of, 36: Lukács disaffection with, 81: Moscow Trials in, 31, 62: *Nineteen Eighty-Four* as imagined reality of, 24: object of radio war, 79: Orientalism and American understanding of, 36: Priestley's criticism of, 31: Pritt's evaluation of, 31: representations of, 11, 34: Shaw's idealization of, 31: social science recruited in struggle against, 79: Stalin's limited ambitions outside of, 36: totalitarianism as abstract generalization of, 46: trope of, 31: U.S cultural strategies to dominate, 11: U.S. psychological warfare against, 43–44; utopia as misrecognition of, 31. *See also* anticommunism; Cold War

Soyinka, Wole, 3, 54, 60, 65; *Dance of the Forest*, 59; *Dear Parent and Ogre*, 59

Spanish Civil War, 36, 62

The Spanish Cockpit (Borkenau), 30

specialization, 73, 91, 106

Spender, Stephen: affiliations with Bloomsbury Group, 53; on American postwar imperial identity, 64; as an asset to U.S. Intelligence, 13; as central to dominant postwar literary formation, 17, 58, 62, 64;

Spender, Stephen (*cont.*)
    as co-editor of *Encounter*, 11, 13, 52–53; and Congress for Cultural Freedom, 1–17, 53; conformity of, 21; and defense of American postwar culture 53, 63; ex-communism of, 62, 64; experience contrasted with Koestler and Silone's, 62; and *The God that Failed*, 64; international recognition of, 21, 58; Orwell's characterization of, 29, 31; and persisting discourse of anticommunism, 64; *Poetry since 1939*, 48; on the postwar European-American divide, 63–64; as subject of Freedom of Information Act Request, 12–16; transnationalization of, 21, 58; on "Western" civilization, 63–64; *World within World*, 55, 62. *See also* Congress for Cultural Freedom; *Encounter*
Sperber, Murray, 25
Spitzer, Leo, 51
Spreading the Word (Coombs)
Sri Lanka, 38, 48
Stalin, Joseph. *See* Stalinism
Stalinism, 31, 36, 44, 56, 71, 73
Stanton, Frank, 74
State of Exception (Agamben), 15
Steinbeck, John, 63–64, 70
Stephan, Alexander, 72
Strachey, John, 30
Strich, Fitz, 109n2, 109n3
Struve, Gleb, 41, 121n16
student movement, 83–85, 131n78
Sudan, 38
Sukarno, 14
surrealism, 114n38
Swift, Jonathan, 120n102
Swingler, Randall, 52

Tamil, 38
Tanganyika, 48
Tate, Alan, 51, 124n40
Taylor, A.J.P., 29
Taylor, Charles, 54
Tempo Presente (Rome): anticommunism of, 52, 53; and changing conditions of humanistic practice, 52; CIA's sponsorship of, 12, 51; consecrating powers of, 9; co-ordinated and regulatory powers of, 53, 54, 57; as a disciplinary mechanism, 13, 54; importance to Cold War, 9, 12; multiple transnational positions provided by,

58; as new mode of articulation, 19–20; origins of, 52; replicating powers, 19, 21; silences of, 12, 53, 54; translations in, 9, 20; transnationalism of, 56;
Thayer, Charles, 42
The Theory of the Novel (Lukács), 4, 100
Third Programme, 9, 20, 49, 61; affiliation with British Society for Cultural Freedom, 61
Third World, 85; Cold War origins of, 38; and non-aligned movement, 53; as physical terrain of Cold War, 20
Thomas, Dylan, 54
Thompson, E. P., contrasted with Williams, 54; *Encounter's* marginalization of, 54; *The Making of the English Working Class*, 33; *The New Reasoner*, 54; on postwar Europe, 34. *See also* British Marxism
Times of India, 38
To the Lighthouse (Woolf), 91
Toller, Ernst, 53
Toptaş, Hasan Ali, 3
totalitarianism, 2, 8, 18, 24, 44, 46, 52, 103, 115n7
Totalitarianism and the Modern Conception of Politics (Halberstam), 115n7
Toynbee, Philip, 55–56, 58
transfer of imperial authority: and anticommunism, 33; and Atlantic Charter, 47; cultural modes of, 12; importance of replication to, 17; and the mobilization of the public writer, 17, 47; modes of transmission in, 17, 45; strategies and techniques involved in, 17
Transition (Kampala): as consecrating circuit, 59; as a disciplinary mechanism, 12, 59; and *Encounter* magazine, 59; importance to Cold War of, 9; as a new mode of articulation, 21; origins of, 59; regulatory powers of, 59–60; replicating powers of, 21; response to emergence of *Présence Africaine*; silences of, 65; translations in, 60; transnationalism of, 60
transitions, 51
translation: asymmetries of, 10; changing conditions of, 45, 58–59; determinants of, 3, 9, 28; and globalization, 10; legitimizing powers of, 3, 45, 58; new modalities of, 45, 58–59; powers of cultural, 5–8; as production of "world writers," 3, 56–57; synchronic aspects of *replication* of,

20–21, 58; and transnationalism, 22, 56, 58; velocity of, 10, 21, 45, 57; and *Weltliteratur*, 3, 45

The Translation Zone (Apter), 28, 94

transnationalism, 56–58, 69, 138n77; alliances and affiliations, 9, 47; alliances and mobilization, 9, 20, 48, 56–57; ; and intellectuals, 9, 20, 56, 58; and literature, 28, 47–52, 57–58; and relations to modes of reproduction, 9, 19, 21–22, 42, 45, 50, 57; temporality of, 21, 57–59

traveling theory, 3, 110n18

Treason of the Intellectuals (Benda), 136n76

Trevor-Roper, Hugh, 62

Trilling, Lionel, 9, 17, 54, 57, 58; affiliations with front organizations, 68; on American exceptionalism, 63, 72; anticommunism of, 63, 73; as editor of *Perspectives*, 67, 70; on the function of the critic abroad, 69–70; illiberalism of, 71; imperial anxieties of, 73; multiple positions occupied by, 69; on national identity, 63, 72; representations of America, 70; on Stalinism and French culture, 71; transnationalism of, 69, 72; U.S. government's support of, 68–69

Trilling, Lionel, works: "Editor's Commentary," 69–71; *The Gathering of Fugitives*, 63; *The Liberal Imagination*, 69; *Opposing Self*, 69; "Outlines of Psychoanalysis," 69

Trinidad, 30

Trotsky, Leon, 114n38

Trouillot, Michel-Rolph, 3

Tucci, Niccolò, 57

Turkey, 39, 91, 94

Tzara, Tristan, 52

Uganda, 44, 60

Ukraine, 42

Ulysses (Joyce), 138n86

U.N. Convention Against Torture, 27

Uneven Development (Smith), 123n22

United Nations, 53, 58

United States: Anglo-American occupation of Afghanistan 5–7, 105; anticommunism in 8, 22, 36, 50, 64, 74; anxieties about boundlessness of, 68; cultural identity of, 50, 53, 64, 68, 73; denervation of *Weltliteratur* as mode of mutual understanding in, 5–7, 15, 96; forms of domination deployed by, 20, 47, 51, 56, 78; heterogeneity of, 104–7; imperial anxieties of, 63, 73; imperial coherence of, 11, 12 50, 53 63; imperial power of, 11, 12, 17, 47, 73; intellectuals in, 18, 21, 22, 49, 50, 53, 55, 58, 61, 63–64, 68; invasion of Iraq by, 5–7, 105; militarization of Orientalism as tactic of armed conflict, 5–7; modes of articulation in, 2, 10, 12, 18, 45, 46, 47, 50, 56, 59, 61, 78, 96; official narrative of, 104, 106; oppositional intellectuals in, 27, 88, 90, 107; place of displacement, 68, 73, 106; representations of, 54, 63–64, 68–72; resistance in, 15, 28, 40, 86, 89, 90, 100, 104, 106, 107, 136n75; strategies of domination used by, 5, 12, 20, 47, 50, 63, 66; suppression of dissent in, 8, 20, 21, 52 53, 54, 55 56, 64, 114n28; transnationalism of, 56, 57, 58, 59, 63, 69, 106, 138n77

United States Department of Defense, 5, 69

United States Department of State, 42 69

United States Information Agency (USIA), 20, 68–69

Universities and Empire (Simpson), 114n28

University of Chicago, 78

The Unnamable (Beckett), 105

Uruguay, 39

USIA. *See* United States Information Agency

U'Tamsi, Felix Tchikaya, 60

Vico, Giambattista, 87, 88, 92, 95 97–98. *See also* philology

Vietnam, 85, 111n28

Visson, André, 63

Voice of America, 42

Voices. *See* Orwell, George

Volney, Constantine, 88

Vossler, Karl, 91. *See also* philology

Wagner, Geoffrey, 55

Wagner, Richard, 88

Wain, John, 54

Walcott, Derek, 3

Wallerstein, Immanuel, 111n28

Warburg, Fredrick, 37

Warner, Rex, 48, 56

The Waste Land (Eliot), 52

Watson, Adam, 34, 40

Weber, Max, 79

Weil, Felix, 54

Wellek, René, 51
Weltkultur, 3, 5, 28, 95, 117n30
Weltliteratur: abstract theories of, 2; aesthetic domain of, 105; Auerbach on, 8, 94, 95–98; CCF's influence on, 8; challenges to the philological study of, 98; changing terrain of, 95, 100; Cold War conditions of, 8; cultural conditions for transmission of, 3, 22; cultural determinants for translations of, 22, 28; dialectical development of, 96, 101; discrepant experiences concealed by evolutionary theories of, 4; economies of power as determinations of, 28; erosions of modes of, 96; eschatological conceptions of, 97; Eurocentrism of, 2, 95; existing modes of, 3; false realization as the expression of the disappearance of, 95; false unity of, 3, 106; fears of ethnocide implied by, 97; German idealism of, 95–96; globalization as threat to, 95; Goethe's definition of, 1–2, 8; historical perspective demanded by, 96; human history as particularities of, 98, 101; intertwined histories as comprehension of, 102; mode of circulation necessary to potential fulfillment of, 3; mode of mutual understanding as Goethean ideal of, 1–2; modernity of, 106; neoliberal illusion of, 3; new geographical realities obscured by, 100; non-identity of, 106; as Orientalist project, 4, 5; as a phase of historical transition, 2; "Philology and *Weltliteratur*," 8, 91, 95–98; philology dedicated to research of, 96; plurality and multiplicities of, 106; political disengagement in abstract models of, 4; questionable relevance of, 28; secular history suspended in unified models of, 3, 101; secular humanism as the philological investigation of, 97; silences as existing condition of possibility for, 10, 13, 107; temporal assumptions in dominant conceptions of, 2, 100–101; *Weltkultur* as global condition of, 3, 5, 28, 95, 117n30
West Germany, 42, 57, 80–82; Allied Control Commission postwar occupation of, 62, 82
What Europe Thinks of America (Burnham), 64
What Is World Literature? (Damrosch), 4

White, Hayden, 92
The White Man's Duty (Padmore), 31
Who Paid the Piper? (Saunders), 1, 11, 12
Why Communism Must Fail (Russell), 37
Wiggershaus, Rolf, 75
Wiley, Arthur, 62
Williams, Raymond, 54; on asymmetries of cultural transmission, 126n82; *The Country and the City*, 89; on the emergence of *Encounter*, 52; on George Orwell, 33; on the methodological breakthrough as trap, 89; on multiple sites of cultural transmission, 125n52; on representation, form, and absence in literature, 89; romanticism of, 89
Winks, Robin, 1, 11, 109n1
Wittfogel, Karl, 74
Woolf, Virginia, 47, 52–54, 56; *To the Lighthouse*, 91
world history: Auerbach's historicist view of 93, 98; dialectic synthesis of, 99; Eurocentric assumption underlying investigations of, 93; potential knowledge of "whole" of, 97
world literary space, 4, 5. *See also* Casanova, Pascale
The World Republic of Letters (Casanova), 4, 21, 45, 46, 56, 111n21
world systems theory, 4, 135n63
The World, the Text, and the Critic (Said), 89–90
World War II, 8–9, 12, 18, 21, 51
World within World (Spender), 55, 62
worldliness: 94, 99; 101,106–107. *See also* secular criticism
The Wretched of the Earth (Fanon), 60
Wright, Richard, 17, 21, 54, 57; cooptation of, 64–65; *God that Failed*, 72, 125n71; and *Présence Africaine*, 65

Yeats, William Butler, 46, 56–57
You Must Set Forth at Dawn (Soyinka), 63
Young, Edgar P., 30
Yugoslavia, 36, 65

Zilliacus, Konni, 29, 54
Zinoviev, Grigory, 31, 54
Zionism, 25, 131n78
Žižek, Slavoj, 10

Writing Outside the Nation by Azade Seyhan
The Literary Channel: The Inter-National Invention of the Novel edited by Margaret Cohen and Carolyn Dever
Ambassadors of Culture: The Transamerican Origins of Latino Writing by Kirsten Silva Gruesz
Experimental Nations: Or, the Invention of the Maghreb by Réda Bensmaïa
What Is World Literature? by David Damrosch
The Portable Bunyan: A Transnational History of "The Pilgrim's Progress" by Isabel Hofmeyr
We the People of Europe? Reflections on Transnational Citizenship by Étienne Balibar
Nation, Language, and the Ethics of Translation edited by Sandra Bermann and Michael Wood
Utopian Generations: The Political Horizon of Twentieth-Century Literature by Nicholas Brown
Writing Outside the Nation by Azade Seyhan
Guru English: South Asian Religion in a Cosmopolitan Language by Srinivas Aravamudan
Poetry of the Revolution: Marx, Manifestos, and the Avant-Gardes by Martin Puchner
The Translation Zone: A New Comparative Literature by Emily Apter
In Spite of Partition: Jews, Arabs, and the Limits of Separatist Imagination by Gil Z. Hochberg
The Princeton Sourcebook in Comparative Literature: From the European Enlightenment to the Global Present edited by David Damrosch, Natalie Melas, and Mbongiseni Buthelezi
The Spread of Novels: Translation and Prose Fiction in the Eighteenth Century by Mary Helen McMurran
The Event of Postcolonial Shame by Timothy Bewes
The Novel and the Sea by Margaret Cohen
Hamlet's Arab Journey: Shakespeare's Prince and Nasser's Ghost by Margaret Litvin
Archives of Authority by Andrew N. Rubin